The Code of Love

ALSO BY ANDRO LINKLATER

The Black Watch (with Eric Linklater)

Charlotte Despard: A Life

Compton Mackenzie: A Life

Wild People: Travels with Borneo's Head Hunters

THE TRUE STORY

OF TWO LOVERS TORN

APART BY THE WAR

THAT BROUGHT THEM

TOGETHER

The Code of Love

ANDRO LINKLATER

DOUBLEDAY

New York London Toronto Sydney Auckland

PUBLISHED BY DOUBLEDAY
a division of Random House, Inc.
1540 Broadway, New York, New York 10036

DOUBLEDAY and the portrayal of an anchor with a dolphin
are trademarks of Doubleday, a division of Random House, Inc.

The Code of Love was originally published in hardcover by
Weidenfeld & Nicolson in 2000. The Doubleday edition is
published by arrangement with Weidenfeld & Nicolson.

Permissions appear on pages 288–89.

Book design by Dana Leigh Treglia

Library of Congress Cataloging-in-Publication Data

Linklater, Andro.
The code of love: the true story of two lovers torn apart by the
war that brought them together / Andro Linklater.
p.   cm.
Includes the text of Donald Hill's World War II diary.
1. Hill, Donald, d. 1985.   2. Great Britain. Royal Air Force—
Officers—Biography.   3. Air pilots, Military—Great Britain—
Biography.   4. Prisoners of war—China—Hong Kong—
Biography.   5. World War, 1939–1945—Prisoners and prisons,
Japanese.   6. Hill, Pamela, d. 2000.   7. Hill, Donald, d. 1985.
Diary.   8. Cryptography—Case studies.   I. Hill, Donald,
d. 1985. Diary.   II. Title.
UG626.2.H48 L55 2001
940.54′7252′092—dc21
[B]   00-060115

ISBN 0-385-50115-3
Copyright © 2001 by Andro Linklater

All Rights Reserved
Printed in the United States of America
March 2001
First Edition in the United States of America

1   3   5   7   9   10   8   6   4   2

For Pamela,
with affectionate memories

Contents

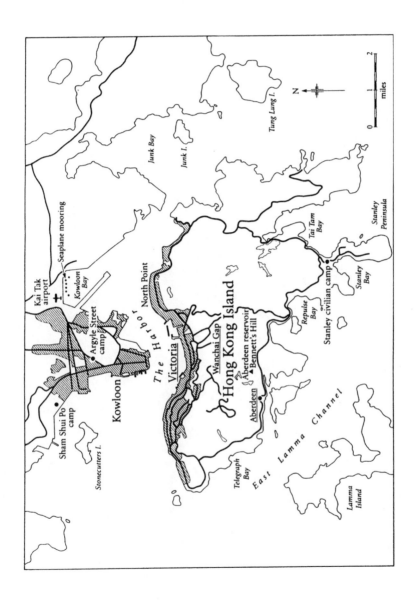

The Code of Love

Introduction

But this is now—you may depend upon it—
Stable, opaque, immortal—all by dint
Of the dear names that lie concealed within't

—EDGAR ALLAN POE,
"AN ENIGMA"

Pamela Hill died on March 22, 2000, sixty-one years almost to the day after she first fell in love. It had been a *coup de foudre,* a blinding revelation, in the course of a dance, and from that moment she was never out of love. She experienced love in many different guises, as joy, agony, despair, renewal, but never did she find it sweet and sugary. There was only one person she loved, and constancy gave to that single attachment a quality that was epic in its depth and passion.

Donald Hill was a young pilot in the Royal Air Force, who had just gained his wings. She was a fashion model with, as she said, no interests "except having fun." They were both in their twenties. Initially, at least, the connection might have amounted to no more than a romantic infatuation, the sort of romance that begins in spring and is finished by the end of the year. But neither of them had ever been in love before. And this was March 1939. What happened between them when they first danced together was to shape her life up to its very last days.

The shadow of war hung over them. There was nothing strange in that. It was the fate of an entire generation to live with the knowledge that the world was out of control. Like other lovers, Pamela and Donald tried to ignore it, as though the high intensity of their feelings could keep the future at bay. What made them different was not something that could be recognized quickly. It was hardly apparent when war broke them apart, separating and scarring them, and it was only beginning to emerge when they found each other again after peace returned. In a way that later generations, searching for immediate fulfillment, would find increasingly hard to understand, it was a matter of keeping the faith whatever it cost. And that was what finally became abundantly clear in the last days of Pamela's life.

She had found her love in that first giddy dance. He made her feel complete as no one else did. To have him and keep him, she had to create an emotion that was more powerful than war, whose coherence outreached the chaos that drove them apart, whose compassion lasted longer than the madness inflicted by the prolonged cruelty of a prison camp. It had to fill absence, to heal wounds, and to make sense of two mortal, misspent lives. And to do that it had to be constant to the very end.

. . .

There was a mystery about what happened to Donald after the fighting swallowed him up in December 1941. Barely three months after meeting Pamela, he had been sent to join British forces in the Far East. On that infamous day when Pearl Harbor was bombed, the Japanese also invaded Hong Kong, where he was stationed. Here, too, they achieved surprise, and after seventeen days of fierce battle the garrison surrendered on Christmas Day. The surviving defenders, including Flight Lieutenant Donald Hill, were taken prisoner.

Among the possessions he carried with him into captivity was a diary. He had begun it the day before the Japanese attacked. "Much talk about war with Japan," he wrote, and then added guardedly, "but no one seems to think anything will happen."

His opening words offer a misleading clue to the writer's enigmatic character. Almost all Westerners thought, as he did, that however warlike the Japanese might appear, they did not want to fight quite yet. Thus anyone able to read what he had written might reasonably have concluded that this was the work of a conventional man. That impression, of being quite ordinary, would have suited Donald Hill. For most of his life he had attempted to disguise himself, hiding his feelings, concealing his ambitions, narrowing the scope of his desire to what was reasonable and attainable. After a childhood overshadowed by tragedy, and a deeply inhibited upbringing, he had dutifully begun his adult years by training to become an accountant. Nevertheless, if only for the intensity of the passion and sensuality that he had begun to sense within him, he could not be called a conventional man.

He had reached his mid-twenties when by chance he stumbled into joy. It came first from learning to fly, and nothing had prepared him for the sense of liberation he felt in the air. Yet even that did not compare with the lightness of being that followed with the discovery that he was in love. The electric moment of their first dance and the golden summer that followed lifted him from the cramped loneliness of what had come before to dizzy heights of happiness. For the rest of his life the sensation was to stay with him as something beyond compare.

Posted to the Far East, he could still fly, but being in love had become less easy when Pamela was six thousand miles away. His instinct was to conceal the power of his frustration. He developed a manner that was very private—the characteristics that his colleagues particularly noticed in him were his quietness and his competence—while his letters to Pamela were cheerful and full of anticipation of their future together. But he could not hide from himself either his unhappiness and his yearning to be with her, or the fact that during his two years' absence he had not been faithful.

When he began his diary, he was in command of a flight of five aircraft which represented Hong Kong's only air defense. Since the planes were old and slow, and had repeatedly been condemned as obsolete, he knew that his chances of survival in combat would be small. He was not yet thirty. If he did not live to see Pamela again, he would at least leave a record to tell her what had happened to him.

By a miracle, he came through the fighting unscathed, and was eventually to emerge alive from a Japanese prisoner-of-war camp. Yet he was not the same. That was the mystery. What had changed him? If there was any sort of answer, it had to be in the diary.

Married and with three children, Donald and Pamela carried their past, with its extremes of emotion, into middle age. Long years had come between their engagement in 1939 and their wedding in 1946. Like many of that generation they coped with the injuries of war by an effort of self-control that seemed alien to their children, growing up in the 1960s. But the pain of what Donald had suffered was not the less for being rarely expressed.

The nearest he came to revealing what had happened was in a tape recording he made not long before his death for his son, Christopher. In it he sets out to tell his life's story. His voice is clear and collected, softened by the burr of his native Devon. It sounds like that of a man who has no secrets to hide, no anxieties to weary him. Yet whenever some awkward memory arises, he avoids it. "There's no point in going back over it," he says again and again. "The past is over." When he reaches the most deeply buried memory, the experience of his time as a prisoner of the Japanese, the usually strong, fluent delivery becomes broken. "I think I've told you about my experiences as a prisoner of war," he says at last, and after a long pause adds emphatically, "In fact I know I have." Then, after several false starts, he concludes by saying, "I think I'll gloss over that." It is clear that the memory is too deeply blocked to be spoken.

Thus it was only in the diary that Pamela could hope to find a clue to explain her husband's mental anguish. But its contents were well hidden. To keep any kind of record in camp was to risk torture, or death. To conceal what he was doing, Donald had buried the entries in numerical cipher, altered their order, and then disguised the long rows of figures as mathematical tables. What he wrote would not be deciphered for half a century. By then the bittersweet tragedy and final reconciliation of their marriage had run its course, and the diary still retained its secret when he died holding Pamela's hand.

Its existence ensured that their love story would not end with his death. It took Pamela another eight years to find someone who could decode the secret that had cast such a shadow over both their lives. When she could at last read what Donald had written, there were no dramatic revelations; the deciphered text covered a mere thirteen pages. But she found there something that had eluded her for almost sixty years. Learning of his suffering in camp, of the shame and humiliation of being a prisoner, and of his profound love for her, she could see him whole again, as though the man she first loved had at last come home from the war.

Soon afterward, and as a result of publicity about the diary, a magazine sent me to interview Pamela. By then she was in her eighties and suffering from cancer. I expected to meet a frail old lady. Instead I encountered a genuine romantic heroine, someone who was beautiful, funny, stylish, hugely entertaining, and at the same time difficult, and temperamental, and utterly beguiling. Those qualities emerged during the interview, and in the following years when we became friends. What I did not realize fully until after I had written this book was her strength of will.

It became apparent soon after the manuscript was delivered to my London publisher that she was dying. The cancer made it difficult for her to swallow, and she grew painfully thin. Nevertheless, whenever I saw her, she declared fiercely that she was going to live to see the book published. It seemed a hopeless ambition. She was taken to a hospice for the terminally ill, but staged a remarkable recovery and came out again. By a prodigious effort, the publishers accelerated production so that on her birthday I was able to put an advance copy in her hands. She could just whisper her pleasure, but it was the look of relief that I really remember. A few days later she returned to the hospice, and it seemed impossible that she would ever leave it alive.

On the actual day of publication, there was a launch party at a bookstore in the town where she lived. To my astonishment, as I stood up to talk about her the door was thrown open and she appeared, swathed in blankets and propped up in a wheelchair pushed by her caretaker. During the next twenty minutes, I told an audience of over one hundred people about her life, but I was aware only of her sitting five feet away, her blue eyes fixed on me with blazing intensity, her face skeletal and as pale as death, yet with her last energies ferociously holding death at bay.

When I finished speaking, there were questions, and someone asked whether she had read the book. Her caretaker replied that she had read it to Pamela. Another person asked what Pamela thought of it. Her caretaker answered that she had been repeatedly overwhelmed by tears during the reading, and kept saying it had told the truth about her and Donald. Not realizing how ill she was, the questioner persisted. "I would like to hear Pamela herself tell us what she feels," he said. There was complete silence. Then with the tiniest breath she whispered, "I feel that now I can let myself die."

Six days later her life was completed.

What follows is her story.

PART I

1

Enigma

All longing converges on this mystery revelation,
unraveling secret spaces, the suggestion that the
world's valence lies just behind a scrambled facade,
where only the limits of ingenuity stand between
him and sunken gardens. Cryptography alone
slips beneath the cheat of surfaces.

—RICHARD POWERS,
THE GOLD BUG VARIATIONS

In his cramped office in the University of Surrey, Dr.
Philip Aston turned off his computer and opened a
large brown envelope that had arrived in the post for
him that morning. Inside it he found about twenty
photocopied pages. The first page had been taken
from the cover of a notebook. The words "Russels

Mathematical Tables" were written on it in block capitals. What caught his eye, however, were twelve pages filled with neat, closely written columns of numbers. They resembled old-fashioned logarithm tables, except that there did not appear to be any pattern to them. Another page contained elaborate handwritten instructions showing how to use the numbers as a ready reckoner for multiplication. To multiply 83 by 26, for example, the reader was instructed to combine numbers from different columns in different ways "so that the answer is found to be 2118."

The calculation did not look right but, just to be sure, Aston checked it. One digit was wrong. It might have been a mistake, but a child equipped with no more than pencil and paper could work out that 83×26 came to 2,158. As a senior lecturer in the department of mathematics and computing science, Dr. Aston allowed himself to make the first, and in some ways most crucial, of what would be many deductions about the notebook: whatever the numbers represented, they were not the mathematical tables they claimed to be.

It was only by chance that the package had been sent to him at all. A few days earlier, he had been copying some notes when the department's secretary looked up from her phone. "There's someone on the line who wants to speak to a mathematician," she said. "Will you deal with it?" There was no one else around, so he had taken the call.

The voice at the other end was clipped and military. The caller was Colonel Ian Quayle from the Soldiers', Sailors' and Airmen's Families Association (SSAFA). He had with him a notebook kept by a young RAF flight lieutenant, Donald Hill, who had been captured by the Japanese after the fall of Hong Kong in 1941. It contained numbers arranged to look like a ready reckoner; conceivably, declared Colonel Quayle, that was what the notebook really was.

"That's why we want a mathematician to look at it," he said briskly, seemingly unaware that getting a top-flight academic to check out what might be nothing more than multiplication tables was akin to asking a general to inspect a box of toy soldiers to ensure that they really were military figures. "Would you be prepared to glance over it, and tell us what it is?"

Aston had an international reputation for his research on such recondite branches of mathematics as bifurcation theory and chaos analysis. Someone of his academic standing might have felt slightly insulted, but instead he was intrigued, a response that marked him out from others who had heard about the tables. They had been sent to both the Imperial War Museum and the RAF Museum, and at neither place had anyone been tempted to give them a second glance before returning them. What interested Dr. Aston was the story Quayle told.

There was a distinct possibility, the colonel explained, that the notebook was in fact a diary. Donald Hill had died in 1985, but he had told his wife and children that the columns of numbers were a code, which concealed the record of his experiences in Hong Kong during the battle for the colony and later as a prisoner of war. What had happened to him then had remained a secret for half a century. Hill rarely referred to his wartime experience, and understandably the family now wanted to discover what the notebook contained. Then Quayle added, "And of course, if it *is* a code, we wondered whether you would have a stab at decoding it?"

Aston had enough to keep him busy. His heavy teaching workload ate into the time he needed for research and, like every academic, he knew that his reputation depended on having his research published. Yet his imagination was caught by the idea of finding out what had happened so long ago. Besides, he thought, if it does turn out to be a code devised by a prisoner of war with nothing more than pencil and paper, it should be easy enough to break. Aston had never really considered what life would have been like in a Japanese prison camp, but Hill had had neither computer nor calculator and, with all the pressures and privations he must have faced, he surely could not have had the time to work out anything too complex. It should not take long to crack the code. Perhaps a weekend would be enough. He could spare a weekend. "Send me a copy," he said, "and I'll see what I can do."

Now he had the notebook in front of him. With it, Quayle had sent some details about Donald Hill. He had been in a prisoner-of-war camp in Hong Kong for three and a half years. At the end of the war, he had been decorated for his conduct in battle and behind the wire, and then had left the RAF with the rank of squadron leader. Quayle did not say that Hill was "a sound man," but the implication was there in those scraps. Studying the tables again, Aston had a thought that was to return more clearly the longer he worked on them. The columns of tightly packed numbers made a direct connection with the man in the prisoner-of-war camp. What he sensed was that in their neatness and order, and their misleading instructions, and their seemingly impenetrable secrecy, they contained not just a record of events, but a flavor of Donald Hill himself.

Most people find numerals at least a little daunting, and so many, crammed on to the page with no clear purpose, might freeze the mind. For Aston, however, they had an irresistible beauty. Even as a child, he had enjoyed the patterns that numbers made, and as he grew older the world that mathematics revealed often seemed more fascinating than the world revealed by sight and touch and smell.

The fascination lies in the way mathematics describes patterns to be found not only in abstract geometrical shapes such as triangles and rectangles, but throughout nature, from the branched structure of a snowflake and the wavelike formation of dunes in the desert to the spiral of the Milky Way. To everything that can be measured, there is a number. When two or more numbers have been found, comparisons can be made, proportions observed, relationships discovered, variations predicted. Eventually, from the multiplicity of numbers a shape and a rhythm will emerge, even where they should not be at all, in chaos.

As a child Aston was brought up to believe in God according to the strict faith of the Plymouth Brethren. The Bible was interpreted literally, and the Brethren's fundamentalist beliefs were diametrically opposed to the questioning, speculative outlook of a scientist. As he grew older, it was hardly surprising that he often found himself deeply torn between the claims of religion and science, but everywhere in mathematics he discovered patterns of such intricacy and beauty that he found it impossible to accept that they were created by chance.

"I cannot believe that all this is the product of some meaningless process," he declared. "What mathematics reveals, at least it seems so to me, is evidence of a creator beyond the scope of human thought or imagination."

And so, while he spent his weekdays working on papers with daunting titles like "Symmetry and Chaos in the Complex Ginzburg-Landau Equation," on Sundays he always made time to play the piano in the university's Baptist chapel.

Now, with Donald Hill's numbers on the page before him, he

instinctively began to search for patterns. Each page was filled with a tight latticework of boxes squeezed into twenty-three columns across and forty-seven rows down; four tiny digits were crammed into each box. On the first two pages, he saw, the numbers ranged from 1 to 26, with a dot placed either side of a single digit. On subsequent pages, a different set of numbers was used. These went from 10 to 35, and he suspected that this set had been adopted because double digits fitted more conveniently into the columns. What jumped out at Aston was that Donald Hill had chosen to use no more than twenty-six different numbers. The first recognizable shape had emerged. If any meaning was to be extracted from the diary, at some point the numbers would have to be translated into words, and it was surely no coincidence that those words had to be made from the twenty-six letters in the alphabet.

If there is one characteristic that mathematicians share, it is the enjoyment of meticulous work. One digit out of place, one equation misread, and the poison kills every subsequent calculation. The penalties are too great to risk anything less than perfect accuracy, and so the otherwise tedious business of achieving perfection becomes an ingrained and even pleasurable habit. The quickest way to transfer the numbers in the notebook to the computer would have been to put the sheets on a digital scanner, which would have recorded them in a form the computer could read. But there was a danger that the scanner's optical recognition software might mistake a tiny 3 for a 5, or a 1 for a 7. In the end the human eye and intelligence were more reliable than a silicon chip, so Aston decided to type the numbers directly into the computer, one by one. It was like a cabinetmaker putting a new edge on a chisel before beginning work.

Tall and lean to the point of being cadaverous, Aston possessed a sublime confidence in the power of numbers. He knew little about codes and ciphers except that there was a relationship between them and his field. This was enough to persuade him that he could master the discipline, and he looked forward to the intellectual challenge it would present. His guide was a book with the drab title of *Elementary Cryptanalysis: A Mathematical Approach,* by Abraham Sinkov. One of the giants of modern cryptanalysis, Sinkov had in 1929 helped to set up the Pentagon's gigantic cryptographic section, now the National Security Agency and the largest ciphering and deciphering organization in the world. He had been recruited from New York University to this position at the heart of the U.S. military machine simply on the basis of his brilliance as a mathematician, and he never quite lost an academic's outlook. By a neat coincidence his most effective work was in cracking the codes of the Japanese air force, which destroyed Donald Hill's planes. For this he was promoted to the rank of colonel and awarded the Legion of Merit, but even after four years of war his response to a crisp military salute was a little wave of the hand and a cheerful "Good morning." For the next few weeks, his book taught Aston the intricacies of his new subject.

Secrecy is the aim of all codes. The crucial word is "crypt," whose Greek source meant "concealed" or "underground"— hence the name for the little chapel hidden beneath the main body of a cathedral. The study of secret writing is cryptology; the creation of codes, ciphers, or any communication containing a hidden meaning is referred to as cryptography, and uncovering the secret messages is cryptanalysis. From the start, mathematicians have been the supreme makers and detectors of this kind of secret communication—indeed, the word "cipher" itself once simply meant "zero," the most basic of all mathematical terms.

There is an important difference between a code and a cipher. A code simply replaces a fragment of information, usually a word or sentence, with another symbol. Thus to send a message from the front line, American troops in the First World War needed only to consult a codebook consisting of lists of letters referring to common situations, such as "YB" for "rifle ammunition needed" and "AF" for "enemy machine-gun fire serious." The most widely used code in history, although many users have no idea they are employing it, is ASCII, American Standard Code for Information Interchange, which is part of the software of nearly all personal computers. Unusually for a code, individual characters are replaced in this case, so that each symbol on the keyboard has its counterpart in a string of seven 1s or 0s; thus the lowercase letter "a" becomes "1100001" and upper-case "A" becomes "1000001."

What makes a cipher different is that when it changes the letters in the original message, it does so according to a rule which is defined by a secret key. The simplest example is the cipher devised by Julius Caesar and used by generations of schoolchildren since, in which "A" is encrypted as "D," "B" as "E," and so on. The key is that each letter is replaced by another three further on in the alphabet. The drawback, as generations of schoolchildren have also learned, is that this key is extremely easy to recognize.

Aston set himself to search for some underlying pattern that would unlock Hill's cipher. It occurred to him that cryptanalysis had at least this in common with mathematics: Communication had rules that had to be obeyed. Meaning depended on word order, verb tense, arrangement of sentences. It was the cryptanalyst's task to find that inner structure, just as the mathematician looked for the numerical relationships that lie beneath the surface of physical events. It was easy to see why the two disciplines were so compatible.

A typical example of pattern recognition in a cipher, and the one that gives away the key to the Caesar cipher, concerns the letter "e," which occurs more frequently than any other in the English language. Thus, if an encrypted message contains more "h"s than any other letter, it is a good hypothesis that "h" stands for "e" in the original message—the plaintext—and that quite probably the key is the one devised by Caesar. In fact, the frequency with which different letters appear in English is astonishingly consistent. In any long text, the five letters used most often will almost invariably be *E, T, A, O,* and *N,* in that order, and the frequency with which the remainder appear can be predicted with the same certainty.

Knowing this weakness, experienced cryptographers try to disguise the frequent appearance of "e" by throwing in complications. A second encryption might transform the first "h" in the Caesar cipher into "i," the next into "j" and the third into "k." They might also attempt to avoid using "e" in the plaintext, following the example offered by Ernest Vincent Wright in his novel *Gadsby.* Summarizing its plot, he wrote, "It is a story about a small town. It is not a gossipy yarn; nor is it a dry, monotonous account, full of such customary 'fill-ins' as 'romantic moonlight casting murky shadows down a long, winding country road.' No. It is an account of up-and-doing activity; a vivid portrayal of Youth as it is today; and a practical discarding of that worn-out notion that 'a child don't know anything.' " Not a single "he" or "she" or "the" or "then" appears, and to show it was possible, he went on to complete his 50,000-word story without using the letter "e" once.

In its final form, what confronts the cryptanalyst is designed to be as impenetrable as the shell on a tortoise. It is as though a secret needs protection as much as a soft-skinned animal out in the open, and codes have evolved as a defense against predators. However farfetched it might seem, the analogy had a particular application to Donald Hill's code, for had his diary been discovered, it could have put his very life at risk.

In *The Codebreakers,* his magisterial study of the craft, David Kahn commented, "Cryptography is protection. It is to that extension of the modern man—communications—what the carapace is to the turtle, ink to the squid, camouflage to the chameleon. . . . The objective is self-preservation. This is the first law of life, as imperative for a body politic as for an individual organism. And if biological evolution demonstrates anything, it is that intelligence best secures that goal. Knowledge is power." Between the codemaker and the codebreaker, Kahn argued, there existed a state of conflict as primal as the basic rivalry between prey and predator that drove evolution forward. "Cryptography," he concluded, "seeks to conserve in exclusivity a [person's] store of knowledge, cryptanalysis to increase that store."

The importance that Donald Hill attached to his secret could be measured by the effectiveness of the protection he created for it. At both the Imperial War Museum and the RAF Museum, the words "Russels Mathematical Tables" had aroused enough doubts in the minds of whoever had examined the notebook to persuade them that it was not worth subjecting to any further scrutiny. In the jargon of codebreakers, this was a successful piece of steganography, concealing the very existence of the coded message. The fact that Hill had not only enciphered his diary, but set out to disguise the cipher as mathematical tables, indicated how essential to his life it was, and how greatly he feared the threat that would come from exposing its contents to outside view.

Aston's initial difficulty lay in deciding where to start. In the end, he decided to find out whether Donald Hill had used a substitution cipher, replacing one letter with another or with a number, according to a secret formula. He chose to begin with the most basic of them all, "Z" = 26. It was simple to write a program for the computer to translate the numbers into letters, substituting "A" for 1, "B" for 2.

It was almost embarrassingly primitive, but the challenge had to begin somewhere. The computer on his desk could process 10 million bits of information a second, sift the numbers for sequences, measure them for mathematical relationships, and compute every possible connection between them, all faster than Aston could read. Beyond that machine lay all the resources of a modern university's math and computing department. It was a formidably powerful hammer to break open the little nut of Donald Hill's code. The date was February 3, 1996, and outside Aston's window the short winter's day was turning to dusk. It was time to go to work.

The news that Colonel Quayle had discovered someone who was prepared to examine Donald Hill's notebook brought a curious kind of hope to Pamela Hill. Throughout the years of their marriage, she had known that the numbers were a code that concealed his diary. Over ten years had passed since her husband's death, and the need to find out what was concealed nagged at her insistently. It was more than curiosity that drove her to search for someone to decode it. Her own past, almost all her adult life, had been intimately bound up with Donald Hill. From the age of twenty-three, when she first saw him, there had scarcely been a day when he had not occupied her thoughts and driven her feelings. What he experienced during the period covered by the diary had profoundly affected their relationship, yet he had never been able to tell her what had happened to him.

At the same time, the sheer weight of expectation made her apprehensive. The contents of the diary were bound to affect her in ways she could scarcely imagine. Its secrets could explain the enigma of the man she had adored, but they might reveal some behavior of his that she would find unforgivable. It was as though one crucial piece in the jigsaw of her own life remained face-down, and the image it hid would change the picture she had of herself.

She was in her eighties now, as fragile as porcelain but still, with enormous blue eyes beneath a wave of perfectly cut and dyed hair, recognizably the beauty she had been in her youth. Half a century had passed since she and Donald first fell in love. He had died in 1985, but still she thought about him every day, and on many nights saw him in her dreams. When she looked back on her own life, its shape was formed by that one relationship. It had not been entirely happy, but it had been all-encompassing, from its first beginning in spring to the final winter parting. They had loved and quarreled, and said everything that could be said both in ecstasy and in anger. Each of them had regretted much, and loved more, and in the end forgiven everything. By the time death halted the dance, they had reached an understanding that united them in a way beyond the power of words to describe.

Yet, at the heart of their relationship, there remained this mystery of what had happened to Donald in Hong Kong. It was not just the experience of war, or even of a Japanese prison camp. There were histories and reminiscences that told of the general conditions the prisoners had endured. What mattered was the particular impact of those experiences on Donald's character. Any explanation he might have provided had been locked away so deeply that he had been unable to say it aloud. That was why Pamela had to know what was in the diary, whatever its consequences. It was the last secret. Before his end, all others had been told and shared. Only this one had remained, literally, unspeakable. Behind the numbers were words that she should have heard while he was still alive. Until they had been spoken, the story was not complete.

In the years since his death, she had repeatedly tried to find someone who could decipher the diary. It had proved to be a frustrating search. Friends had been approached, acquaintances consulted; the notebook had been sent to the sort of organizations that might be expected to crack codes. Some were simply daunted by the dense forest of numbers. Others wondered whether it was worth the trouble, or the risk of stirring up the past. And a few, without ever actually telling her she was being a fool, let it be known that perhaps the numbers actually amounted to nothing more than multiplication tables. None of them ever appreciated how compelling it was for her to know.

With the willful confidence that a beautiful woman learns from her beauty and never forgets, she simply ignored a verdict that did not suit her. Regardless of what the experts might say, she remained certain that sooner or later someone would be found who could penetrate her husband's disguise. Her insistence had led her to SSAFFA, and eventually to the redoubtable Colonel Quayle. When he came up with Dr. Aston, she was delighted that he had succeeded, but not entirely surprised. Men usually did what she asked of them.

Her sublime confidence was a source of wonder to her children. Her eldest child, Joanna, used to marvel at her ability to speak her mind without thinking about the impact of her words, and what was stranger still was that her comments about other people's clothes or behavior, however outrageous, did not seem to matter. People enjoyed Pamela, and they did not appear to mind about the rest.

In her flat, Pamela kept the picture of Donald which a fellow prisoner had drawn shortly before he was released. In it he is still wearing his RAF cap, but he has grown a thick, black beard and his face has a gaunt appearance. There are no other clues about what is happening to him. He is looking down as though to prevent the artist seeing into his eyes and revealing any more than that. The drawing was one of the few items, other than the diary, that he brought back with him when he returned after the war, and it gave away no more secrets than the diary.

Pamela did not have many other physical mementos of him. Some had been destroyed in the turbulent years of their marriage, and more had disappeared in the decade since his death. What remained were the wedding photographs in their leather-covered frames standing on a cupboard by the wall, some letters kept carefully in a torn manila envelope, and a few pieces of furniture. Otherwise there were only her memories of him. Sometimes it seemed very little to show for the intensity of sharing a life for so long.

There was no adequate means of bringing back the past, she thought. The scope of it could be told easily enough—went there, saw them, earned this, did that—but the intensity of living itself had disappeared from view. All that remained of it was in the diary, and the diary came from the very heart of her invisible history.

Protected by the code, it had survived like a time capsule from a moment that was the turning point in their lives. Throughout their marriage its contents had been locked away. She could guess what pain it contained by the insistence with which Donald defended the secret. It was Bluebeard's room, the one part of his life that she was not allowed into.

Sitting in her comfortable armchair, she watched the light drain out of the February day, and wondered how long it would take Aston to break Donald's code. She did not doubt that he would succeed in the end. Or if not him, someone else. What sort of secret might emerge from his efforts? As she pondered the question, she realized the importance of what he was attempting to do. It was not just a matter of decoding a document. For Pamela Hill, it was a matter of decoding a man.

2

First Love

There is no such thing as the State
And no one exists alone;
Hunger allows no choice
To the citizen or the police;
We must love one another or die.

—W. H. AUDEN,
"SEPTEMBER 1, 1939"

Pamela Kirrage and Donald Hill first met on the afternoon of Friday, March 31, 1939. Since the course of her life was irrevocably marked by the events of that day, it was no surprise that in later years she remembered what happened so well.

It was Derry McConnell who set it up. He was Irish in his birth and his charm, but pure pilot by temperament. Flying was what he lived for, and having trained at Cranwell, he was now a flying officer in the RAF. McConnell possessed the easy confidence of someone who had found his rightful place in the world. He could have been a fighter pilot, but instead was posted to Coastal Command at RAF Gosport, where they specialized in torpedo bombing and antisubmarine warfare. His parents lived in Tunbridge Wells in Kent, where he met Pamela Kirrage at a dance and promptly enrolled as one of her impecunious admirers. These were the men who had the privilege of taking her to dances and to pubs, while the moneyed ones took her to dances and the Savoy Hotel in London. Where she was taken was less important than being able to dance and have fun, and for both she liked to sense a certain confidence, an undefinable but instantly recognizable cocktail of zest and savoir-faire, in her escorts. And she could afford to be selective, because membership in both groups was large.

She was just twenty-three. A photograph by the outstanding fashion photographer of the time, Angus McBean, shows her pale, serious face gazing out with enormous eyes from the moody black-and-white shadowed background that was his trademark. There is a vulnerable, almost waiflike look about her delicate features, emphasized by the thick, dark hair tumbling down to her bare shoulders. Not all of this was really her. In reality, the hair was chestnut-colored, the eyes gray-blue, the character assertive, and the look challenging. But the camera told no lies about her beauty.

When she was still seventeen and working as an au pair in France, she had been spotted in the street and offered a modeling contract. It was an occupation she had scarcely heard of, and which, until the 1920s, had hardly existed. Up to then, most new styles were still run up, as they had been for a century or more, by dressmakers and milliners following designs taken from fashion plates, mass-produced prints of the latest fashions. The change started when magazines like *Vogue* began using photographs rather than sketches to illustrate what Worth and Molyneux and the other Paris fashion houses were producing for the new season, and photographers like McBean and Edward Steichen looked for striking models to show the clothes off. Coincidentally, after the First World War a growing number of clothes shops, such as Simpsons and Selfridges, as well as textile companies, produced their own particular look and hired mannequins to display it for their favored customers.

One of the very first models, Lucie Clayton, had just opened a school in London for those who wanted to learn the trade, and in 1936, after she returned to London, Pamela took its six-month course. She was taught how to wear dresses and show them off, and given advice on how to put on makeup. They had foundation creams and rouge, but there was no eye shadow, and for mascara the women learned to dilute black paint with spit, applying the mixture with a large brush. Pamela's first job on the catwalk was for the couturier Maggie Roulf, as desirable a label then as Calvin Klein or Yohji Yamamoto is now.

In the respectable Tunbridge Wells of the 1930s, attitudes to modeling were as old-fashioned as the taste in clothes. According to the historian Richard Cobb, who grew up there during this period, fashion tended toward sensible tweed or Jaeger suits in winter, and vaguely Edwardian, yellow tussore dresses with green parasols in summer. Tunbridge Wells was, he judged, "a town built for leisure, for quiet and orderly enjoyment, for rather dowdy comfort and old fashioned luxury." On the whole, models were regarded as not much worse than actresses and hardly better than chorus girls. "Racy" described their reputation, and raciness is not a quality that Tunbridge Wells has ever greatly cared for.

A handsome old town built on seven hills around a bowl in the Kent countryside, it had known a decent prosperity since the seventeenth century, when its water was found to be chalybeate, impregnated with salts of iron, which were thought to be health-giving. It is less than forty miles south of London, close enough to become a fashionable spa for the capital, and consequently it has never had to struggle very hard for its living. It avoided the raffishness of other resorts, such as Brighton and Bath, missed out on the vulgarity of the Industrial Revolution, and was cushioned against the chanciness of farming life. Insulated from such life-giving turbulence, it had nothing to challenge its settled existence. Retired colonial officials, accustomed to the automatic deference of their inferiors, found Tunbridge Wells an attractive spot for their declining years.

The early frames of *Mrs. Miniver*, portraying the Miniver family's hometown of Bellham, might almost have been taken from prewar Tunbridge Wells. It was the essence of middle-class, respectable England, secure, stuffy, and socially exclusive. As an official guide in the 1920s put it, "The town is never over-run with trippers, nor are its streets ever defiled by the vulgar or the inane. Its inhabitants are composed for the most part of well-to-do people who naturally create a social atmosphere tinged by culture and refinement." To the outside world, Tunbridge Wells became synonymous with comfort and—although there may have been some envy in this—smugness.

Modeling was certainly not the career that Tunbridge Wells would have expected from a member of the Kirrage family. Pamela's father was general manager of the Scottish & Union National Insurance Company, and he had sent his four children to the sort of schools that specified in the prospectus that they catered for the offspring of gentlemen. Their home was a substantial house near the top of the hill, on Queen's Road, where they were looked after by a parlormaid, a housemaid called Sainter, a nanny called Quincy, and a live-in cook called Edith. Faithful to the tenets of an unknown but unquestioned authority, the family ate a roast on Sundays and ensured that the port circulated in a clockwise direction.

From that background of middle-class solidity, Pamela drew the memory of a completely contented childhood. She was the second of the four children, and the household in which she grew up was almost entirely female. Peter, the son and the eldest by thirteen months, had gone to university at Cambridge, and then departed for Burma. Behind him he left three sisters: Pamela; Brigit, who was two years younger; and then, after a gap of seven more years, Sheila. Nanny Quincy and the beautiful Sainter, archly named "The Fairest" by their father, acted as their quasi-mothers, providing an affection that they missed from their real mother.

The picture of middle-class rectitude was not entirely unblemished. Brigit found their family to be respectable, but just slightly eccentric. Their father, Henry, was a clever and determined man, who had gone to the same state school in Nottingham as D. H. Lawrence. He was popular with women and something of a flirt, but it was their mother, Marjorie, who ran things. She was round and fierce with a sharp tongue—what her daughter described as "an outspoken pudding."

Recognizing that the girls had inherited their mother's force of character, Henry Kirrage did not try to oppose their ambitions too strongly. When Pamela announced that she was going to be a model, he restricted himself to expressing his relief that she was not going to be an actress, and paid her Lucie Clayton fees. And when Brigit declared that *she* was going to be an actress, he paid the fees for her training at the Old Vic without a murmur, no doubt silently relieved that she had not wanted to be a chorus girl.

Perhaps the desire to show off was partly inherited, for very often Mr. Kirrage would play the piano in the parlor while Mrs. Kirrage sang something from Gilbert and Sullivan. Frequently her selection included "Three Little Girls from School Are We" with her daughters encouraged to join in, followed by "Come into the Garden, Maud" from the *Popular Home Songbook*. Rather less often they organized musical evenings in a village hall, where young men were expected to sing romantic or silly songs. In 1930 the local paper, *The Courier,* noted Miss Brigit Kirrage's performance as Mustardseed in Hamilton House's "admirable production" of *A Midsummer Night's Dream,* and sometime later commended Mrs. Kirrage's "remarkable concert" at St. Barnabas Parish Hall where there had been humorous musical sketches and a Scotch dance, and Mr. Elphick had contributed "Old Barty" and "The Skipper of the Mary Jane"—which, the reviewer noted approvingly, were "two very breezy songs." Among their neighbors, the Kirrages were regarded as arty and rather odd.

As often happens, each daughter was deemed to have one quality only; thus, Pamela was the pretty one, Brigit the clever one, and Sheila the sensible one. But regardless of character, each in turn was sent to school at Hamilton House. It was only five minutes down the road, but the two elder girls were taken as boarders because there was something ever so slightly common about being a day girl. The school was run by two lesbians, Miss Ferguson and Miss Body, known as Fugs and Bods, whose rigid sense of caste forced them to exclude any child with parents suspected of being engaged in trade, and at the same time prevented any but the most sordid minds imagining their sex life. No one much cared that Miss Ferguson and Miss Body taught the girls little beyond some elementary Scripture, the offside rule in hockey, and how to imitate the dashing Suzanne Lenglen's forehand drive on the tennis court. Sooner or later they would get married to a young man who would provide for them while they brought into the world another generation like themselves.

Buttressed by servants and convention, the prewar family was a small society of its own, headed by the senior male and descending by gradations of age and sex and wealth to the youngest scullery maid. Consequently its values, particularly its respect for hierarchy, property, and comfort, had an unmistakably municipal flavor. Tunbridge Wells liked to imagine itself reflecting those same values writ large.

The two elder Kirrage girls had a glamour that did not quite fit these surroundings. Richard Cobb, who for all his intellectual boldness was socially timid, remembered admiring them hopelessly but until the war broke out never plucked up enough courage to talk to either of them. First Pamela found her way on to the catwalk; then Brigit started to train as an actress; and, while Brigit was still at the Old Vic, her elder sister was offered a lucrative contract by the British Celanese Company. Men might not know what this bland name implied, but every woman could make the association, and it was certainly not one that any decent Tunbridge Wells family would choose for its daughter.

Although she worked regularly, Pamela was not ideal for her career. At five feet nine inches tall, she only just met the requirements for height, and her figure was slightly too full. Her official model sheet described her measurements as 35 inches at the bust, 25 at the waist, and 37 at the hips. The boyish look of the twenties had never quite gone away, and mannequins were required to be flat-chested or at least to bandage their breasts, with no hint of cleavage allowed. Such considerations did not apply to underwear, however, and underwear was what the British Celanese Company manufactured. Tunbridge Wells preferred not to think of such matters.

When *The Courier* carried its first advertisement for corsets and bodices, in the form of a discreet sketch of a nubile young body, the reaction was furious. Among other protesters, one reader wrote to tell the paper that the picture would encourage depravity and throw open the floodgates to unbridled lust, and in his outrage he signed himself simply "Disgusted of Tunbridge Wells." In the rest of Britain the phrase quickly became a joke which epitomized small-town values, but to those living in the town it was a serious matter.

Henry Kirrage, in particular, was shocked by the idea of his daughter parading up and down the catwalk in a skimpy bodice. For some weeks he forbade her to take up the contract, but his daughter would not give way. In the end, he swallowed his misgivings—Pamela gave her mother the credit for persuading him— and as it turned out, the job could hardly have been more respectable. She traveled the country to model Celanese camisoles, underpants, and bras to a select clientele in upmarket department stores like Selfridges in London, Jenners in Edinburgh, and Binns in Manchester. When Princess Marina became engaged to the Duke of Kent and went to Simpsons in Piccadilly to select her trousseau, Miss Kirrage was hurriedly summoned to model the underwear.

What persuaded Mr. Kirrage to change his mind was probably more than his wife's advocacy. The nice conventional girl who was hopeless at schoolwork and adored tennis and dancing had developed a will of her own. It was a characteristic that remained apparent throughout her life. Convention depended on a young woman knowing her place and relying on her parents to support her until a husband arrived, but the attention that Pamela's looks attracted, and the income she earned, allowed her to insist on her own course. Compared with other girls, who became secretaries or schoolteachers, she had a glamorous career. She still lived at home, and still kept the same friends, but the narrow world was inexorably broadening.

There had always been a rivalry between the pretty sister and the clever one, made worse, according to Brigit, by their mother's clear preference for Pamela. It encouraged what her younger sister regarded as an already disagreeable expectation of getting her own way. Thus when they went to Stratford to see a production of *Richard III* and had to share a room, it seemed to Brigit typical that Pamela should claim the best bed, strew her clothes all over the place, and on the night of the play pinch for her own use a pair of deeply desirable black stockings that Brigit had reserved for the occasion. Her mood was not sweetened by the crowds of young men who clustered around her sister. They came in all kinds, from a handsome curate called Guinness to a smooth lounge lizard with greasy hair and a flashy style of dancing, from the charming, confident Derry McConnell to the bashful, brilliant Richard Cobb, whose hopeless adoration ultimately turned to a more realistic passion for Brigit. Meanwhile Pamela danced and flirted with them all, but emotionally remained utterly unmoved.

Watching with a jealous eye, Brigit decided that Pamela was like ice cream. Innumerable young men were queuing up to marry her, and on the outside she was sweet to them, yet on the inside she remained quite cold. Pamela would not have tried to defend herself against the accusation, for she found her own behavior equally perplexing. She adored dancing with her admirers, and longed to fall in love, but never found any of them physically attractive. It seemed as though deep down in the supremely confident Miss Kirrage there were a huge pit of timidity.

She was, however, far warmer than Brigit gave her credit for. It was, after all, the intensity of the sisters' feelings for each other that made their relationship so volatile. And Sheila, the youngest of the girls, remembered that it was Pamela rather than Brigit who helped her with all the problems of clothes and boys and growing up. In fact, it was because Pamela was a good sister that the meeting that was to change her life took place.

In 1938 Brigit suffered terrible injuries while she was ironing a dress. A short circuit in the wiring produced a flash that set alight her clothes. The right side of her body was so severely burned that for months her life was in danger. It was only the work of a pioneering plastic surgeon, Raynsford Mowlem, who took strips of skin from her thigh and cultured them before applying them to the suppurating wounds, that she survived at all. It put a halt to her theatrical ambitions. When she came home to convalesce, the two sisters began to establish a new relationship. Despite her injuries, Brigit resented being treated as an invalid, and she was grateful to Pamela, who went out of her way to make sure that any invitation to a party or a dance also included her sister. In the swirl of sibling rivalry and affection, inner tensions still occasionally blew up into spectacular quarrels, but increasingly the sisters were allies against the world.

Above the din of big bands blaring out "The Black Bottom Stomp" and the chatter of gossip about Charlie Chaplin's new film, the drone of politics had become so insistent that no one could ignore it. Events in Europe were significant for some reason, and if the intricacies of treaties with France and guarantees to Czechoslovakia and Poland were too hard to understand, the threat of military aggression was something that young men instinctively responded to. Some volunteered for the Royal Navy, others enlisted in the army, and a minority put themselves forward for the Royal Air Force, the youngest service and until then the least fashionable. But for those who thought about it, warfare in the sky represented the last opportunity for single combat, in which one person pitted his fighting skill against another. And compared to army discipline and naval anonymity, flying offered freedom and self-expression.

Long before war actually broke out, a new aristocracy had emerged among the young of Pamela's generation. They wore ashy blue uniforms with white wings sewn above the heart to show that they were pilots. They had to be pilots. However much the experts tried to insist that the navigator or the station commander or even the engineer was equally important, civilians, especially female civilians, recognized only one hero in the lineup.

Derry McConnell had that mark on him, and he spoke the cool RAF slang that diminished danger to a joke. When he "pranged the kite," he'd had a crash that could have killed him; "daisy-picking" was coming in too low, and the day he "bent the landing kit" referred to a slewed landing with sparks cascading from the plane's collapsed undercarriage. Nothing was that serious, not even death. And to ride the air at over a hundred miles an hour, to see the world as an eagle saw it, looking down on the dusty lanes of Kent picked out from the green fields and plowland by hawthorn hedges dusted in white blossom, to follow the silver snake of a railway line through the blackness of a night flight, to sideslip through the indigo canyons that twisted between mountainous bronze thunderclouds, that was—what was the right word?—it was absolutely wizard.

On the twenty-first anniversary of the founding of the Royal

Air Force, the Gosport aerodrome decided to host a dance. It was to be a grand affair, and Derry invited the most glamorous girl he knew. He would come and pick her up on March 31, then drive her down to Gosport. But Brigit was at home, and under the terms of their new alliance, Pamela was not going to let her be left out. Besides, it was not absolutely certain that she would be allowed to spend a night with a godlike pilot unchaperoned.

Oblivious of what the future held, Derry happily accepted her conditions. "Alright," he said, "I'll get a date for Brigit as well."

In the summer of 1937 the government had begun belatedly to prepare for the worst. At that late stage, the priorities had finally become clear, however impossible they were to achieve. War would come in Europe. Defense must begin at home, and the first line would be in the air. It was not only girls in their twenties who thought pilots were gods. In the huge program of rearmament which began that year, over two thousand new aircraft were ordered for immediate construction, a string of radar stations was to be built around the south and east coasts, and an accelerated training schedule was set up for pilots. As an added inducement, they were allowed to sign on for only four years instead of the normal twelve. By 1942, it was estimated, Britain's air defenses would be in good shape to deter German aggression.

Even then, there would be gaps. As Alexander Cadogan, later the permanent undersecretary of state for foreign affairs, wrote in his diary in early 1937, "We shall come to no good, and I don't see how we're to defend our interests here, and in the Med or in the Far East. Most depressing." In other words, even in 1942 it might not be possible to defend Hong Kong. A Japanese army had already invaded Manchuria and northern China, and showed every intention of moving south, but it appeared that the colony would have no air defense for the foreseeable future.

Among the first of the "short service" pilots was a tall, silent young man from the West Country who enlisted in 1937. He was sent to Perth, on the edge of the Scottish Highlands, where he was taught how to fly a Tiger Moth, training plane; having mastered the basics, he was sent to a training squadron in Wiltshire to learn about more powerful military aircraft like Ansons and Harts with their five hundred horsepower Rolls-Royce engines. Day after day, he practiced landings and approaches and sideslips and spins and aerobatics and night flying, and on September 11, 1937, he was awarded his pilot's wings. For Donald Hill, that was the highest point of his young life, a moment he would never forget.

What made it especially unforgettable was that it represented a double escape. When he first walked into the RAF recruiting office in London, he had been a trainee accountant living with his mother in a flat in Swiss Cottage. He had scraped through his preliminary and intermediate exams, but the thought of his finals depressed him almost as much as the prospect of a lifetime poring over account books and preparing tax returns.

Donald was not born to be an accountant. It was a realization that had only just crept up on him. The career had been thrust upon him, that was the phrase he used—"It was thrust upon me"—as though he had had no choice in the matter. He was not happy about it.

The person who had thrust it upon him was his mother, and becoming a pilot meant release from both accountancy and his mother's domination. What gradually dawned on him was something even more fundamental. In the air, he was in his element. In such a large man, and one so matter-of-fact, it was a surprising discovery. He did not have a pilot's flair like Derry McConnell; his instructors consistently marked him "average," and when he came through his Tiger Moth training, his report noted that he was "quiet, hard-working, and very keen, with high average results, but needs more spirit in his flying." Nevertheless, he had the balance and speed of a good athlete, and, more important, the desire to roam the vastness of the sky. In the brief happiness that was about to enfold him, one crucial ingredient was the pleasure he took in that newfound freedom.

In January 1938, after six months with a training squadron in Wiltshire, he was posted to the drably named Coast Artillery Co-operation Unit at Gosport. It was part of Coastal Command, and provided airborne spotters for earthbound gunners aiming at targets in the Channel. The task demanded exact calculation and suited his temperament. On his first flight at the base, he met Derry McConnell and their friendship was as immediate as it was unexpected. Donald was a mere pilot officer, the lowest form of flying life, and on a short service commission, while Derry was a regular, one rank higher, and had an extrovert dash that was the opposite of Donald's reserve. Nevertheless, they became the closest companions, and in March 1939, when Derry needed someone to take Brigit Kirrage to the RAF's twenty-first-anniversary dance, he turned automatically to Donald. Rather to his surprise, his friend's response was not enthusiastic.

It took some getting at the truth. Donald muttered that he was "not very keen on girls," but the fact was that in his mother's inhibiting presence he had hardly had any opportunity to become keen on them. Emotionally he was as ignorant about women as he had been about double-entry bookkeeping.

"You can't come to the party without a girl," Derry pointed out forcefully, "so you've got to get a girl, and here is one."

It was irrefutable logic, and gilding the lily Derry added that she was bound to be good-looking because her sister was utterly ravishing. In fact, as he made plain, the situation left a real friend with no choice. Derry's only transport was a sporty two-seater, but Pamela would only come if Brigit was invited, and with two girls to transport, a larger car was needed. And his quiet friend had just laid out £13 on a piece of kit that any pair of girls would be proud to be seen in.

On the afternoon of March 31, a huge car the size of a Bentley drew up in front of 2 Queen's Road in Tunbridge Wells. Even without the croaky, bullfrog rortling from its big three-liter engine, it would have been hard to miss. It had an immodestly huge chrome radiator grille, swollen silver headlights, and running boards wide enough to hold a sheep, and it weighed rather more than two tons. A company called Whitlock had built it, but the expense left them with no profit and they had gone bankrupt, survived only by a few hundred of their giant cars. Gleaming and engorged, this example dwarfed the thin Austin and Morris sedans in the street. Unfortunately its owner did not yet have a driving license, and so Derry had driven it for all but the last hundred yards.

Watching from the window, Pamela saw Derry get out of the passenger seat, followed by the driver, a tall, dark-haired young man wearing the blue uniform of the RAF. He was standing beside Derry when Pamela opened the front door.

"This is Donald," said Derry. "Donald Hill."

She would always remember how white the pilot's wings had appeared against his uniform.

They were invited in so that her mother could inspect the young men who were to look after her daughters. It gave Pamela the opportunity to satisfy her own curiosity. She liked Derry, but there was nothing new to learn about him. His friend offered more scope for imagination. The wild car, the romantic wings, the big shoulders—those were enough to catch her thoughts like wisps of candyfloss wrapping around a stick. She liked his quiet self-possession, and even her mother was reassured when he told her how careful he was about driving. He had a faint Devon accent, which sounded rural and trustworthy.

They quickly found out that the stuff about his driving was nonsense. Donald drove them to the end of the street, and there they switched over so that he was in the back with Brigit, his date for the dance. "He's barely been driving more than ten minutes," Derry said as he took the wheel.

She saw him smile, a sudden boy's grin as though he had got away with something. The road to Gosport curled over the chalky back of the South Downs and offered them a sight of the English Channel merging into the gray winter sky beyond, before they plunged down to the coast. They talked of friends and flying and films. The Gosport aerodrome specialized in gunnery and torpedo bombing, where the pilots had to approach low over the water to launch their weapons. It was possible to tell from the jokes about being overtaken by slow-moving seagulls that they had to sacrifice speed for precision, but there was nothing to suggest that what they did was particularly dangerous. Or perhaps events had now put all their lives in danger.

A fortnight earlier Hitler had annexed another of those middle European nations, and every newspaper in the land had printed the long list of his broken promises—in 1936, Saarland had been all Germany wanted; in March 1938, they had taken Austria and assured everyone that this satisfied their final requirement; then it was the Sudetenland, in September 1938. For a week, they had all been digging trenches and trying on gas masks, certain that the bombing would start at once. The prime minister had gone to

Munich, and Hitler had given a solemn promise: "This is the last territorial claim I have to make in Europe." They could all remember the relief when Neville Chamberlain flew back waving the agreement and saying it was "Peace in our time." Now Hitler's forces had taken over another gallant little nation, and everyone in England was living in a split world, with the present going on as peacefully as before and the future unwatchably violent. War was going to happen, and nothing could be done about it.

At the top of the Downs, Donald told Derry to stop and announced that he would drive the rest of the way. It alarmed Brigit to see how wobbly the Whitlock's steering was, but Pamela enjoyed watching Donald drive. The car was too big for the narrow strip of tarmac, but any cars they met hugged the verge at the sight of their bulging bonnet, and he barely slowed as they passed. His confidence was catching. Long before they arrived at Gosport, Pamela began to wish that she, rather than her sister, would be Donald's partner.

The girls were dropped at a hotel near the base so that they could change. Pamela had a strapless dress, silk taffeta in midnight blue, cut low in the back, boned to the waist, with a full, ruched skirt. It was a dress that bred confidence, that any girl would look good in, and Pamela knew she looked terrific. The question was, Would he think the same?

Presumably Derry was with him when they picked the girls up from the hotel, but only the most important details of that night were to survive through all the trials of a long life. Donald was in full evening dress: black tie, air force blue mess jacket with gold braided epaulettes and black satin lapels, and evening trousers. As was proper, they danced the first dance with their partners, and then changed over.

"Do you like dancing?" he asked.

"I love it," she said eagerly.

He smiled back at her. "So do I."

Standing six feet two inches tall, he towered over her, but it did not matter. He danced beautifully, and she felt herself floating in his arms. Telling the story, she laughed at herself for using such a tired phrase, but insisted that it was exactly how she had felt—dancing with him, she had floated. They danced a fox-trot, then a waltz, then a Charleston, and as dance followed dance, each of them found that it was only the other who would do as a partner.

There are moments that never fade. As it happened it etched itself into her being. "It's like a dream," she told herself. "It doesn't happen like this in real life." And to the end of her life those were the words she would always use to describe what she felt.

There was no point in pretending to keep up the formalities. What was happening was so electric that even those on the sidelines felt its intensity. "It's something that remains absolutely vivid in my memory," Brigit would say sixty years later. "I can see Pamela in her evening dress, it was dark blue taffeta, I can see the two of them walking very close together, Donald and her side by side, it's something I've never forgotten. And then they disappeared."

The fox-trots became more frenetic, the waltzes a little closer, but in public that was as far as one went. What hands spoke and eyes read had to be understood without other signals. If they could dance for long enough, they might never have to explain anything. Then there was a break for a buffet supper, and voices were needed again. She found herself laughing too loudly and trying to balance a tongue salad on her lap and at the same time say something eloquent enough to tell him how happy she felt. But afterward the band played louder, and they turned and whirled in each other's arms until every secret had been exchanged and he led her out into the privacy of the night and kissed her, sealing up the inadequate words in her mouth.

The national anthem had been played, the last dancers were leaving, and Brigit and Derry were sitting in the front of the vast Whitlock, when Donald and Pamela emerged from the darkness and climbed into the backseat.

The next day was April 1. When the two young airmen came to the hotel to pick up the sisters they had so carefully left there in the early hours of the morning, the porter informed them with suitable gravity that the Miss Kirrages had already left. Leaning over the banisters, the girls could hear their dates' confused voices—Was he sure? They were supposed to meet—had they left a message?—but as they ran down the stairs shouting "April Fool!," Pamela saw the look on Donald's face; she never forgot it. It was an expression of pure relief. Oh, she thought, sharing the emotion exactly, he *does* care.

Tunbridge Wells exacted its dues. Having returned the two girls to the safety of 2 Queen's Road, Donald was taken through the ritual of the middle classes at dinner, the need to address Mr. Kirrage as "sir," to pick out the correct fork, to reassure Mrs. Kirrage about the RAF's efficiency, to pass the port from right to left, while every atom of his being was concentrated on the hot hand clutching his beneath the tablecloth. It was a qualifying ritual. There would have been nothing dramatic had he failed, just a corrosive perception that he was not quite what he seemed to be.

Anxiously Pamela noted the obstacles, and admiringly saw him take each in his stride until at last the decanter of port came around. It would have been easy to push it over to her on his right, and if he did a social chasm would open up between the two men she loved most deeply. Everything that was really important to that generation was contained in silence. She willed him to do the correct thing, to show that he belonged there.

He pushed the port to his left. It seemed as though there was nothing he could not do utterly perfectly.

When she saw him to the door, he said quietly, "Can I ring you?"

"Yes," she whispered, "please ring." And she gave him what she hoped was an adoring smile.

He kissed her. There were maids and parents and sisters about and the kiss was quick and polite. She watched him walk down the path, then ran upstairs to her bedroom and hurled herself on her bed and burst into tears. It was the smile that was wrong. Gawping at him like a lovesick schoolgirl. And the hand-holding under the table, that had been completely wrong. How he must despise her for being so forward. She had shown no poise, no dignity, no self-restraint. Nothing she had done was worthy of him.

All through the next day, the black Bakelite telephone, Tunbridge Wells 744, stood squat and silent on the hall table. But that was a Sunday, and perhaps the RAF did not permit frivolous calls on a Sunday. There had to be a different reason why he did not ring on Monday. Or on Tuesday. Or on any other day of the week. It was not his fault. In all that he did, he had shown himself to be honorable and well-behaved. It was she who had behaved so badly. Now he would find someone else. It would not be difficult. There would be no shortage of girls to snap up a man like Donald.

A week passed. In memory the party grew even more vivid, as though it were a perfect work of art, from the opening discovery that the blue of her dress went so well with the color of his mess jacket, through the excitement of the dance, to the sunlit world laid open by his kiss, and the knowledge when she ran down the stairs to him in the hotel that he shared her feelings. For a few hours it had created a happiness higher and wider than any she had experienced. Now it was over. And she was to blame for ending it. Every day that the telephone did not ring made its ending more final. And it was her stupidity that kept it from ringing. Another week passed. Every day the distance between the happiness she had known and the misery she lived grew greater. It was all her fault.

At long last, in the middle of April, the black phone rang.

The voice at the other end was tentative. "Is Miss Pamela Kirrage there?"

She was, but hardly able to breathe. Like a fisherman who had thought the catch of a lifetime was gone but now felt the faintest tug on the end of the line, she had only one thought: not to frighten him off. "Oh it's you," she said as though the memory had almost lost itself among a multitude of distractions. "I did enjoy the dance, such fun." Her voice was light, bright, false.

His remained unsure. He had thought that perhaps she was only being polite when she had said he could ring her. "I didn't know whether you really wanted me to," he said. Then a hell of a flap had broken out, he explained, and life had suddenly become hectic. She jumped at the excuse. Of course that was the reason; she should have guessed. Apparently the international situation was getting worse. In the race to prepare its pilots for war, the RAF had extended training to fill every available hour of flying time. But she could not care less about the international situation. All she knew was that his not calling her had not been her fault.

"I thought you might have found someone else," she burst out.

"I'm not like that," he answered, and the reply was something else she never forgot. She believed it, partly because she wanted to, but partly because she sensed that it was true.

Yet on his side it had been a little more complicated than he suggested. He had been touched as deeply as she by the magic of the evening, and it had come as no less of a surprise. Finding himself with Brigit, he had been appalled to discover that she could be as bossy as his mother and was far sharper-tongued. Then, as he would in time tell his son, "before I knew what had happened I was dancing with Pamela, and I suddenly realized she was the most beautiful girl I had seen in my life." As he told the story, a note of wonder would enter his slow Devon voice. "I don't think I have ever seen a more beautiful girl. She had the most glorious eyes, and I completely fell for her. We spent the whole time dancing together. She was a beautiful dancer, and we danced all night."

The sheer force of the emotion stunned him. What he never admitted to Pamela was that he could have telephoned her earlier. It was true that the training schedule was being accelerated, but that was not the whole reason. A fortnight after the dance he faced a crucial exam in order to be promoted to flying officer, and his flying duties were canceled to allow him time to prepare for it. There had been nothing to stop him getting in touch with her except his own caution. He must have realized that once he saw Pamela again, he would have no more thoughts of study. If so, it was his last hesitation.

He told her that he had some leave due to him that weekend, and arranged to pick her up. They would drive somewhere. It did not matter where.

He arrived with an orchid in his hand, a piece of extravagance that she learned to appreciate over the weeks ahead. A pilot officer's pay on the brink of war was £17 a month, and once the petrol and the car's fiendishly expensive repair bills had been paid, there was little left for lavish gestures.

The details of where they went that day merged into the glow of the golden summer. Barely a weekend passed when they were not together. Crowding close to each other on the Whitlock's benchlike seat, they drove off into the country, to the seaside, to the cool shade of Epping Forest and the long sunlit rides of the New Forest. In 1939, the southeast of England was enjoying its finest summer in years, with day after day of sunshine. The May blossom came early in the hedgerows and the apple and cherry blossom in the orchards. Then the white flowers gave way to green leaves, and in the summer heat the hop vines climbed their poles with tropical speed until the gardens looked like jungles.

They drove down narrow lanes where the dust rose in a cloud behind them, and stopped at village shops with painted signs advertising tea and scones with strawberry jam and clotted cream for 1/6d. Occasionally, when only the best would match their mood, they took the Whitlock to the Criterion restaurant in Piccadilly Circus and invested a week's pay in the best American highballs. Eating there was out of the question, but just down the street there was the Lyons Corner House, in the Strand, where they could have a three-course meal served by a smart, white-aproned waitress for the price of a Criterion highball.

They held hands and kissed, and began to find out who they were and what attracted each to the other. His quietness seemed endlessly appealing. At twenty-six he was older than most of the RAF's young guns, but his reserve made their puppyish enthusiasm seem adolescent.

He had come late to flying, but there was another reason for his more adult manner.

His family came from south Devon, near Sidmouth, where they had farmed for generations. Samuel Hill, his father, had bought Leighs Farm, a large dairy farm, overlooking Lyme Bay and had become one of the most successful milk producers in the area. Donald was the second of three children, with an elder sister nicknamed Billie and a younger brother called Ralph. Numbers had always come easily to Donald; at the local school in Branscombe he was recognized as something of a math prodigy, taking every available prize. To Maud, his mother, this was evidence that he was a genius, too good for a life on the land. Perhaps for that reason, or perhaps because she herself was desperate to escape, she insisted that they give up the farm so that he could receive the best education money could buy. In 1924 Samuel Hill reluctantly sold his beloved farm, and the family moved to a large house in Honiton; eleven-year-old Donald was sent to Mount Radford, a prep school in Exeter with a reputation for high academic standards. Barely a year later, his father went out rabbit shooting and did not return alive. It was one of the earliest secrets that Donald confided to Pamela.

"The story was he was trying to get over a hedge, and he slipped and the gun went off," he said. "I just don't know, I've always had a feeling at the back of my mind it wasn't an accident—that possibly he shot himself. He was only forty-seven and a crack shot, not the sort of person to have an accident like that. It's possible that there might have been trouble between my father and my mother, but I just don't know."

Donald's doubts were justified, for although the coroner ruled that his father's death was accidental, that verdict hardly tallied with the evidence. Samuel had been found on hands and knees in a stream, with his shotgun underneath his body. A shot had been fired against his right temple from a range close enough to singe his hair, and it had blown away the top of his skull. The court's sympathies were accorded to the victim's family, and a huge crowd filled St. Michael's Church in Honiton for the funeral, but once the facts emerged local opinion arrived at a different verdict. Samuel Hill, it was generally agreed, had put the barrel of his gun to his head and killed himself out of despair at losing the farm he adored.

Not surprisingly, the boy's educational career failed to flourish. At sixteen he was brought back to Honiton to go to the local private school, All Hallows, but when he was eighteen, Maud decided on a new ambition for him. Samuel had left a substantial sum of money in trust for the education of his children, and there was enough, too, for his widow to buy her own home. In 1932 she boarded Billie out with relatives, sent Ralph to a boarding school in Sussex, and took Donald to live with her in London. It was not a move he wanted to make. His memories of his Devon childhood were of freedom, of stealing apples from a nearby orchard, of being endlessly indulged by a father whom he loved. Samuel had been no disciplinarian. He never lifted a hand to his son. Sometimes Donald thought he should have, especially after their neighbor caught him pinching the apples. But his father was too gentle. His mother, on the other hand, was something different. No one in the family, least of all his father, was able to resist her forceful character. Like the others, Donald passively accepted the plans she made for him.

"I imagine my father wanted me to become a farmer," he told Pamela, "but my mother's very ambitious, and she had other ideas."

Determined to make the best use of his gift for numbers, she had him apprenticed to a firm of accountants, Clemons Midgely, and there he might have remained had it not been for the country's sudden need for pilots. His father's death had required him to take on the role of senior male in the family. To cope with his mother's domineering nature, he had learned to suppress his own wants and inclinations. The ugly rumors about his father's death had taught him not to dwell on the emotions it aroused in him. Flying revealed a romantic streak he had never suspected in himself, and now a beautiful woman who loved him as he loved her was revealing depths of feeling of which he had known virtually nothing until then.

In the next few weeks, they realized how improbable it was that they should have fallen in love. They were like reverse images of one another: Pamela had come from an extraordinarily secure background and grown up volatile and passionate, while Donald had developed solidity and maturity against a background of anxiety and rootlessness. In the course of a single summer, each appeared to borrow something from the other, she growing more adult, he learning to relax.

One Saturday, they found themselves driving through Epping Forest. Impulsively he swung off the road down a forestry track, which bounced through the green-dappled shade. Showing off with one hand on the steering wheel and the other around her waist, he failed utterly to see a tree stump, which tore away the Whitlock's running board with a hideous clatter of exploding rivets. A younger Donald would have been made distraught by his carelessness, but this one laughed. The big car began to look its age. A few days later, while reversing into a parking space, he happened to catch Pamela's eye as he turned to look over his shoulder. One passing glance was not enough. He could not tear his gaze away, and with his eyes locked on hers ran gently into the car behind. The bumper absorbed most of the impact, and it did not matter that the chrome was scratched or the metal buckled. So long as they were together, nothing mattered.

Through the heat of summer, the inexorable descent into war accelerated and every moment together became more precious. They had disagreements. Accustomed to having her own way, Pamela resented furiously the time that the RAF demanded of its pilots, and for all Donald's protestations refused to believe that it could not find other officers to undertake the mundane chores of inspecting stores or filing reports.

His frustrations were no less powerful and irrational. The thought of Pamela modeling lingerie, parading half-naked up and down beneath the eyes of strangers, provoked his jealousy, and more than that—a feeling that his girl should not have to display her body to earn her living. For the first time in her adult life, Pamela acknowledged a will stronger than her own. She tore up her modeling contract and, with the impetuosity of a romantic heroine, took up the most self-denying work she could find: cooking in a youth club in Bermondsey.

"How I must have loved him," she sighed, looking back. "I adored modeling and the freedom it gave me—nobody else could have made me give it up."

With the cool appraisal of hindsight, she could see that their opposites fitted. Emotionally, she was the more extravagant, he the more stable, but while she drew confidence from his calmness, it was apparent that with her he expanded and let himself give expression to feelings which might otherwise have remained buried. It was as though in her he had found an element that welcomed him as completely and unexpectedly as the air. He was learning to let go, to fly emotionally.

Years later, when he wrote to her recalling their summer together, each tiny incident had become charged with the romance of that golden season: "The evening you drank too many highballs and developed girlish giggles—early morning cups of coffee in some snack bar—I lost my hat in a tea house—nearly got chewed up by a pack of hounds. Our last few days in London. I remember everything as if it were yesterday."

Others were struck by the quality of the man who had fallen in love with Pamela. Although the youngest of the sisters, Sheila had an intuitive good sense that carried weight in the Kirrage family, and Pamela waited anxiously for her opinion. Fortunately, her reaction was favorable. It helped that Donald was tall and good-looking, but what struck her most was how quick his mind was. His quiet, reserved manner made it easy to miss, but Sheila grasped at once that Donald was a very clever man.

Once she had given her approval, he was adopted as part of the family. He would stay with them for the weekend, playing tennis on the court in their garden, and on Saturday night take Pamela to a dance. The next day, flying out of Gosport, he would detour over Tunbridge Wells, and swoop low over the rooftops until one of the girls ran out into the garden to wave at him.

He might almost have been regarded as an extra brother, except that an unbrotherly problem grew inexorably from their pleasure. Until they met, neither of them had found a partner who excited them physically. Now their kisses grew longer and more passionate. In the heat of one of the hottest Julys on record, fingers grew heavy and would not lift unaided from a breast or a thigh. In the dark, limbs stretched involuntarily, and by day desire weighed on the brain like a thunderstorm.

One evening they went to a dance in Windsor, and when it ended they could neither leave each other nor satisfy what they wanted. They kissed until their lips were sore, and drove slowly through the sallow dawn clutching hands as though something might turn up which would relieve the terrible longing. For an hour they escaped it in the unromantic surroundings of a transport café, where they drank mugs of tea and stifled desire in a vast plate of bacon and eggs. The ordinariness of the meal brought them back to reality, and they smiled at each other as though they had come through an ordeal. But when they went outside again, the sun had risen above the horizon, and they could feel its rays relight the warmth of their dangerously combustible bodies.

It seemed hardly possible that they would not soon fall into bed or simply lie down where they were and make love. But it was 1939, and most brides were virgin when they married. Nowhere was that more true than in Tunbridge Wells, where it was unthinkable that a well-brought-up girl should have had sex before marriage. Pamela was terrified of becoming pregnant. Nothing could have been more dreadful for her and her family, and for Donald. It would have been a disaster.

Although the consequences for men were less drastic, they were expected to observe the same canons of behavior. An officer who made an unmarried woman pregnant would have to resign his commission. A gentleman would lose his reputation and be branded a rotter. Sexuality itself, so openly discussed today, was scarcely talked about except in medical terms or as a music hall joke. Smart young people could earn a reputation for raciness by referring to Krafft-Ebing or Freud.

"I can remember the embarrassment when an older woman told me that Miss Ferguson and Miss Body were lesbians," Pamela exclaimed. "I didn't even know what 'lesbian' meant until she explained. I was so innocent."

By itself the sexual restraint might seem inexplicable, but it was part of a much wider pattern of self-restraint. Rules which had been shaken by the slaughter of the First World War, and by the consequent imbalance of the sexes during the 1920s, were reestablishing their power. Throughout the Western world, the Jazz Age was in retreat before the forces of conformity. The retreat was epitomized by the censorship imposed on Hollywood by the Hays Office, which prohibited any displays of nudity, or even the portrayal of a woman in a bedroom unless she had at least one foot on the floor. In the newly fascist and communist countries, even more than in the old kingdoms and republics, there was pressure to regulate individual behavior in what was seen as the wider interest of society.

The films they watched carried the same message. In *The Drum,* Roger Livesey, as a beleaguered British colonial officer, leaves the safety of the fort knowing that he will be killed by the wicked khan, but prepared to make the sacrifice because his death will inspire others and thus save the empire. In the United States, Jimmy Cagney played a condemned killer in *The Public Enemy* who agrees to fake cowardice as he is taken to the gas chamber so that his contemptible example will dissuade impressionable kids from following his criminal career.

Fashion mirrored the restoration of the old rules. Women's clothes had almost abandoned the hard tubular shape of the 1920s. Now fabrics were soft and clinging—crepe, sharkskin, and silk; dresses were calf-length, cut on the bias to show off the curve of the body, and nipped in at the waist with a sash or belt. The last remnant of the masculine look was a jaunty line in fedoralike hats with tilted brims. Meanwhile men's clothes had drifted toward an almost defiantly uncivilized male look. Suits were made of tweed, preferably hairy and Harris; beneath their jackets they wore Fair Isle sweaters and loosely knotted ties, and on their feet, solid brown brogues. The sexes knew their places once more.

It was this unspoken pressure toward conformity that constrained Donald and Pamela. Later generations sometimes look back on the 1930s with a nostalgic envy for its innocence and honesty, but the era was all of a piece. The sexuality and the clothes, the attitudes of Hollywood and Tunbridge Wells, the same moral values ruled them all.

Nevertheless, before the summer was over, it had become evident that either a wedding must take place or convention would be blasted apart. One Sunday as Donald was having breakfast in Queen's Road, Pamela's mother asked him bluntly what his intentions were. Between themselves, he and Pamela had talked vaguely about marriage, but now a definite answer was required. He felt nervous, and stuttered over the crucial phrase, "We want to get married." She countered with the traditional question, "What are your prospects?," and he began to feel that it was all slipping away. On £17 a month he could hardly support the Whitlock and his mess bill, let alone a wife as well. But he need not have worried. For the first time in her life, Mrs. Kirrage's eldest daughter was in love. It would take a lot to persuade Pamela's mother of his unsuitability. Not even when he careered off the tennis court and destroyed a bed of fragile peonies did she object.

On a walk over the South Downs, Donald asked Pamela to marry him. It came as no surprise, but she cried all the same before she could say yes.

The next weekend, he drove her with more than usual speed up to London, and stopped outside Gieves, tailor and jeweler to the armed forces. He left her outside while he went in himself, and emerged a few minutes later with a small box. At a quiet table in the Criterion he produced the ring, a gold hoop with a single diamond surrounded by diamond half-circles. It was far too expensive for a newly promoted flying officer to pay for outright, but Gieves knew that an officer would not fail to pay a debt, and it was put on his account. As it turned out, the bill was not settled until after the war.

For one blissful week, Pamela and Donald tasted the delight of being an engaged couple. Her family and his mother were told, and gave their blessing. Congratulations frothed up from friends and relations, and plans were made for a wedding in the autumn. To cement the bond, she bought him a gold ring and slipped it on his little finger. Then, unexpectedly, he was given a fortnight's leave.

It should have been good news, but she knew by his expression that it was bad. It was preembarkation leave, because in July he was being posted to Singapore. Nothing could have prepared her for the total extinction of all her happiness. In desperation, she clung to him tightly as though that might prevent him going.

"We'll be married whatever happens," he promised. "Next year you will come out to Singapore, and we'll have the wedding there."

It was all she had for comfort. They spent the last days of his leave together in London. All she wanted to do was cry. To keep herself from bursting into tears, she joined in his elaborate plans for what they would do after they got married. They would have a vast wedding, and a sumptuous honeymoon, but most important of all, they would spend their wedding night in the Savoy Hotel. It was a dream to which she would cling for many years.

On July 12, 1939, he drove for the last time to the Bermondsey youth club where she worked. The only place they could find to be alone was a room at the top of the building. All the kisses and unvoiced desires had to be compressed into one final embrace; then he pulled himself away and walked downstairs. Outside the front door, he looked up and through a blur of tears saw her on a small balcony waving to him. He waved back and went down to the street. A policeman was examining the Whitlock's out-of-date license and jotting down details in his notebook.

"I'm sorry," Donald said. "I've been ordered abroad, and I had to come and say good-bye to my fiancée before I left."

The policeman looked at him and the sight of a young pilot with tear-reddened eyes must have touched him. He put away his notebook. "I don't know if you'll get away with it," he said, "but the best of luck."

From the balcony, Pamela watched the man she loved get into his big black car. It began to move. A hand waved from the window. Then the car rounded a corner and he was gone.

3

Ciphers and Codes

. . . those obstinate questionings
Of sense and outward things,
Fallings from us, vanishings . . .

—WILLIAM WORDSWORTH,
"INTIMATIONS OF IMMORTALITY"

The opening sentence of Parker Hitt's *Manual for the Solution of Military Cyphers* lists the four ingredients needed to break a code. In order of importance, they are "perseverance, careful methods of analysis, intuition, luck." As events were to show, Philip Aston had an abundance of the first three qualities. It was the last that he lacked.

The weakest point of a code is the key. Since this must be known to the person who is to read the message, the lucky codebreaker may find help at two points: the encoding stage and the deciphering stage. Even in the most famous, sustained, and demanding exercise in cryptanalysis—the reading of the Enigma codes used by the German navy during the Second World War—the codebreakers at Bletchley Park outside Cambridge relied on this sort of luck. They had versions of the Enigma encrypting machines, and thus knew the technology used to create the constantly changing codes, but at crucial periods they acquired codebooks retrieved from damaged U-boats. It was Aston's bad luck that the encoder and intended reader of Russels Mathematical Tables had been the same man, and he had died taking the key with him. If he was to find a way into Donald Hill's mind, he would have to rely on perseverance, analysis, and intuition alone.

Aston understood numbers almost aesthetically, and derived a deep satisfaction from their undeviating logic. Almost the only decorations in his drab office with its gray linoleum floor and cream walls were the photographs of his wife and two children on his desk and the rows of books with titles like *Chaos and Fractal Theory* and *Complex Analyses and Applications* arranged on shelves above his computer. At thirty-six, with chronic lung problems, and a young family to bring up on an academic's salary, he might have been forgiven for worrying about health or money. Instead, mathematics seemed to give him the serenity of a priest secure in his faith.

His first attempt on Donald Hill's code was aimed at discovering whether he had merely substituted numbers for letters. Knowing the frequency of letters in English makes it simple to test for a substitution cipher. Aston wrote a quick computer program to list the frequency with which different numerals appeared on the first page. The top five were 5, 20, 1, 14, 15. It seemed almost disappointingly simple. "E" was the fifth letter in the alphabet, "T" the twentieth, "A" the first. Could Donald Hill simply have used the basic schoolchild's substitution, $1 = A$, $2 = B$? Using that key, he programmed the computer to substitute letters for the numbers on the first page of the diary.

It took seconds for the numerals on his screen to be replaced by letters, and for their frequency to be computed. Sure enough, the order was E, T, A, O, N, and so on, following the characteristic order almost exactly. With his first effort, Aston had blown away part of Donald Hill's code. He was almost embarrassed.

Then he tried to make sense of the letters that now filled the mesh of tiny boxes on his screen. They should have made up words. Unlike numbers, which may contain many different patterns, letters resolve themselves into just one pattern that makes sense: words. And if words did not appear in the usual fashion, read from left to right, then a reader had to find them reversed, or running vertically or diagonally. It was like a puzzle. Somewhere in the chaos, the letters would become orderly and could be read and a meaning could be understood. But that meaning was not to be found in their present arrangement. However much Aston studied the screen, and later the printout of the diary's opening page, no words appeared. When he switched off the computer on that first evening, it was with a sense of something like satisfaction. This might turn out to be a task worthy of a mathematician.

The basic substitution cipher was only the outer covering. Inside it, Donald Hill had evidently constructed another. The problem was to identify it. The computer's gray screen offered no clues, so Aston decided to go back to the diary itself. Its neatness was remarkable. Row after meticulous row of numerals running across the full width of the page, split up by columns exactly half an inch apart to make a grid of 1,081 tiny boxes. And each box held four minute numerals.

As he examined the first page, his attention was caught by some faint pencil marks. Some numbers had been marked out with a little square penciled around them. He counted along the rows. The thirty-fourth number had a square around it. With mounting anticipation, he discovered that so did the 68th, the 102nd, the 136th, and so on. Each square enclosed a multiple of 34. Then, in the margin, he found an almost obliterated arrow pointing to the right, with the number 340 written beside it.

Aston drew breath and considered the possibilities. The 340 might refer to something else, but the coincidence of that 34 was too great to be overlooked. Cautiously, he let himself hope that Donald had simply added a zero as another part of his camouflage. In which case, he thought, trying to contain his excitement, the arrow must indicate that the numerals are to be read from left to right, with some sort of limit being reached at the thirty-fourth. What then? For want of anything better, he decided that then a new row would begin below the first. He went back to the original page of numerals on his computer screen, and tentatively rearranged the dense forest into this new, neater shape, with each row restricted to thirty-four numerals. As the pattern imposed itself, he almost gave a whoop of triumph. Another part of the jigsaw had fallen into place.

At the end of the thirty-third row, there was a box with four zeroes, as though it marked the end of a section. He made another block with thirty-four numerals in each row, and sure enough the thirty-third row ended with 0000. He was certain now that this was the way the diary should be arranged. As though he needed the confirmation, he found on the margin of the first page a second faint arrow, this time pointing down and with the figure 330 beside it.

Now the pattern he had was a block—thirty-four numbers in a row, thirty-three rows in a block. If he could believe the evidence, he had cracked Donald Hill's code. It was time to run again the program to translate numbers to letters. Once more the magical transformation took place on the screen, and again Aston scanned the arrangement of letters, hoping to find that they had made themselves into words. As he studied the screen, his excitement faded. The diary kept its secret. The pattern had changed, but the letters still made no sense. There must be yet another step built into the code.

When Aston first mentioned the code to his wife, Linda, he had described it as a diversion, an interesting little challenge he had set himself. By the middle of March, she guessed from his increasingly abstracted silences that it had grown more important. Without Aston's realizing it, the diary was gradually working its way into his mind until he could not shake it free. The longer he worked on it, the more intently his mind would return to the problem of the cipher, and the more obsessed he became.

In fact, any code sets a special trap for its would-be breaker. Making sense of a perplexing world is what the mind has evolved to do. When it is confronted with something strange and incomprehensible, it strives to perceive a pattern in these random stimuli. In psychological terms, the moment at which it recognizes a pattern is called a Gestalt perception—literally, a shape perception. The urge to make that mental construct is so deeply rooted that neuropsychologists today believe it to be innate. Thus someone who sets out to decipher a code is engaging in a highly specialized version of what people do constantly in everyday life, but in this case failure carries a particular danger. To be perpetually frustrated in the search for a pattern is to feel that the brain is failing or that the world is mad. A cryptanalyst who knows that apparently meaningless letters must contain a meaning is especially vulnerable. William Friedmann, head of the U.S. Signals Intelligence Service, which eventually broke the "Purple" machine, Japan's version of the Enigma, suffered a complete nervous breakdown in December 1940 and spent almost four months in the hospital; he was never able to work at the same intensity again. At Bletchley Park, codebreakers were closely monitored, yet frequently worked themselves to the point of mental collapse before they could be taken off the job. Even after being relieved, they found it hard to stop their minds from churning away at the problem.

There was at least a third step built into Hill's code. Of that Aston was sure. The text was somewhere among the scattered letters on the screen. His task was to find out the key formula Hill had used to mix them up, and use it to rearrange them into their original sentences.

Now began long hours of painstaking work. Since single letters offered no clue, he began to search for digraphs—pairs of letters. Centuries of research had shown that in normal English, the letter "h" was to be found paired with two other letters, "t" and "e," more often than in any other combination. From the ubiquitous "the" through pronouns like "she" and "that" and adverbs like "though" and "here," the digraphs "th" and "he" appear again and again. Aston tried to pair off the letters in different ways, reading them forward, backward, and up and down. When this produced nothing, he searched for less obvious links. He counted the letters between each "t" in a block of letters and each "h," hoping for a regular number of intervals that would indicate another pattern. When this failed, he tried to re-late the position of each "t" in one block to every "h" in the next. Through the last weeks of February and the first weeks of March, he wrote program after program, sweeping electronic nets through the clutter in an attempt to catch its invisible patterns. Time after time the net came in empty, and on each occasion he tried to imagine another way in which the natural pairing could have been concealed.

As his frustrations increased, Aston began to think more about the man who had unknowingly set him this task. The care he had taken to conceal his message went much further than the straightforward disguise that he had expected of someone in a prison camp. This, the most frustrating step he had encountered, was the third that Donald Hill had built into his code. It was the work not of an amateur but of a person who enjoyed the intellectual challenge of concealment for its own sake.

4

The Battle for Hong Kong

She tells her love while half asleep,
In the dark hours,
With half-words whispered low:
As Earth stirs in her winter sleep
And puts out grass and flowers
Despite the snow,
The falling snow.

—ROBERT GRAVES,
"SHE TELLS HER LOVE WHILE HALF ASLEEP"

Nobody knows how he or she will react to a violent attack until it happens. It calls up responses buried too deep for normal use. Even in war, where violence is the norm and participants are specifically prepared for it, the first attack reveals depths of character which no other situation evokes. For Donald Hill, as for every other person in Hong Kong, the Japanese onslaught that took place in December 1941 was to reveal aspects of his inner self in a manner which could not be camouflaged.

When he said good-bye to Pamela, the pain of leaving her had plunged him into savage despair. An unsuspecting young airman with whom he shared a cabin on the troopship to Singapore made the mistake of trying to tease him out of his gloomy mood. Suddenly Donald leaped across the cabin and, as he later confessed, "hammered the hell out of him." The days at Gosport, and especially the few months with Pamela, had been like no other. Even golden childhood could not compare. To the end of his time, he would always say quite simply, "Those were the happiest days of my life."

Before leaving he had traded in the Whitlock to pay for its last lot of repairs. To remind him of his happiness he had only Pamela's photograph, the ring she had given him on their engagement, and her cigarette case. As the troopship plunged through the Bay of Biscay, sweated into the Red Sea, and rolled across the Indian Ocean, he went morosely about his duties, seasick and depressed.

It was in Singapore that he discovered how much he had been changed. He who once was "not very keen on girls" suddenly found them irresistible, and the attraction was mutual. He was tall and good-looking, with an inexhaustible appetite for dancing, and, as married women seemed to sense more hungrily than others, there was a banked-up reserve of sensuality in him waiting to be released. His most frequent partner beneath the slowly turning fans in the ballroom of the Raffles Hotel was the thirty-five-year-old wife of a naval officer who had the misfortune to be away at sea on night patrols.

He was not proud of himself. His behavior in Singapore embarrassed him. He could not shake off the misery of parting from Pamela, and in her absence grasped at the opportunity of a purely physical affair. "I loved dancing, and this woman she loved dancing too—her husband was always on duty at night," he said by way of excuse. On the tape recording, there is a short uncomfortable silence, then: "I'm afraid I was a rather naughty young man."

Their relationship could not be kept secret in Singapore's expatriate community. Gossip there was such a finely developed art that when Somerset Maugham came to stay in the 1930s, he was able to lift chunks of it almost verbatim to serve as the basis of some of his best short stories. Word of Donald's affair reached his superiors. Frequently he was sent upcountry to the airfields being opened up in Malaya to deter the Japanese, but whenever he returned the relationship blazed up again. In less dangerous times, the scandal might have ruined his career, but he was recognized not only as a pilot whose skill was now rated "above average," but as a first-class officer. Promoted to flight lieutenant, he was transferred in June 1941 to Hong Kong.

To his embarrassment the naval officer's wife followed him there, swearing that she would never leave him. Firmly he pointed out to her the central reality of all his thoughts, that he intended to spend the rest of his life with Pamela Kirrage. "There were a lot of tears," he remembered, "but I was engaged and I was going to stick to that."

It did not prevent him having an affair with another married woman, the Chinese wife of a Hong Kong police officer. Her name was Foo Ling, which became Florrie. Born into a Westernized family, she too was in her mid-thirties and loved dancing. This was a deeper relationship, about which Donald felt guilty and confused for years afterward. In Hong Kong's last, pleasure-filled months of peace before the Japanese invasion, what seemed important was that she had great beauty and sophistication, and danced superbly. It was when war came that her other qualities emerged—courage, ingenuity, and an inexhaustible capacity for love. Yet despite her attractions, his underlying sadness did not lift. When he looked back on those six months before war broke out in December 1941, he confessed that he was "not too happy," and the opening of his diary showed that it was intended to be the record of his actions rather than of his own gloomy feelings.

Until war came, Hong Kong was the solid outpost of an empire that covered a third of the world's territory and contained a quarter of its population. Or so it seemed, for the reality was that Hong Kong's defense depended on Japan's fear of provoking such a formidable enemy as Britain. At the highest military level, the Committee of Imperial Defence in London, strategists had accepted that the colony lay too close to Japan and was too unwieldy to be defended. Thus British policy toward Japan was simply to avoid provoking her hostility unnecessarily. In 1940 Winston Churchill had bluntly written, "If Japan goes to war with us, there is not the slightest chance of holding Hong Kong or relieving it. It is most unwise to increase the loss we shall suffer there. Instead of increasing the garrison, it ought to be reduced to a symbolic scale. We must avoid frittering away our resources on untenable positions."

Nevertheless, among all the overseas postings that the empire offered, Hong Kong was the serviceman's favorite. The climate was almost tropical—steamily hot in summer and merely cool in winter. Although nothing like the commercial powerhouse it became after the war, the colony was successful enough to maintain two luxury hotels, a range of superb restaurants, and, closer to the military heart, pubs, beaches, brothels, and dance halls without number. In the words of a 1930s tourist brochure, visitors would find there "the exciting and the exotic, the breathtaking and the colourful—everything in fact that typifies the Wondrous East, hand in hand with the comfort of an up-to-date British Colony."

As such, Hong Kong illustrated in graphic fashion the empire's strengths and prejudices. Its governor was invariably British, as were most of the members of its Executive Council, but commercially its mixture of races competed on equal terms. Apart from the great trading names, like Jardine Matheson and Swire, the richest families in the colony were Chinese, and several had been appointed to the Council. Nevertheless, the underlying power structure could be deduced from where people lived. In Kowloon, all but the wealthiest Chinese had their homes at sea level; farther inland and a little higher were the Japanese; then came the Indians, and after them the continental Europeans, beginning with the Portuguese and ending with the French. Above them all lived the British. The same distinction existed on Hong Kong island. There the crucial frontier was a street in the foothills called May Road and, in the only slightly ironic words of one Hong Kong history, "from May Road upward to heaven was the exclusive preserve of those who gloried in the name of Briton."

A similar form of unofficial racial segregation separated the working areas of prostitutes, courtesans, and bar girls. The Europeans operated farthest up the hill, mostly in Lyndhurst Terrace, which was known from its string of brothels simply as the Line. Their acknowledged leader, a beautiful Russian blonde with the impeccably Anglicized name of Ethel Morrison, became so wealthy that she was accepted as readily in the cathedral as at the racetrack. This combination of administrative rectitude, social hypocrisy, and commercial license gave Hong Kong life an extraordinary intensity that mesmerized its inhabitants. Outside the frontier, the Japanese had been occupying the neighboring province of Kwangtung since 1938 and evidence of their tightening grip in China came from the steady stream of refugees coming into the colony. But inside, the parties and the moneymaking only grew louder and more frenzied. When they ended, they did so with a suddenness which took everyone by surprise.

On the morning of Saturday, December 6, Flight Lieutenant Donald Hill joined a farewell party for his retiring commanding officer. The talk turned to the endlessly deferred possibility of a squadron of fighters being sent out to give protection to the airfield and their tiny force of two Walrus seaplanes and three Vildebeeste torpedo bombers. As with so much of the British empire's defenses, the chief function of these aircraft was display. A Walrus surging up from the sea between curtains of foam, or the immense span of the Vildebeeste—almost 50 feet from wingtip to wingtip—roaring low over the rooftops made an impressive spectacle for those who had never seen any other plane. Put up against the latest generation of Japanese fighters, which could fly at more than 300 miles per hour, they would be death traps. The Vildebeeste, which was a biplane with an open cockpit, had a top speed of 156 miles per hour, and the firing rings for the torpedoes it was designed to carry had been removed. Instead it was used mainly for reconnaissance, although it could carry two small five-hundred-pound bombs. A year earlier, the Air Ministry had declared it obsolete, but its replacement had not yet arrived. There were rumors that some fighters would be sent to protect their antique bombers, and an Australian pilot called Frank Hennessy had arrived to set up a fighter operations room. No one quite believed reinforcement would arrive, but at the beginning of December the Air Ministry in London authorized the construction of a new five-hundred-yard runway. Work was due to begin on Monday, December 8.

That Saturday afternoon, Donald Hill and his new commanding officer, Wing Commander Sullivan, ran through the details of what needed to be done. Obstacles that had been placed on the existing runway to prevent its being used by enemy aircraft would have to be moved, and a detachment from the Hong Kong Defence Force Volunteers taking over guard duties had to be warned that there would be contractors on site.

Physically, the two officers made an incongruous pair as they surveyed the airfield—Sullivan, stocky and red-haired, nick-named, inevitably, Ginger; Hill towering over him, with dark hair and black hawk's-wing eyebrows—but in character they were still more unlike. As his appearance and nickname indicated, Sullivan was energetic and quick-tempered, with an unquenchable desire to spur up people and ideas. Hill appeared to possess the solidity of a big man, slow to show his mood or even his thoughts. His fellow officers regarded him as "a sound man," conscientious and careful, though a little remote. Despite these differences, he and Sullivan worked well together.

By mid-afternoon their work was finished, and the weekend began. Some of the small RAF detachment went racing at the Happy Valley racetrack, but for others there were rugby matches, football, swimming, and sailing. All of these were mixed up with preparations for Christmas. Later, the atmosphere of shopping and partying struck many people as unduly frenetic—"like Brussels before Waterloo," one participant later commented. At the colony's most luxurious hotel, the Hong Kong, the famous

Gripps restaurant and ballroom were booked solid until Christmas for dances and parties. Those were the smartest events, but the colony's prosperity could be seen, too, in the fantastic entertainments put on at the Rose Room and Roof Garden at the Peninsula Hotel, and the dances organized at private homes.

"The evening ended at a typically bright young colonial party with discreet flirtations everywhere, sleek beautiful women and dashing young men in uniform," wrote Emily Hahn, a sharp-eyed American-born resident of Hong Kong, "all being incredibly childish, so it seemed to me . . . we played our charades, we drank at the funny little bar, we giggled."

In the red-light district of Wanchai, the bar girls in their thigh-length cheongsams offered more adult entertainment, and most of those among the six-thousand-strong garrison who preferred alcohol to sex were crammed into the bars along Nathan Road.

Despite the general refusal to believe that the colony faced any real threat, Donald Hill took two measures which suggested that he viewed the situation more seriously, or at least more conscientiously. On Sunday morning, he loaded one of the Vildebeestes with two five-hundred-pound bombs, climbed into the cockpit, and went out on a reconnaissance flight to see what targets the colony would present to an enemy pilot.

In the clear sunlit air, the scene looked too peaceful to be easily imagined as a battlefield. The streets were filled with traffic, ferries carved white wakes through the blue water, and a green-and-red tartan of intensively cultivated fields decorated the countryside. From three thousand feet the three parts of Hong Kong were quite distinct. Disappearing into the haze of the Chinese mainland was the crumpled countryside of the New Territories. It was from here that any military force would attack. Directly below Donald, the sprawl of Kowloon stretched inland, from the long waterfront lined with tall brick-built stores and warehouses to a dense cluster of streets packed into a narrow coastal strip and eventually to straggling suburbs and steep hillsides dotted with the substantial red-tiled houses of the wealthy. A few hundred yards offshore lay Hong Kong island, consisting of a crest of jagged hills with Victoria, the colony's capital, at its southern end.

For years, there had been plans to build a defensive line to separate the New Territories from the mainland. Stretching from Gin Drinkers' Bay on the south coast to Tide Cove on the north, it would consist of pillboxes, barbed wire, and trenches, but there had never been a great sense of urgency about it. After three years only one short section by the Jubilee Reservoir had been completed. Nevertheless, the colony's defense required the enemy to be held up in the New Territories for perhaps a week. Then the defenders would start to withdraw through the hilly countryside, where several commanding peaks offered the chance of slowing the attack still further. The next line of defense was in the crowded streets of Kowloon, and finally the defenders would fall back across the narrow strait and make their final stand on the island of Hong Kong itself. There they would hold out for as long as was needed for a British or American fleet to appear over the horizon, or a Chinese army to attack the invaders from the rear. The plan was to keep the Japanese at bay for as long as three months.

In the previous month, Donald had taken up both the governor, Sir Mark Young, and the commander of the colony's forces, Major General C. M. Maltby, to show them what they might have to defend. But this time he made himself view the scene as a Japanese pilot might, and beside the short landing strip of the airfield, a target immediately presented itself. The two other Vildebeestes were lined up in the open side by side; farther out, in the blue waters of Kowloon Bay, the fat Walruses swung close together at their mooring buoys. When Donald landed, he ordered the old torpedo bombers to be dispersed to opposite corners of the airfield, and he parked the one he had flown out of sight under the trees by the tennis court. There was nothing to be done about the seaplanes. Then he took another precaution.

The diary was his secret. During the First World War, soldiers on both sides had kept journals and when these were captured the intelligence services had found them an invaluable source of information. In consequence the Ministry of War in London had made it an offense for a serving soldier to keep any sort of daily record of his activities. The prohibition was not popular and thus was widely ignored. Officers far senior to a flight lieutenant kept personal diaries, and few even attempted to disguise their contents.

Donald Hill took a different approach. He would record what happened to him, but do so in such a way that no enemy would be able to read what he had written. Hiding his true feelings was second nature to him, and it was understandable that he should now have thought of using a code or cipher to conceal what he wrote. In the first instance, he wrote in a crude shorthand. But over the months ahead, as the danger of discovery grew, he responded by devising new layers of camouflage. One cipher overlaid another, and eventually he tried to mask his secret so that it was impossible for anyone even to recognize it as a diary, let alone be able to read it. Finally he locked it with a keyword which no enemy could guess unless he knew for whom the diary was written.

Long after the other officers went to bed, he remained awake, writing in a stiff-backed notebook. By chance, December 7 was his night to act as duty officer, the one who would be woken if any urgent message had to be passed to the colony's air force. Shortly before dawn an orderly shook him awake. The colonial secretary, Franklin Gimson, was on the telephone. Donald listened to his dry, tired tones, acknowledged the message, then put the phone down. In the early hours of December 8, Tokyo Radio had interrupted its shortwave news broadcast to Southeast Asia with a special announcement. It could hardly have sounded more innocuous: "Allow me to make a weather forecast at this time: west wind clear." But Donald was not the only one to disguise his secret in code. On the other side of the International Date Line, where it was still December 7, the attack on Pearl Harbor had just begun. Now Tokyo was sending a radio warning to its embassies that it proposed to wage war against the enemy in the west, Britain.

Even after the other officers had been woken with the news, there was no urgency in their response. It was as though the imaginative jump they needed to make from the orderliness of a peacetime existence sheltered by the power of empire to the savagery of fighting for existence was too great for them even at that late hour. At eight A.M. some of the aircrew were strolling out to the airfield, but others were still eating breakfast, when everyone heard an ominous roar to the north. Someone foolishly suggested it might be the long-awaited squadron of fighters arriving.

Donald began to run to where the Vildebeestes had been parked, but if there had ever been anything that could be done with such ancient aircraft, it was too late now. Nine bombers escorted by more than thirty Japanese Zero fighters came in low from the north, heading straight for the airfield. While the bombers droned on toward the docks and strategic targets like oil depots and electrical power stations, the Zero fighters wheeled round in a tight turn over the airfield, and began to machine-gun the aircraft below.

Within minutes, one of the three Vildebeestes was in flames, and another badly damaged. In the bay were the two seaplanes. Again and again the waters were whipped up by lines of bullets, which eventually smashed into the canvas-covered Walruses. The big seaplanes rocked with the impact, then quite quickly began to sink. The first lesson of the war was being demonstrated: it was not Japan that had been bluffing, it was Britain.

In the relative quiet left by the departure of the attacking aircraft, it was the roar of flames from the burning Vildebeeste parked by the tennis court that attracted the airmen's attention. There was nothing to be done about the Walruses. One of the Vildebeestes had survived the raking bullets untouched, while another had been damaged. It was the fire that caused most anxiety. The burning aircraft was the one Donald had taken up the day before loaded with two bombs. In anticipation, perhaps, of war breaking out, he had left them on board after the flight. Now there was a good chance that they might explode in the intense heat produced by burning aviation fuel.

The danger was such that Ginger Sullivan asked for volunteers to help extinguish the fire. It was an awkward moment because the risk was so obvious and he was so new to his command. He never forgot that Donald was the first person to volunteer. Through most of the morning, they attempted to put out the flames. The heat made it impossible to bring the hoses near enough to dowse the fire, and soon they could see the two bombs glowing white in the heart of the inferno. Miraculously neither did go off, but the plane was reduced to twisted metal spars and lumps of engine fused to the bombs.

Later that afternoon, the men of the RAF detachment watched helplessly as the Japanese bombed the docks on Hong Kong island and the crowded tenements in Kowloon on the other side of the hills from the airfield. But by nightfall, they had made one gain. The damaged Vildebeeste was repaired.

The pilots made an oddly homogeneous group. Each had a nickname: Donald Samuel Hill became plain Sammy; Flying Officer Donald Gray, the next most senior, was named Dolly after an actress of that name; the Irish pilot Baugh was christened Wimpey (misspelled "Whimpey" by Donald) after the construction company, which relied on Irish laborers; Crossley, the youngest, was simply Junior; but Hennessy, who had only just arrived, was still Frank. They favored RAF mustaches and the obligatory slang, and all had envied their counterparts back in Britain for the experience of flying in combat.

Now they, too, had an enemy, and just two serviceable aircraft. All the Japanese fighters could outfly them, but with the courage of young men, Donald and Dolly decided that the night offered them one small chance of using the ancient machines to some purpose. They had no night-flying equipment, but there was half a moon and the railway line between Hong Kong and Canton would reflect enough light to guide them there. A stocky man with an absurdly luxuriant mustache, Gray had come up through the ranks. Like Donald, he was older than most pilots and felt somewhat apart from the others. What they shared above all was a passion for flying; indeed, Gray had won fame five years earlier by taking part in a record-breaking flight from London to Sydney.

Looking at the two Vildebeestes, they came to the same conclusion. Japanese troops would be congregated by the railway station, ready to reinforce the Hong Kong attackers, and they would present a good target. Between them they would be able to drop just four of the five-hundred-pound bombs, but the chance of striking back in any way at all made it worth the risk. As they argued forcefully to Sullivan, anything was better than sitting on the ground doing nothing. Sullivan supported them, but standing orders required all air operations to be cleared by General Maltby. Fearing that a bombing raid might provoke reprisals against civilians in Hong Kong, Maltby curtly refused permission, and the two old bombers stood unused on the ground.

Hong Kong had other defenses. Six battalions of infantry were posted on its frontiers, their composition reflecting the empire's scope. They included Canadians, Punjabis, Rajputs, Scots, and English. With almost a thousand artillerymen, British and Indian, and three thousand men of the Hong Kong Volunteer Defence Corps, representing seventeen different nationalities, the garrison was multicultural to a fault. The naval defenses consisted of two warships from the First World War and a flotilla of six torpedo boats.

Yet little more than a fortnight after the first aircraft roared in over Kai Tak airfield, the great outpost had gone, and with it the mystique that had sustained the world's largest empire. Trying to convey the shock of it to her fellow countrymen and -women, Emily Hahn wrote of the last peacetime party, "Half the men I remember that night horsing around are dead, and the girls are standing in line at Stanley [detention camp], cup in hand waiting for a handout of thin rice stew. Does that sound banal? It isn't. It strikes me sometimes like a slap in the face."

On Tuesday, the Japanese 23rd Army under General Sakai Takashi launched its attack on the Gin Drinkers' Line. The assault troops consisted of the 38th Division, that is, three regiments of infantry numbering almost 9,000 men, with perhaps 3,000 artillery and other support units. The Hong Kong garrison was also about 12,000 strong, being made up of about 5,200 infantry, with some 7,000 artillery and auxiliary units. But the raw numbers counted for little compared to morale and training. The Japanese had been fighting as a unit since October 1939, and had known nothing but success. They were battle hardened and confident, supported by total air superiority and naval dominance, with around 27,000 troops in reserve.

Most of the regular troops among the defenders—two battalions of British infantry and four of Indian artillery—had spent years on garrison duty. Two Canadian battalions, which had arrived weeks earlier, had little more experience than a recruit's basic training, and the Hong Kong Volunteers were part-time soldiers ranging from young students to fifty-five-year-old businessmen.

The ground assault began on the New Territories; within twenty-four hours the attackers had broken through the Gin Drinkers' Line, and were threatening Kowloon. There were pockets of individual resistance, often mounted by old soldiers, in one case a veteran of the Boer War of over forty years before, who already knew the shock of battle. The Indian battalions, which had experienced real conflict in the North-West Frontier, held their shape. For many of the others, the onslaught of the Japanese forces, particularly at night, advancing silently in rubber-soled boots and under cover of heavy artillery and mortar bombardment, was simply overwhelming.

As the scale of the collapse emerged, the RAF detachment was among the first mainland units to be ordered to retreat to the island. None among them were in any real doubt that their eventual fate was to be killed or captured. They still had two workable aircraft, and again the two Donalds, Hill and Gray, volunteered to put them to some use. This time they pleaded for the chance to bomb Japanese airfields at Canton. Once more Sullivan begged permission for the raid, pointing out that if they were not destroyed the planes could be flown on to Nationalist Chinese airfields and thus save two pilots from captivity. Maltby, facing the worst nightmare of any commander, the certainty of defeat, forbade them to take off and ordered the planes destroyed. Nothing must be done to inflame the temper of the eventual victors.

From day to day the fate of anyone caught up in the great destructive machine of war is so precarious that each moment might be regarded as decisive. But for Donald Hill, who had trained for years to perform this single task, that order shaped quite crucially the subsequent course of his life. Maltby's consent would have allowed him a chance to put his special skill to use, and possibly to escape capture and continue fighting. The refusal condemned him to captivity.

War alters more lives than it ends, but Maltby's refusal led to Gray's death in extraordinarily brutal circumstances. Perhaps he would have died in the war anyway, but the courage with which he faced his terrible fate lent a particular poignancy to the order from his commanding officer that prevented him from finding an alternative, more merciful end.

That day Donald for the first time did not keep up his diary. Even for someone of his self-discipline it was a forgivable lapse. The evacuation of the airfield meant that every bit of machinery that could not be carried had to be destroyed in order to deny it to the enemy. The two serviceable planes, one undamaged, the other laboriously repaired, needed now to be sabotaged irreparably. There were huge quantities of papers to be burned, men to be sent across to the island, and final checks to ensure that obstacles scattered across the airfield had put it out of action. Finally Donald himself left Kai Tak with the last party of airmen carrying all the detachment's weapons and ammunition.

At the docks, the makings of a small Dunkirk armada was assembling to ferry troops to the island. Bent under the weight of kit bags and weapons, the first evacuees filed aboard the ancient destroyer H.M.S. *Thracian* and the innumerable ferries, launches, and sampans. The group of airmen clambered onto a lighter, but as the boat pushed out into open water, a British artillery battery began shelling them. Quickly a Union Jack was hoisted and the shelling ceased, but the confusion of battle was growing. Eventually it enveloped everything so thickly that when defeat came, its clarity was a relief. The RAF detachment had been sent to Aberdeen on the south side of the island, where a huge building for handicapped children, known as the Industrial School, had been requisitioned for their use. To reach it, they had to push their way through crowds of evacuated troops searching, like them, for food and accommodation. By the time Donald at last found a bed, he was too exhausted to do anything but fall on it and sleep.

The news from the Far East was all bad. Pearl Harbor had been bombed and the Americans' Pacific Fleet crippled. The core of Britain's naval force in the region, the battle cruiser H.M.S. *Repulse* and the battleship H.M.S. *Prince of Wales,* had been sunk. Japanese troops had landed in Malaya and were advancing on Singapore, and now it was evident that Hong Kong's defense was disintegrating. The BBC put the best face that it could on this last item. "The evacuation of the mainland is now complete," its announcer said in clipped, unemotional tones on December 11. "Hong Kong is now settling down to an old-fashioned siege."

That "old-fashioned" was masterly. In Tunbridge Wells, Pamela's alarm at the thought of what might happen to Donald diminished immediately. Britain was good at old-fashioned things, and the suggestion of castles, and thick stone walls, and hunkering down until the siege was lifted was distinctly reassuring. Then early the next morning, Friday, December 12, she received a cable from Hong Kong. It was from Donald, telling her simply that he was well and alive, and that he loved her. Relief drove out any lingering apprehension. Clearly the BBC had got it right again; he was "settling down" to the siege.

There was indeed a lull in the fighting. Success bred its own problems and the Japanese needed to regroup before the assault on the island. Meanwhile, within the siege lines fragments of peacetime life continued. The banks cashed checks, the cable office sent out cables, and restaurants on the island still served European dishes like grilled steak.

The RAF detachment had brought over its own heavy machine guns, which could in a pinch be used against low-flying bombers. At first the RAF men were drafted as stand-in antiaircraft gunners on the roof of the Aberdeen Industrial School so that they could defend the nearby docks, which were certain to be a target for Japanese bombers.

Among the besieged troops, rumors began to fly. It was firmly reported that Chiang Kai-shek's Nationalist Chinese army was about to attack the Japanese from the rear. But it was also said that the Japanese success was due entirely to the work of Chinese collaborators. Then came a news item that indicated the sheer scale of their Pacific campaign. First had come Pearl Harbor, then Hong Kong; now it was reported that they had attacked Malaya, aiming at the great fortress of Singapore.

Waiting for the Japanese onslaught, the young airmen realized that the whole world was at war and that anything could happen. In the crowded surroundings of the Industrial School, they discussed their own part in the great conflagration. Soberly they accepted that in the short term they were doomed—"Hong Kong is only a very small fry in a tremendous issue," one of them said—but with a last flicker of prewar optimism they agreed that in the long term civilization would surely triumph. It was easier to think of that than of the more immediate reality.

A few hundred yards away, on a small island just outside Aberdeen harbor, Michael Wright, a young architect who had joined the Hong Kong Volunteers, was arriving at a similar conclusion with his colleagues on the artillery battery they manned. None of them doubted that Hong Kong would be taken by the Japanese. "I don't think it was spelled out," he said later, "but we knew that sooner or later, and probably very much sooner, we would either be captured or killed. There was no other outcome."

So far no Japanese attempt had been made to land on Hong Kong island, but the fighting on the mainland had demonstrated the difference between a force trained in peacetime parades and one used to the ferocity of war. The defenders had seen the quality of Japanese soldiers and understood how formidable they were individually and how effectively they coordinated massive artillery and mortar fire with infantry attacks. On the mainland, where the defense had been unprepared and overconfident, courage before the event came easily. Knowing exactly what the future held required a deeper, more complex response.

So confident of success were the Japanese that on December 13 they sent three officials across the water under a truce flag to offer terms of surrender. The offer was rejected out of hand. Then loudspeakers on the mainland began broadcasting Christmas carols and pop songs mixed in with appeals to the troops to give themselves up if they wanted to see their families again. Despite knowing what lay ahead, no one responded, and the next day the Japanese began to bombard the island from two sides. Patrolling the open sea to the south, their warships pounded the town of Aberdeen and the hilltops, while from the mainland heavy guns fired on the northern coast.

Running the length of the island from east to west was a line of steep hills, divided almost halfway by a pass called the Wong Nei Chong Gap. The main road connecting the north and south coasts of the island ran through the pass. West of it lay the island's two principal towns, Victoria on the north coast and Aberdeen on the south, while most of the reservoirs on which the inhabitants depended for their water were in the east. Both sides understood that whoever held the Gap would dominate the island. It was here that Brigadier John Lawson, the commander of the Canadian forces, had his headquarters.

The problem for General Maltby was to decide from which direction the attack would come. An invasion from the north was the more likely. Here the victorious Japanese forces on the mainland were separated by barely five hundred yards of water from the island, but on the south side the Japanese navy, backed by waves of bombers, continued to pound Aberdeen harbor as though preparing to make an assault from the sea. With fatal indecision, Maltby chose to spread his forces thinly across the entire island instead of concentrating them on the most vulnerable sector opposite the mainland.

Most of the small RAF party under Donald Hill was sent up into the hills just above Aberdeen to hold a section of line, measuring almost a mile, from Bennets Hill to Mount Nicholson, whose peak almost overlooked the strategic Wong Nei Chong Gap. This was controlled by a company of the nearest Canadian battalion, the Winnipeg Grenadiers. Its commander was a friendly, enthusiastic major called Baillie. Concrete pillboxes had been sited near the top of strategic hills, but elsewhere men who had been trained to fly and service aircraft had to become infantry soldiers, digging trenches as well as they could on the rocky, scrub-covered slopes. It was, according to Donald's commanding officer, "a task that was utterly foreign to them."

On December 16 a probing attack by a small force in sampans and junks was driven off, and the next day a surprising second offer of a truce was made to Sir Mark Young, the governor of Hong Kong. Japanese intelligence had many well-placed agents and fifth columnists on the island, and must have known that many civilians wanted the authorities to accept the reality of the situation and capitulate at once. Despite this pressure, his response was unequivocal. "The Governor," he wrote, "declines most absolutely to enter into any negotiations for the surrender of Hong Kong, and he takes this opportunity of saying that he is not prepared to receive any further communications on the subject."

His meaning could not have been plainer and, on the night of December 18, the expected invasion began. It came at the most obvious point, on the north corner of the island nearest the mainland. Brushing past the thin line of defenders, the Japanese fanned out east and west, but with the main central force driving inland straight for the Wong Nei Chong Gap. Most of the defense was wrong-footed. Hastily the RAF machine-gunners, like others in the central mountains, improvised new lines to face an attack coming not from the west but from the north and east. At the same time, troops stationed on the southern coast were hurried up into the hills.

Among the latter was Major Robert Giles of the Royal Marines, who had been on duty at the naval dockyards in Aberdeen; he was now sent with naval reinforcements to strengthen the defenses around the Gap. A seasoned regular, with a strong, almost fussy belief in discipline, he took over Donald's part of the line and set about trying to strengthen their position. He had no illusions about the hopelessness of the task, but refused to acknowledge it except by ensuring that his section posts knew their job and remained where they were. In Donald he found a kindred soul, who despite his youth and lack of experience had the steadiness of a veteran.

"He kept completely calm under all circumstances," Giles wrote later, "acted with energy, and did all he could to help me. In fact he gave me what I valued most, an officer I could leave at HQ when I was out at the section posts, who I knew could be relied upon to carry out any instruction I had given, or to act on his own if a situation I had not foreseen arose."

As the sounds of battle approached through the hills, steadiness became a diminishing quality. Reports of the Japanese tactics emphasized their skill at infiltrating enemy lines. Advancing stealthily under cover of night, they took up positions as snipers so that in daylight they could pick off unsuspecting troops from vantage points in trees or behind rocks. Using any ground cover available, they crept up undetected on troops sheltering in concrete pillboxes from snipers or artillery attack, and several sections had been wiped out by grenades dropped down the ventilation shafts. None of the defenders had been prepared for fighting like this. Raw troops, as the Canadians were, became jumpy, and the strain of their sudden frights added to the unspoken anxieties of detecting the rustle of the enemy's approach against a constant background of crackling small-arms fire and thudding artillery exchanges.

Within twenty-four hours of landing, the enemy had come so close to taking the Gap that the nearest Canadian troops were sucked into the battle. Donald and his Royal Marine commander remained in position through the night, listening to the firefight. No one could sleep. At midnight, an exhausted sergeant from the Canadian section stumbled back to the pillbox, almost weeping from the impact of his first experience of the sudden slaughter of battle, the screams and hideous dismemberment of living bodies. Another followed him a few hours later in the same state. To add a final twist to the misery of living through what might be their final hours, the weather had changed, and a cold rain whipped on by a sharp wind chilled them to the bone. Throughout the night, the steady issue of Navy rum was all that kept alive the spirits of the weary, frightened soldiers.

In the morning, the encircling Japanese were thought to be threatening the dockyards, and Giles together with his naval detachment and his naval rum was called back to help in their defense. Now there were only the main Canadian party and the dozen or so RAF men. A constant bombardment from warships and mainland artillery prevented them from sleeping or getting rations. The next night, starving and exhausted, they were suddenly ordered off the hill by the Canadian company commander, who was convinced that their position had been surrounded. At two in the morning, they were told to fall back to Aberdeen, about five miles away. They groped their way through the dark, and once they had reached the town fell asleep in makeshift barracks until a fresh artillery barrage crashed into the building the following morning.

There was nothing now but confusion. The Japanese had taken the strategic Gap, and repeated counterattacks had failed to shift them or prevent their further advance. Each part of the island was isolated from the other. The nightmare that had been pushed to the back of the defenders' minds was coming true. Yet even as the inevitable was becoming real, extraordinary acts of bravery were still performed.

As the invaders swarmed into his headquarters by the Gap, Brigadier Lawson sent one brief but memorable message to General Maltby: "They're all around us. I'm going outside to shoot it out." No more was heard from him, but six days later, a burial party found his body with two empty revolvers beside it, and eight enemy lying dead nearby. On Mount Butler, another Canadian, Company Sergeant Major John Osborn, made that same choice to confront danger head on. Leading a company reduced in strength from 200 to 30 men, he drove the Japanese off the hill and held it for over eight hours before he himself was killed and the last five men alive were captured.

"The man who can most truly be accounted brave," said Pericles in his great funeral oration over the Athenian dead in the Peloponesian War, "is he who knows best the meaning of what is sweet in life and of what is terrible, and then goes out determined to meet what is to come."

The reality was that everyone had a choice about how he would react to the violence of battle. Perhaps he had no more than a moment to make it, and in its form and extremeness the occasion might have been overwhelming; but waiting for the attack to come, the men had had days to appreciate what might happen. At that point, when the violence came—"in the death," to use a good expression—a quality emerged that others called courage.

"Much talk about war with Japan, but no one seems to think anything will happen," Donald had written when he began his diary barely a fortnight earlier. At that moment, he still enjoyed a uniquely privileged existence: he was in love, he was an officer in a powerful, undefeated military force, and he was a servant of the greatest empire on earth. By Pericles' definition, he knew what was sweet in life. In the few days since the Japanese had invaded, that had been swept away, and he had begun to taste what was terrible. When he was woken early on the morning of December 24, 1941, with news that the order to retreat had been a mistake, and that he was to return to Bennets Hill, he could hardly have been ignorant of what was to come.

His RAF section, strengthened by a dozen Canadians, was still armed with machine guns, together with as many grenades as each man could carry. They struggled up the steep slope, hauling their packs and weapons. As they reached the top, they were seen and the Japanese opened up with mortar fire from a neighboring hill. Caught out in the open, they threw themselves flat, but the enemy had the range, and immediately shells landed among them. Several men were hit by splinters of metal, including the man lying next to Donald. He himself was showered with pebbles and dirt from the explosion, and some shrapnel clanged off his helmet. Out in the open, they were perfect targets for the mortars, but standing up they would be vulnerable to rifle fire. Between two bad options, one was certain, the other only potential. Shouting above the sound of explosions, Donald ordered his men to disperse and take cover lower down the hill.

Miraculously they all made it into the shelter of some undergrowth out of sight of the Japanese, but at the top of the hill, just as the mortar shells were coming in, he had noticed farther along the slope a little group of soldiers wearing the pale khaki of the Canadian forces. Clearly they had not received the order to retire given the night before. So far the Japanese had not spotted them, but it was only a matter of time, and then the mortars would start exploding among them. They were not his responsibility, but he knew they had to be warned. Shouts would attract the enemy's attention. To reach the stranded party, someone would have to crawl out into the open.

Perhaps Donald felt that he had no choice: there were Canadians in his section, and he had been alongside the Winnipeg Grenadiers for almost a week. Perhaps he felt lucky: seconds after he had got up that morning, a bomb had landed on his makeshift bed in the Industrial School, blowing the room to pieces. Whatever he felt, the reality was that he could have left the outpost to its fate.

A Canadian, Corporal A. C. Blueman, volunteered to come with him. Crawling through the thickest undergrowth, they climbed out of the shelter they had found and wormed their way up toward the isolated troops. The movement of the bushes caught the attention of Japanese snipers, who repeatedly fired at them, but each time the bullets flew wide. When they were close to the concrete pillbox the Canadians were defending, Blueman called to them. There was a hurried conference. They could take only what arms they could run with. Once they had been spotted, speed alone would save them. The heavier weapons and ammunition were piled inside the pillbox, a couple of grenades were tossed in on top, and everyone began to run back down the hill. Before they had gone more than a few yards, the grenades went off, and suddenly there were bullets flying everywhere. Donald found himself running with his head ducked down as though that would protect him, but the commotion distracted the enemy and the rescued troops reached safety unscathed.

Unable to find out where they should go, Donald led his little band of twenty-two soldiers—ten RAF and twelve Canadians—back into Aberdeen where a distracted Canadian command post admitted that they had no idea what was happening. The Japanese had taken the vital Wong Nei Chong Gap, but then their troops had spread out in all directions. In the east of the island they seemed to be everywhere. In the west, Aberdeen had so far escaped attack, and Victoria was still not taken. Perhaps a new line could be established between the two towns. In that case, the Aberdeen reservoir, the last supply of water in the area, would be strategically important. Wearily, the men marched up into the hills again, and in late evening took up position on a bridge that carried a road across the reservoir.

As night came an eerie silence fell. The artillery ceased firing once the light faded. Elsewhere on the island, the quietness made it seem as though the enemy had taken a rest. But across the water, sounds carried clearly. Twigs snapped, pebbles rattled down rocks, branches suddenly rustled although there was no wind. They had experienced enough in the past week to know that the Japanese were far from asleep.

Suddenly, just after midnight, the dark night was split by flashes of yellow flame and the silence broken by the crack of small-arms fire and wild cries of "Banzai! Banzai!" The attack seemed to happen on the farther shore, and quite soon they could distinguish black shapes running across the bridge toward them. Warning shouts showed that they were Canadian. The Japs had broken through, they yelled; they had crept up on them and blasted them apart. There was an officer with them, trying to get them under control, but they were too demoralized to listen. The Japs were right behind them, they claimed, just the other side of the bridge. As though they could actually see the enemy's silhouettes, Donald's party opened up with every weapon they had— machine guns, rifles, revolvers—shooting into the darkness down the road.

The firestorm provoked an immediate response, and once more Japanese mortar shells began to explode around them. It was too much for the jumpy Canadians. To Donald's horror, they began to run off down the road, but before they had gone far they were brought up short by Major Baillie, who drew his revolver and threatened to shoot anyone who retreated another step. With operatic timing, the shooting stopped everywhere, so that only Baillie's furious voice, cracking with emotion, could be heard swearing at his men.

It was not the voice of leadership. There was too much fear in it. Even when he called for volunteers to go back across the bridge, it was not with authority. In the silent night, the Japanese must have heard every word and known exactly where he was. None of his own men moved. Waving his pistol, Baillie went on himself, striding on into the dark, cursing the men who were supposed to be under his command.

Donald watched for a moment, then could not bear to watch the solitary figure any longer. Everything indicated that Baillie was walking into a Japanese ambush, but even so Donald could not let him die alone. Jumping to his feet, he ran after the major. Together they reached the other side, unharmed, whereupon Baillie was violently sick. Only then did Donald smell the alcohol and realize that he had risked his life to accompany a man who was hopelessly drunk. Oddly enough, he found himself feeling sympathy rather than anger. The poor major, it was clear, had simply been unable to cope with the intolerable stress of commanding untrained troops in battle.

A little foolishly they returned through the darkness to their own side only to find that more of Baillie's men had taken the chance to slip away. Paradoxically, in the lottery of warfare, they might in fact have been safer staying, for in the stillness Donald could hear Japanese circling around the far side of the reservoir, evidently having decided not to attack the bridge. Instead of letting them go, Baillie decided that the sound of the enemy made a target too good to miss. A mortar was hauled into place on the road, aimed across the reservoir, and a shell dropped down the tube. The men were shaken by what they had gone through, and no one had checked the positioning of the mortar tube with sufficient care. The shell was fired, but instead of flying out across the water, it hit a branch of a nearby tree and fell back to the ground among the firing party. The explosion blew off the mortar operator's right arm and almost severed another man's leg, besides wounding several others.

The casualties were carried to a dugout, where the others made unavailing efforts to stop the bleeding. They had no painkillers, only bandages, but however tightly they ligatured the shattered limbs, the blood kept welling out. Above the cries of pain, Donald tried to call up an ambulance, but none arrived. By now the remainder of the force were totally demoralized. The bridge had been left unguarded, and there was no pretense of being other than frightened men. Although not the senior officer, Donald was evidently the only one left able to take command. For a long time, he laid into them. He must have told them about the need for self-discipline, the importance of hanging together, and their duty to behave like soldiers, because they began to go back to their posts. "His powers of leadership were outstanding," his commanding officer, Ginger Sullivan, later observed, and the fact that Donald carried weight in a situation where rank no longer counted was proof of that judgment.

Before dawn, the ambulance came, and with it two young subalterns from the Winnipeg Grenadiers, who were so shocked by Baillie's inebriated state they wanted to arrest him on the spot. But there was no time left to restore order or normality. It was Christmas Day, and the surrender for which the previous fortnight had been a preparation was at last about to come. At ten o'clock, a rumor went around that a truce had been declared, but the Japanese artillery barrage that followed did not encourage belief. In his last act as a combatant, Donald decided to take his RAF platoon away from the reservoir and rejoin the main British force, which he thought must be farther west. They trudged up the long slope of Mount Butler and at the summit came upon the main road between Victoria and Aberdeen. It was crammed with retreating troops.

They bore the unmistakable air of defeat—heads down, moving wearily—and above all, they had no weapons. Beyond them, the sky was filled with columns of black smoke as ammunition and fuel dumps were torched. Shells whistled and screeched overhead and exploded into houses scattered along the peaks. Suddenly the barrage ceased, and from the windows of the battered buildings white flags began to appear. The time was four-thirty P.M. The surrender of Hong Kong had taken place one hour before.

PART II

5

Prisoner of War

Love seeketh not itself to please,
Nor for itself hath any care,
But for another gives its ease.
And builds a Heaven in Hell's despair.

—WILLIAM BLAKE,
SONGS OF EXPERIENCE

The "old-fashioned siege" had lasted a fortnight. In
Tunbridge Wells, the news of Hong Kong's fall de-
molished the fragile confidence that Pamela had sustained on the reassurances of BBC news bulletins. In
the next three months, the rest of Britain's Pacific possessions, from Malaya to Borneo and New Guinea
along with a string of island colonies, all surrendered,
including most shatteringly, on February 16, 1942, Sin-

gapore, the rock on which the whole defense of the Far East rested, together with a garrison of 120,000 men.

At first it was impossible for Pamela to separate her own bitter anxiety from the mood of recrimination and doubt that settled on the country. She wept and blamed herself for not somehow having found a way out to Hong Kong so that she could have been with him. On a national level, *The Times* blamed the catastrophes on the "easy-going routine of colonial administration," while censors noted that servicemen's letters were filled with criticism of outmoded attitudes in government. Attempting to shore up morale, an MP, Captain Leonard Gammans, reminded the critics that "we cannot expect Asiatics and Africans to believe in us as a colonial Power unless we believe in ourselves."

That old imperial certainty never did recover, but quite soon the country's temper solidified into a narrower conviction that in Europe, at least, Britain would not be defeated. In the stirring words used by Pamela's local newspaper, *The Courier,* in 1944, to sum up Kent's resistance to Hitler's onslaught: "There was seldom a day that enemy planes were not overhead, but no note of terror was struck in the hearts of a people who had long since steeled themselves to these wanton attacks on the towns and villages of rural south-east England."

In similar fashion, Pamela's own volatile feelings eventually settled into a stubborn faith that somehow Donald must have survived. It was difficult to explain why she should have been so certain. For over six months, she had no news of him. He had simply disappeared. The RAF's official notice was that he was "missing, believed PoW [prisoner of war]," but no one knew for certain. Normally after a battle, each unit would find the time to call a roster; survivors would pool information about who had become casualties or been taken prisoner, and the news would be passed back to families. After a surrender, nothing could be known about the fate of individuals until the enemy chose to release the names of those it held in captivity. The Japanese did not begin this process until the summer of 1942.

Stoicism was not one of the qualities that Pamela's family associated with her, but she had started to learn it almost from the moment that she waved good-bye to Donald in July 1939. In the days after his departure, she took to her bed, and wept for the misery of life without him. When she got up, it was only to write him a long, tear-stained letter saying that life hardly seemed worth living if he was not there. His reply took weeks to arrive, but it transformed everything, for it contained plans for a meeting in Singapore where, he promised, they would be married. With their wedding on the horizon, her spirits soared as extravagantly as they had earlier plunged. Now she had something to live for. It was something strange, which her sisters remembered with startled clarity amid the explosive impact of the declaration of war, that Pamela—who had never cared about any of her other boyfriends enough to scribble a note—now regularly sat down to cover pages of Basildon Bond writing paper with her open, looped handwriting.

Day after day, she wrote to him. She suspected that everyone else thought her more than a little mad. "I missed him so bitterly," she said. "This was the one way that I still had of talking to him."

On September 3, 1939, much of the United Kingdom heard on the wireless the thin, beaky tones of Neville Chamberlain explaining that Germany had attacked Poland despite Britain's guarantee to protect the integrity of her borders. Hitler had been asked for an undertaking that his forces would be withdrawn, but no such undertaking had been given. "As a result, I must tell you," Chamberlain declared in his plaintive voice, "that this country is now at war with Germany." Almost at once, air raid sirens began to wail in London—a false alarm, as it happened, but an appropriate response. To the general apprehension, Pamela added her own fear. A voyage to Singapore might no longer be possible, and the wedding would have to be postponed.

While the Far East remained at peace, Britain wearily braced itself for the second half of the conflict that had begun in 1914. The Kirrage girls responded to the outbreak of hostilities as most well-brought-up girls did, by taking up work of national importance. In Sheila's case, this was farm work. Brigit organized files in the Ministry of Defence, but Pamela understandably aimed at something a little more elegant. She chose the Red Cross, expecting to become a nurse, but when she told her interviewer of her previous work in Bermondsey, she was briskly informed that the organization stood in far greater need of cooks. Her first job was at a convalescent hospital in Ascot called Winkfield Place.

In Donald's absence, her parents provided an emotional refuge, and it became a habit to spend every weekend with them. There was just time after lunch on Saturday to get a lift from the hospital into London and then take the uncertain train from Charing Cross to Tunbridge Wells, to be in time for supper before going to sleep in the same bedroom she had occupied since she was a child. At the center of the drama and self-display, it might be seen as a small steady cry for security. When the real war finally burst on the country, she stubbornly persisted in her routine.

In Kent they had a grandstand seat at the cataclysm. They saw the defeated army that had been taken off the beaches at

Dunkirk to be landed at Ramsgate and Dover. They heard the desperate whine and staccato gunfire beneath the vapor trails as the Brylcreem boys of the RAF countered the Luftwaffe in the Battle of Britain. In the night the drone of bombers passed overhead, carrying the Blitz to London and Coventry and the Midlands. The Kent coast was lined with antiaircraft guns, observer posts, and the mysterious radar stations, and every flat expanse of ground that might take a glider attack was peppered with concrete pillboxes. Sometimes *The Courier* would describe Kent as being "in the front-line of the war," though by the middle of 1940 there was in truth no front to be lined in Western Europe. Except for fascist Spain and Portugal, all the landmass from Brittany to Stalingrad was controlled by Nazi Germany.

Through it all, like Mrs. Miniver refusing to let Hitler's bombs change her habits, Pamela insisted on traveling to and from Tunbridge Wells, so that she could walk up the hill from the Central Station to arrive at the peace of her parents' house in Queen's Road. But even there, the effects of war were apparent. All but one of the servants had disappeared to join the forces or work in war production, and the great house, so full of life in peacetime, was almost empty. Her father had joined the Home Guard and cultivated an allotment. Her mother had become an air raid warden, responsible for ensuring that the blackout was observed. For a brief period the street's closed doors and gleaming windows shielded by the neat white net curtains that in peacetime kept out prying eyes were opened to her as she checked on the blackout arrangements. For Tunbridge Wells, giving up so much of its cherished privacy must have counted as, next to the bombs, the ultimate hardship of the war. Nevertheless, the town remained Pamela's home, and if she timed it right she could stay until Monday morning before catching an early commuter train back to London and a connection out to Ascot to be in time to prepare lunch.

She specialized in what she called "good English cooking." When rationing began, it became impossible to get the right ingredients, but she learned to stretch whatever beef or lamb she could get, and made sure that at least once a week the patients got a really delicious dessert. In the tattered pages of her menu book, shepherd's pie, mince and potatoes, and whale-meat stew appear repeatedly, along with "Resurrection Pie," in which all the previous week's scraps returned in a single dish. The strongest flavor the recipes convey is one of austerity. It was not until the summer of 1942 that she found a setting better suited to her temperament.

The Political Warfare Executive was one of the war's more shadowy organizations. Nominally it was part of the Special Operations Executive, whose mission, in Winston Churchill's magical phrase, was to "set Europe ablaze" by acts of sabotage. The PWE aimed to achieve the same end by feeding false information and sabotaging the news organizations of occupied Europe. Increasingly it developed its black arts independently of the SOE, but it shared the same smart headquarters in the Riding School at Woburn Abbey, the Duke of Bedford's ancestral home.

Apart from its size, the very beauty of the place served a propaganda purpose. Many of the men and women who arrived there were French, Polish, or Dutch nationals who had escaped from Nazi domination. In Woburn Abbey, once a medieval Cistercian abbey and finely restored as an eighteenth-century mansion surrounded by a three-thousand-acre park, they had a picture of the civilization for which they were now fighting. It was a reminder that they stood for the good against the evil. Everything served the same end—even the food, which was good, and largely exempt from rationing. The staff, including the cooks, were expected to be as stylish as their meals. A Polish member of SOE training for a sabotage operation in his native country was particularly struck by the women who looked after him and their effect on morale: "You couldn't have found a finer type of Englishwoman anywhere," he wrote. "Cultured and friendly, hardworking and smiling, they created the relaxed, happy atmosphere so necessary before the coming adventure."

When a friend suggested she come to work at Woburn, Pamela did not hesitate. It was the perfect setting, beautiful and glamorously secret. In fact, it was so secret that officially she was still at Winkfield Place. That remained the address to which all her post was sent, and the return address she put on the letters she continued to send, week after week, to Flight Lieutenant Donald Hill, addressed first to Singapore and then to Hong Kong. Through those first ferocious years of the war, she gradually accepted the postponement of their wedding until he could return to Britain. Time drags slowly for any twenty-three-year-old who is waiting to hear from a lover. For one who was living through the sudden death of the Battle of Britain and the nightly destruction of the Blitz, the antlike progression of the days was interminable. Then came the battle for Hong Kong, and silence. Donald disappeared. He might have been killed or wounded. Pamela had no way of finding out. Still she wrote to him, and still she waited, but now with agonized apprehension. She never knew how she got through that time. All she would say of it was "I thought I would go insane."

The surrender of the Hong Kong garrison took the Japanese by surprise. Although they had twice called on the island's inadequate forces to give themselves up, they had made no preparations for that eventuality. At 3:25 P.M. on Christmas Day, Sir Mark Young finally accepted the advice of General Maltby that further resistance was pointless, and ordered commanding officers in the field to cease fighting, "it being abundantly clear any further resistance meant the useless slaughter of the remaining Hong Kong garrison." Most troops, including Donald Hill's small party, stopped firing soon afterward, but a few pockets of troops had still not heard the news twenty-four hours later. Even then, the Japanese were still not ready to deal with them.

On their outlying island, Michael Wright and his Hong Kong Volunteer battery did not know that any change had taken place until Christmas night, when they saw cars driving through the streets of Aberdeen with their headlights on. A party was sent ashore to find out the reason, and was told of the surrender at the Industrial School. Wright's feeling, like that of most soldiers, both amateur and professional, was predominantly one of relief that he had survived the ordeal. The choice had always been between death and captivity, and he was thankful to have arrived at the lesser of the two evils.

Elsewhere on Hong Kong island, the realization that they were still alive prompted many of the garrison to celebrate. There had never been any shortage of alcohol on the island, and those who did not fall asleep took the chance to drink themselves into oblivion.

"Discipline had vanished," according to an anonymous private in the Middlesex regiment. "We scrounged, looted and stole, ignoring the respect we owed to each other. We fought and argued over trivial matters and behaved like untutored and inexperienced children."

Donald Hill's reaction was different. After almost a week with only broken sleep and the constant tension of moving warfare, he was physically exhausted. However, his immediate instinct was to escape. With four burly RAF colleagues, he grabbed the first car that they could find, a tiny Austin Seven, determined to drive back down the hill to Aberdeen and find a boat with supplies to get them to the mainland of China. Night had fallen and the engine would not start, but unfazed they freewheeled down the steep narrow road, crashing through flimsy roadblocks on the way, and eventually came to a halt in Aberdeen itself without having seen any of the enemy. They jumped out and ran to the Industrial School to get their kit. Inside, they found a Chinese man who promised to find them a boat and to provision it for them. It was late at night at the end of a long day, and evidently they were slowing down, or the conference with their helper had taken longer than they thought. When they finally assembled in the hall ready to leave, they found to their horror that the door was locked. The Japanese had arrived in Aberdeen, and orders had been given that no one was to leave the building. Their chance had gone.

Hong Kong was the first territory the Japanese captured, and the actual business of dealing with its defenders and inhabitants had to be improvised. Initially civilians were held in requisitioned hotels, until, on the advice of the British director of medical services, Dr. Selwyn-Clark, they were interned in Stanley, a peninsula in the very south of Hong Kong island. Here, the healthiest spot in the colony, existing large buildings made it possible to house a population of almost 2,500 men, women, and children. More complex arrangements had to be made for the combatants. A week was to pass before they were ready.

When they awoke on Boxing Day in the badly damaged Industrial School, Donald and his companions tasted first the luxurious sense of being alive on the first sunny day since hostilities had begun. There was no artillery barrage, and no prickling tension of listening for the furtive sound of a bomber or sniper creeping up unobserved. But almost immediately came the realization that they were about to become prisoners of an enemy renowned for ill-treating its captives.

Throughout their campaign in China, some Japanese practiced all the barbarities of war. From the notorious Rape of Nanking in 1938, when the fall of the city had been followed by medieval scenes in which up to 300,000 male prisoners had been killed, many by being made targets for bayonet practice, others by beheading, while tens of thousands of women were raped and imprisoned in military brothels, it had been clear that the armed forces of Japan condoned behavior designed to terrorize the civilian population.

Fearing that drunkenness might aggravate these murderous tendencies, the senior surviving officers decided to destroy all supplies of alcohol, and most of that sunny morning in Aberdeen Industrial School was spent smashing bottles of beer and spirits. Units that had lost men in battle sent out burial parties, while others were ordered to destroy weapons. The five RAF officers commandeered a car to drive over the hill to military headquarters in Victoria to find out what they should do next. In the bright sunshine they passed through groups of Chinese looters, but still the victors were not to be seen. Donald had been fighting them for a fortnight, he had been defeated by them, but still he had not seen them.

At headquarters, he learned of the terms of surrender. All units were to assemble by Victoria docks to be shipped to a camp on the mainland. Until then the men of the RAF detachment were to be held in detention barracks, while the officers were confined to headquarters.

Donald's old life had effectively ended, but his new life as a prisoner had still not begun. The conquerors were not yet in command, the defeated not yet captive. On both sides, a drunken chaos reigned. Poised on the cusp, Donald had enough time to reflect on what he needed from the old, ordered, privileged existence in order to survive in the new, uncertain impotence into which he was about to be delivered. Materially, he needed his kit, clothes, food, toothbrush, and razor. At a deeper level, he needed something more important: the mementos of his old existence.

The most precious of these were the presents that Pamela had given him during the brief three months they had known each other: the gold ring, her photograph, and a cigarette case. Even when the bomb exploded in his room, he had rescued them from the rubble. To be deprived of them would have seemed like losing the last memory of happiness. But there was something else he needed: the diary.

Only he knew why it had to come with him. The evidence of Japanese atrocities was clear to everyone. At headquarters, numerous reports had already been made of prisoners who had been beheaded and of wounded men beaten to death. When he and the other officers talked of what would happen to them as prisoners of war, one constant piece of information that entered every speculation was the knowledge that the Japanese regarded surrender as shameful, and prisoners as consequently expendable. Obviously, to continue keeping a diary while in Japanese hands was to run the risk of being killed. Yet when he decided to go back to Aberdeen Industrial School to retrieve his belongings, the diary was one of the things for which he returned.

Once more he would have to make the absurdly beautiful journey over the spine of the island from Victoria to Aberdeen. He took with him two other pilots who wanted to collect their kit—Frank Hennessy and Wimpey Baugh. This time the only suitable vehicle he could find was an abandoned milk lorry. There was one other change: for the first time they encountered the enemy, thousands of Japanese soldiers plodding wearily down the road toward them. It was impossible to turn back, and so they drove on through the ranks of their conquerors. The Japanese were small, in some cases almost dwarfed by their rifles. Many wore wire-rimmed spectacles, and their uniforms were coarse and ill-fitting. Faces looked up, registering their strange blue uniforms and Western appearance, but no one interfered until one officer more alert than the others stepped out and signaled them to stop. This was the moment when they would discover for themselves how the Japanese treated their prisoners.

The officer gestured at them to turn the lorry around, then loaded his men into the back. He seemed bemused by the uniforms, but more interested in having his soldiers carried to their destination in Victoria than in finding out why they were driving the lorry. Having unloaded the Japanese in town, the three pilots set out again. This time, by dint of turning a blind eye to the gestures of other officers, they made it through the lines of marching soldiers to Aberdeen. Hurriedly they picked up all the supplies of food and clothing they could carry, and Donald carefully packed away his diary and Pamela's gifts in his bags. One more journey would see them home. Hardly daring to believe that their luck would hold, they drove the ancient lorry back over the hill, and down again to headquarters in Victoria. Not until they piled out of the milk lorry did the tension lift. At that moment, a Japanese officer approached Donald and ordered him peremptorily back behind the wheel. Quietly, Frank and Wimpey let themselves out, taking the precious kit bags with them.

As much as at any time in the battle, Donald was now in the grip of forces beyond his control, and the way he reacted offered as good an insight into the depths of his personality as his response to the physical danger of bombs and bullets. For hour after hour, he and his lorry were passed from one inebriated Japanese to another to transport troops around the island. The streets were filled with soldiers, and the seriousness of their intentions was made obvious by the corpses of Chinese civilians that littered the road. In the immediate aftermath of victory, most of the Japanese officers were good-humored, but not all, and there was never any room for misunderstanding. One jabbed a bayonet into Donald's buttock when he reacted too slowly; another group began gesturing angrily at him; and when one Japanese pulled his long officer's sword out of its scabbard, Donald recognized the gesture. It was part of the samurai ethos to see whether one could decapitate an enemy with a single blow. He resigned himself to what was to come. But instead of execution, the officer produced a bottle of beer, and with the point of his sword neatly flicked the cap off, then handed Donald the bottle. He drank it showing neither fear nor relief.

Late at night he was still ferrying his dangerous and unpredictable enemies through the black streets. One officer gave him a loaf of bread, another shared beer opened on the lorry's mudflaps, while others shouted and swore at him. In Aberdeen, two drunken Japanese volunteered to drive him in a car without headlights, and crashed into a traffic island in the middle of the road. Bowing politely to his stunned fellow passengers, Donald walked quietly back over the hill to the safety of his bed in Victoria.

The cusp was not a comfortable place to be. For three more

days, they waited for instructions from the Japanese about their future. In that time troops from other parts of the island were gradually assembled in Victoria, each of them bringing more news about the fighting and increasingly detailed reports of atrocities. The worst came from Stanley, where the Japanese troops had entered St. Stephen's Hospital, murdered the doctors, bayoneted patients in their beds, then raped and killed the nurses. That was when the extent of the survivors' impotence first began to strike home. However dreadful the events, there was nothing they could do. Not even an officer whose wife had been one of the nurses could be allowed to respond. When he attempted to assault the nearest Japanese, it was his brother officers who held him back. They were powerless. For Donald Hill, this was a new challenge. He had discovered that physical danger produced in him a response unlike most others around him. He became cool and clear-sighted, able to take effective action to counter the menace. Now there was nothing he could do physically. He had to learn how to be passive. And for someone of his size, the lesson was to be taught with particular harshness.

The small Japanese guards felt challenged by the physical size of their prisoners. The largest, including Donald, seemed to become a focus for their aggression and were singled out for ferocious beatings. "I think the Japanese disliked big men," he once said, but that was all he would say.

On December 29, the prisoners were told to be ready to leave at first light the following day. There was to be no transport for personal possessions. They would walk, and they could take with them only what they could carry. The rule held good for General Maltby and the youngest private. In a country where face and public appearance counted for so much, the significance of the arrangements could not be mistaken: the conquered were to be

A page from Donald Hill's
coded diary.

Brigit Ferguson (née Kirrage), Pamela's sister, taken in 1937 prior to the accident that caused her burns.

Maggie Roulf's summer collection of 1938, modeled by Pamela Kirrage.

The golden summer of 1939. Donald photographed by Pamela in a village on the South Downs.

The dispirited survivors of the battle for Hong Kong on their way to
Sham Shui Po prisoner-of-war camp, December 30, 1941.

A gaunt, withdrawn Donald
in April 1945, sketched
by a fellow prisoner.

Hong Kong's front-line air defense,
the obsolete Vildebeeste
torpedo bomber.

To: Miss P.S.Kirrage,
    Winkfield Place,
       Windsor Forest, Berks.

From: Donald. S.Hill,
      Prisoner of War Camp N,
         HongKong.

Date: 17th. April 1943.

My Darling One,
                Last week a miracle happened, I received a letter from
you, dated 11/7/42. My first letter Darling and what a difference it
made. I was so excited that I started reading it upside down. To know
after all these months that you are safe and well. Darling what more
could I ask.
                Ginger and I were delighted to hear that you had met
Beryl. We have started to plan the reunion party when this is all over
Incidentally it's the first time I knew that you had a passion for red
heads darling. He's in great form and has been absolutely grand.
                Nearly four years of separation darling and I love you
as much, if not more, than ever. I remember so well how the prospect of
three years away from you seemed a lifetime. It has been an eternity
Darling. But having stood that test we can be sure of the future. I
just live for the day when I shall see you again my darling. I shall
probably be struck completely dumb.
                I have just about used up my 200 words. I would need
another 200 to tell you how much I love you darling. You are for ever
in my thoughts.
                Take great care of yourself my Darling.

                        I love you,

                                Always have and always will.

                                        DON.

Rules For Correspondence.
1. Use one side of the paper only.
2. Letters must be typed or written in Block Capitals.
3. English language only to be used.
4. Use simple words and phrases.
5. Do not use code or secret marks.
6. News about Military, Political, Commercial and Industrial affairs
   is not allowed.

Scorched, torn, and fragile from much reading,
the letter that told Pamela she was at last
in touch with Donald once more.

Eric Maschwitz, secret agent, eternal romantic, and Pamela's dancing partner.

January 13, 1946. The end of six and a half years of waiting.

Donald at ease on the lawn in 1946. A moment of peace before his experiences in camp returned to haunt him.

Pamela (right) and Donald (third left) in 1947 with friends
in Tunbridge Wells. His pensive look hides the inner turmoil
that overcame him that winter.

The growing family:
Pamela with (from left) Joanna, Christopher,
and Carolyn in Kirkuk, Iraq, 1952.

The code cracked at last:
Philip Aston, the man who
provided Pamela with the
story that Donald had
hidden for fifty years.

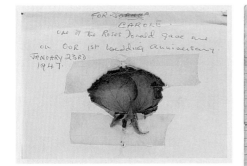

FOR ~~JOHN~~
CAROLE.
one of the Roses Donald gave me
on OOR 1st wedding anniversary.
JANUARY 23RD
1947.

10 NOV 1983

In replying to this letter, please write on the envelope:
Number J52H7 Name HILL
H.M. PRISON,
NEW NORTH ROAD,
EXETER,
EX4 4EX.   R L

WAS TOUCHED BY YOUR CARD - FULL
WARMTH & AFFECTION
NEVER FELT SO WELL - ARIVE
VACATE YOUR FLAT   NOW
AM ONE   TO THE CROFT
YOUR NEW PERMANENT HOME
WHERE WE ALL TADMIRE
LOVE YOU
BURN ALL HOT WATER BOTTLES
WE HAVE SUPER LOG FIRES
ROLL ON JANUARY . I LOVE YOU
BUT CARE FOR CYNTHIA

香港停唐收

To: Miss Pamela Kirrage,
    Winkfield Place,
    Windsor Forest, Berks.

From: Donald S Hill,
      Prisoner of War Camp N HONGKONG.

Date: 12th July 1943.

Darling One,
              Yesterday I received my second letter from you, written
on the 2nd Oct. 1942, in which you say you had just received my first letter.
My Darling it was like water to a man dying of thirst. Ginger had three from
Beryl written a little later than yours. He was very disappointed as she
had'nt heard from him-officially. So far I have'nt heard from Mother.
              My own sweet Darling to know that you are well and still
love me after four years of waiting is almost too much to believe. Often at
night I lie awake thinking of you,wondering when I shall see you again. I
know fully all the sacrifices you have made because of me, and I'm overwhelmed
with love for you. Heaven knows it's going to be a crazy world when this war
is over; families broken up and everyone seeking new ideals. But you are all my
ideals rolled into one sweetheart, to work and to live for, and to try to make
up to you everything that you have sacrificed for me. I live for two things;
to be free, and to hold you in my arms again. Four years ago today we were
together for the last time. Those few days and nights we spent together have
been with me all these years darling.
              I'm very fit; have'nt had a days's illness since I left
England. I read a lot and take plenty of exercise. I miss my flying terribly
and, when I'm not thinking of you, my thoughts turn skyward. I'm very proud
of the Service and regret deeply not being an active member of it. How's
Mac? and I often wonder where Ralph is. I dont suppose you have met Douglas.
              My alloted space is up darling. Your letter has given
me added strength to face things cheerfully. Please give my love to the Family.
              Here's to our future my darling and until then I sha'
but have to dream about you. I love you so much that it hurts.

              All my love darling one,
                I love you now and always,

                              DON.

RULES FOR CORRESPONDENCE
a. Use one side of the paper only.
b. Use block capitals or type.
c. Use simple phrases only.
d. Do not use code or secret marks.
e. News about Commercial Industrial or Military matters is forbidden.

Letters from prison.
Separated by over
forty years, two of
the impassioned
messages Donald
sent to Pamela.

Pamela Kirrage, age twenty-two, photographed
by Angus McBean. "I don't think I had ever
seen a more beautiful girl," Donald Hill recalled.

publicly humiliated. There was nothing they could do about that, either. Any resistance had to be on the inside. To himself, Donald made one silent promise. Whatever happened, however much humiliation was heaped on him, he would bear it without a murmur. His captors would never have the satisfaction of knowing his inner fury and despair.

Donald had come to value the laconic humor of the Australian fighter pilot Frank Hennessy. Together they decided they could take more of their belongings if they shared the burden. They slung their kit bags from a pole which they carried on their shoulders, and tied blankets around their necks. There were six thousand men on Hong Kong island, and all of them had to be taken across to the mainland. At dawn the next day, they marched through the streets of Victoria to the ferry, and the effect of their new status could be seen reflected in the outside world. Crowds of Chinese lined the streets to see those who had been rulers and were now prisoners pass by. Some jeered, but most were silent, as though the change were too momentous for immediate reaction, and Donald noticed that a few wept.

At the ferry they were forced to wait again until they could shuffle aboard, and then they were paraded up Kowloon's major street, Nathan Road, through a maze of roads, then down again. Either their guards were lost or the prisoners were trophies being put on display by the victors, much as a Roman general would have made a spectacle of a vanquished army. Officers rode by on horseback, bands played, and photographers ran beside them to record their downfall. The day was warm, the hills steep, and soon the shuffling columns were leaving a trail of discarded coats and blankets. The pole on which Donald and Frank Hennessy carried all their kit grew heavier and bit deeper into their shoulders. Neither dared discard items on which his life might depend, and so they stumbled on until they could go no farther. A Japanese guard came up, but instead of shouting at them, he compassionately let them transfer the burden to professional bearers. The incident almost passed unnoticed, yet amid the crushing sense of shame, even that little kindness rubbed its own grain of salt into the wound.

Their eventual destination was Sham Shui Po Barracks. Before the war it had been home to an infantry battalion, and much of the camp was occupied by parade grounds. The accommodation consisted of concrete huts and a large block of flats which had been the married officers' living quarters, all surrounded by a barbed-wire fence. The camp was built on land reclaimed from the harbor, with sea on two sides and a road on the other two. It had never been luxurious, but a brief occupation by the victors and subsequent looting by inhabitants from the neighborhood had left it looking, as Donald remarked, "as if a typhoon had hit it." Only the shells of the huts were left. The doors, windows, tables, and beds had all been stolen, and among the ruins they found two members of the Middlesex regiment who had been captured at the beginning of the battle. They had been stripped of their clothes, then tied up with wire, and after three days without food or water were barely alive.

There was a rush to find huts and anything at all that would make a bed. Donald discovered some hanks of horsehair which he used as stuffing inside a knotted blanket to make a thin mattress, and the first night of genuine captivity passed in numb discomfort. Over the next twenty-four hours, each one of them became miserably aware of the reality of their new existence. Almost six thousand men were housed there with no sanitation, no power, and no fuel. Their only food was watery rice served twice a day. And so ended 1941. The next year, Donald told himself, had to be better.

Donald shared his small hut with five others including Frank Hennessy, their commanding officer, Ginger Sullivan, and the two young pilots, Wimpey Baugh and Junior Crossley. Their first task was to patch up its windows and door with planks of wood and any scrap material they could find. They had no cups or plates, and so had to improvise from empty tins or discarded bits of crockery. Around them in the huge camp, the first semblance of organization began to take shape.

Their twice-daily meal of rice was cooked in large oil drums with the tops cut off, which retained a lingering flavor of fuel. Latrines were dug, but the overcrowding and open sewage pits attracted swarms of flies, which helped spread dysentery. The doctors set up a makeshift hospital in an empty hut and, despite the lack of medicines, attempted to treat gaping wounds and the first outbreaks of disease. But when over a hundred Indian soldiers were brought in suffering from dysentery, lack of beds meant that they had to be placed on the hut's concrete floor where, unable to move, they were soon covered in feces and blood. The prisoners' torment was compounded by the violent, seemingly haphazard punishments handed out by their captors. The offenses might seem trivial—failure to salute a guard, walking too close to the wire—but they would be rewarded by punches to the face, or a rifle butt repeatedly slammed into the ribs.

Yet within a week, every other tribulation paled into insignificance beside the lack of food. It was estimated that the two rice meals contained less than 900 calories, about one-third of the recommended daily intake for an adult male. One night as they were going to bed, a lorry roared into the camp, and the men heard the squealing of pigs. Those still up saw Japanese soldiers herd some thirty pigs out of the back of the lorry and drive off. Within minutes the animals were rounded up and penned in an empty hut. The next day they were slaughtered and divided up among the camp's inhabitants. Donald found one small lump of fat in his rice.

As the scantiness of the diet took effect, their thoughts turned insistently to food. They began to shiver and constantly feel cold. Every hut had to provide buckets for use as nighttime lavatories because the lack of vitamins and constant supply of polished rice produced bouts of diarrhea. In the morning, columns of working parties went around the camp collecting the buckets to empty in the sewage pits. To add to their misery, the swarms of flies attracted to the open latrines settled on the men's food and buzzed around their mouths as they ate.

Compared with the prisoners who worked on the Burma Railway—inspiration for *The Bridge on the River Kwai*—those in Hong Kong got off lightly. Although work parties had to be provided for labor on the extension to the Kai Tak airfield, the conditions were not as hard as those in the jungle. It was simply that they were being slowly starved to death by a shortage of food and medicine, and the lack of vitamins. In the first six months, over a hundred of them died as the result of poor feeding. Many of those who survived owed their lives to the courage of the Chinese, and in Donald's case to the courage of his girlfriend, Florrie, in particular.

"That girl probably saved my life," Donald admitted many years later. "My God, she smuggled food in to me. It's something I'll never forget. I think she saved my life."

It was the only direct reference he ever made to what she had done for him in camp, and it was no more than the sober truth. At the end of the first week of captivity, Florrie arrived outside the barbed wire surrounding the camp, accompanied by her *amah*, or maid, and carrying a basket of food. Already some market traders were selling food across the wire to the hungry prisoners, but the unpredictable attitude of the guards made this a risky business. On some days they seemed to regard it as a useful and cheap way of feeding the inmates. On other occasions, and even in the course of an afternoon, the mood changed and they would charge into the crowd flailing their rifle butts. At those times, if they caught anyone, man or woman, the victim was stripped and beaten in full view of the camp. Yet the traders not only returned but were joined in growing numbers by the Chinese wives and girlfriends of men in camp.

"It was surprising to me how many came," observed David Bosanquet, a sergeant in the Hong Kong Volunteers, who later escaped, bringing with him some of the first news of conditions behind the wire. "It was wonderful how loyal some of these girls proved to be. After all, there was no need for them to run the risk of being beaten up by the Japanese for a boyfriend who was no longer able to be with them. Food and money were very short outside."

On that first occasion, Florrie and the others were chased away by the guards because a Japanese general was expected to inspect the camp, but a few days later she was back with a parcel of bread, butter, milk, and tomatoes. No nutritionist could have chosen more carefully the foods he needed, and for the next fortnight she brought supplies every few days. To find food in a city where the normal markets had broken down must have taken hours of effort. The food was shared with the others in his hut, and even with the extra rations he felt cold and listless. Without them, he would have been in a serious state. For a few weeks Florrie was interned in the civilian camp at Stanley, and although his hut pooled their money to buy from traders, he immediately felt the loss of her parcels.

Even in the first few weeks of Sham Shui Po, it was clear that some would not survive. Malnutrition was only part of the cause. In the formless but high-anxiety environment of the camp, each individual had to find his own way of resisting the corrosive effects of helplessness. Michael Wright, the architect, saw it in stark terms. Within the first few months of captivity, he could tell that some people had given up and lost the will to live. His conclusion was simple: "If you wanted to survive you had to take a positive attitude, to assert yourself in some way, however small."

It was now that prison character began to form. Small things counted disproportionately toward survival. In the damp atmosphere, for example, clothes and shoes rapidly began to disintegrate, but when a man had so little resistance against cold and wounds, it was important to protect both body and feet. Utterly undomestic though he always had been, Donald methodically taught himself both to sew and to cobble, and in time became so adept as a cobbler and clog maker that he could earn cigarettes by repairing other prisoners' footwear. He was careful to get his hair cut short. He was conscientious about distributing the hut's precious supply of cigarettes so that no one could complain. He took pains to make his provocative size as inconspicuous as possible, so that fifty years later those who still remembered him as a prisoner also remembered how quiet and withdrawn he seemed. Above all, he made sure that his feelings were thrust so far out of sight that no one could even guess at his profound sense of humiliation.

The weak spot in his defenses was his love for Pamela. He thought about her constantly, and fretted bitterly that he could not tell her that he was still alive. Images from their brief time together kept returning, yet he dared not dwell too much on them for fear that the emotion would break him up altogether. The more powerful the feelings, the more dangerous they were.

Next to their hunger for food, the men's sharpest need was for news, and just as they imagined fantastic feasts to satisfy their empty bellies, so they began to conjure up extraordinary rumors to fill the void in their minds. The most persistent was that Chiang Kai-shek's Nationalist Chinese army was massed nearby and could be expected to attack at any moment. The Pope, it was said, had gone to negotiate peace in Berlin, and an equally definite account held that Hitler had in fact committed suicide. No less encouraging were the reports from Malaya about massive British victories over the Japanese. Quite soon they could expect to be liberated, ran the unspoken message, and each man would again be needed by his unit to help in the war against Japan. Donald appreciated that these were only rumors, and wild ones at that, but he could not help observing that their news was always good. Cautiously he allowed himself to conclude that things must be going well.

The reality began to emerge by the end of January. There were enough radio experts in the camp to assemble sets, and gradually it became apparent from the BBC, despite the brave face put upon the news, that the Malayan campaign was a disaster. This information had a devastating effect on spirits already battered by personal defeat and constant lack of food. In camp tempers were lost for little or no reason, and on one occasion a full-scale fight between British and Indian soldiers flared up. In many units discipline was in danger of breaking down completely, and, perhaps most seriously of all, the rules on sanitation and hygiene began to be ignored. The latrines were often not emptied and the few lavatories that functioned were not repaired, increasing the risk of a dysentery epidemic. Early in February Maltby felt obliged to issue the ultimate threat: unless men obeyed their own officers he would hand over direct control of them to the Japanese. It was a confession of his own incapacity to give a lead in those difficult circumstances, and since it implied a final betrayal of those under his command, it made the task of creating internal discipline harder than ever.

Michael Wright was not alone in thinking that Maltby was a broken man by then. "The surrender was a terrible blow to him," he judged, "and he did not lead well as a prisoner." Only the sudden relief from overcrowding as first the Indian troops and then the Canadians were moved to different camps prevented the camp from descending into chaos.

Once early hopes of victory evaporated, prisoners started to think of escape. With only a wire fence to penetrate, the real problem was not so much getting out as getting away. Europeans were conspicuous, and unless they spoke Chinese or had contacts outside the wire, they were not likely to get far. But perhaps the biggest obstacle was the psychological sense of not knowing where safety lay in the immense space of China. The first man to go over the wire was Lindsay Ride, who had taken the precaution of bringing a map into camp. Yet even he, who as a university professor had twenty years' experience of Hong Kong and was accompanied by one of his Chinese students—reckoned the odds were ten to one against success. As it turned out, the presence of Communist guerrillas operating in the countryside improved the odds considerably, and many escapees, including Ride, were led to safety with their help. Nevertheless, when two of

Donald's young pilot officers, Junior Crossley and Wimpey Baugh, decided separately at the end of January to try to get out, they were venturing into what continued to be unknown and dangerous territory.

Japanese sentries were concentrating on the landward side of the camp to keep trading across the wire in check. As a result, an increasing number of Chinese traders had taken to sailing up at night in junks and sending small boats to sell food through the wire along the seawall. It was from this side that the RAF men hoped to go. The would-be escapees were in different parties— Junior with a group that had bribed a trading junk to take them across the bay, and Wimpey with two others who proposed swimming with a makeshift raft from the shore.

Independently each group had planned to go on the same night, since they needed a full moon in order to travel. The remaining RAF officers stayed up late to give them a last meal before they made the attempt. On their first effort, the moon was so bright that Donald and the others were able to pass the time playing cards. Both attempts were frustrated, one by the junk failing to turn up, the other by the collapse of the makeshift raft built of firewood scrounged or given by friends. Undeterred, they tried again two nights later, and this time slipped away. A little later, bursts of rifle fire left their friends fearing the worst. Though no one in camp knew the outcome, both pilots did succeed in reaching freedom. Each flew again in combat, although Baugh was killed before the end of the war.

All those left behind were prey to regrets—and to relief that they were still within the relative safety of the camp. Something of their confused feelings could be found in a comment from Major J. N. Crawford, a doctor who had been a colleague of Lindsay Ride's and refused the chance to escape with him. "First my duty seemed to be to remain with the men," he explained. "Secondly I felt that anyone of my unusual height would minimise the chances of anyone getting through; and third I was damned scared and preferred to remain with the devil I knew. I deeply regretted my decision on many occasions subsequently."

Although Donald was no doctor, his sense of responsibility for the men in his unit was unmistakable, and one of the reasons why he was later decorated. Like Crawford, he must have felt that his conspicuous size was a handicap. On the other hand, as he was to make plain, he was desperate to be free, to see Pamela again and to fly. Since his courage was not in question, his preference for the devil he knew to the unknown beyond the wire must have been a matter of psychology. As their accounts unconsciously reveal, each of the escapees had a streak of self-belief amounting almost to arrogance. It was not a quality that Donald possessed, and without it no one was likely to launch himself into the hostile void of China.

The Japanese, so contemptuous of their prisoners, at first seemed almost oblivious to the escapes. There were extra parades, and long confused counts of their numbers, but although the sentries shot at junks that approached by day, they seemed to notice nothing amiss at night. Discussing their apparent indifference, Donald and his companions concluded that their captors must regard escape as somehow despicable, like deserting. What they failed to appreciate was that for Colonel Isao Tokunaga, the camp commandant, the prisoners' disappearance amounted to a loss of face.

A week after the two escapes, every RAF officer except one was ordered to pack his kit. At dawn on February 6 they were put on a lorry and transported to Shanghai, to be held for six weeks in a French colonial prison. The one left behind was Donald.

Suddenly he was on his own, responsible for the welfare of sixty men in a situation that could hardly have been worse.

For the only time in camp, his composure almost cracked. Perhaps there was an echo of that sense of being abandoned which he must have experienced at his father's sudden death, for not even battle had provoked such anxiety. He recorded his despair in his diary, then buried the words in the crude letters-to-numbers code he still employed. Over time the secret was to be concealed more and more deeply, and what he felt at this crisis, the gut emotion that emerged from the inner core of his being, was to remain a mystery for half a century.

After six weeks in a Saigon prison, the RAF officers emerged gaunt and starving and so badly diseased that the worst affected spent months recovering in hospital. But none died. Many of those left behind in Sham Shui Po fared worse. Barely a month after the RAF escapees, another party of four, led by Lieutenant Douglas Clague, also got away. This time Tokunaga was furious. He demanded that every prisoner sign an oath not to escape, and as punishment the rice ration, which had gradually increased, was cut back to its original starvation level and all trade through the wire was forbidden. For men hovering on the verge of malnutrition, the consequences were immediate and catastrophic. Donald noticed in himself the preliminary signs of beriberi, which is caused by a lack of vitamin B. Edema swelled his ankles and legs like balloons, but the residual effects of Florrie's parcels saved him from the next stage, agonizing shooting pains that sufferers called electric feet. The agony could reduce victims to tears, and to escape it they would sit for hours with their feet soaking in water until the sodden skin split across the soles.

But everyone's skin was erupting and suppurating as the vitamin deficiencies returned with renewed violence. Diphtheria made the throat swollen and septic. Pellagra left the skin roughened and itching as uncontrollably as eczema, usually around the groin. Sufferers' inflamed genitals swelled to the size of tennis balls, a condition known as strawberry balls, and were so itchy that one man literally scratched himself to death. The deadliest consequence of the malnutrition, however, was dysentery, which affected almost half the camp that April.

A few days after his friends were removed, Donald himself was taken out of camp for questioning. It was not a reassuring prospect. Escorted by an unusually large guard, a Formosan sergeant known simply as George, who stood over six feet tall and was notorious for the beatings he gave with his sword, Donald was marched in front of the commandant Lieutenant Hideo Wada, whose protuberant teeth and character earned him the nickname Ratface. Instead of a beating, however, Donald was offered a cigarette, and George asked him how the Japanese air force compared with the RAF. Donald took the opportunity to steal a handful of cigarettes and offer his forthright, and largely mistaken, opinions about the slowness of the Zero fighter.

Although he did not know it, he had failed a little test. The Japanese had decided that the number of escapes would be reduced if the officers were transferred to a more secure camp. Some, however, would have to remain at Sham Shui Po to be in charge of the servicemen still there; one would be appointed to be in overall command, and thus directly responsible to the Japanese. Donald was only one of several officers surveyed before they found their ideal candidate in Major Cecil Boon. Notoriously inept and soon christened Major Disaster, Boon proved himself so ready to do anything to ingratiate himself with his superiors that after the war he was court-martialed on a charge of treason. Yet even before his appointment, the starving camp had produced a flock of informers ready to sell their friends' secrets for extra rations.

The exception to this rule was the RAF unit, and much of the credit for its high morale was due to Donald's work during these weeks. From the start, he had ensured in his meticulous way that his men were able to cope with the trials of prison life. He lectured them on the need for discipline, but singled them out for praise because unlike other troops they had kept up their standards. When the existence of the camp's clandestine radio was betrayed to the Japanese by informers, Donald took the RAF signals specialists aside, warning them that they would be questioned but that they were to deny all knowledge of the set. As it happened, a total of three radios had been constructed, of which the guards discovered two, the third having been dismantled before it could be found. Although they had certainly been involved with at least one of them, Donald's men admitted nothing and escaped punishment. Amid the debilitation of malnutrition and the unvarying news of military defeat, this tiny triumph helped to keep their spirits up.

Among so many demoralized units, the example of the RAF was sufficiently striking for Maltby to remark on it when Sullivan returned from his prison cell. Five years later Sullivan reminded Maltby that he had "complimented me on the high morale and good behaviour of the Unit, a state of affairs for which Flight Lieutenant Hill was largely responsible." Taken with Hill's courage in battle and his attempt to save the burning Vildebeeste, he suggested that it warranted a decoration. Across the bottom of the page Maltby scribbled "Recommended," with a decisive flourish that showed how vividly he recalled what Donald achieved in camp.

In April, he was forced to leave the men he had cared for

when all but about twenty officers were transferred to a camp on Argyle Street. It had been built for internees before the war, and its relative security could be measured by the fact that only one person successfully escaped from it. There was no furniture, and nothing in the long wooden huts except their concrete floors, but the compensations made up for the renewed discomforts. Ginger Sullivan, Frank Hennessy, and all Donald's other friends were sent there, too. They had space. But most miraculous of all, the Japanese had at last responded to Red Cross pressure to allow prisoners to write home. They were allowed just two hundred words, which had to be printed out.

Very carefully, as though any mistake might prevent it being sent, Donald wrote:

To Miss Pamela Kirrage, 2 Queen's Road, Tunbridge Wells, England.
From: D. S. Hill

Then came the date, "3rd June 1942," and after that a large gap.

My darling,
The Japanese authorities are allowing us to write and this is to assure you that I am safe and well. Would you communicate with mother telling you have heard from me. I shall be writing to her soon.

Well my darling perhaps by now you have given me up as dead. I dont know. But through all these months you have been always in my thoughts. Whatever happens I shall always love you. When you write darling please stick to the rules I have set out below.

All my love darling. I love you. Always have and always will.

Don

The rules, designed to help Japanese censors, required the correspondent to write in capitals, use only simple words, omit political or military information, and restrict herself to one side of each sheet of paper. In addition there was rule five: "Do not use code or secret marks." For someone who was keeping a coded diary, that must have been cause for at least the ghost of a smile.

6

Disguising the Truth

It is impossible to obtain real privacy in
the information age without
good cryptography.

—PHILIP ZIMMERMAN,
AUTHOR OF PGP ("PRETTY GOOD PRIVACY")
SOFTWARE FOR EMAIL ENCRYPTION

Early in March, it occurred to Philip Aston that although Donald Hill had had neither a computer, nor privacy, nor security, he had possessed one priceless advantage that his decoder lacked. He had an abundance of spare time. Aston had begun to ransack the university library for books on prisoner-of-war camps in the Far East, and the more he read, the better he understood the conditions under which Donald must

131

have been working. For Donald, the problem would have been how to spend time rather than how to find it.

There were fewer people and a greater degree of organization at Argyle Street than at Sham Shui Po. On the other hand, there were the same huts filled with long lines of beds, and a parade ground with the same long-drawn-out inspections. When they arrived the huts contained nothing, and so there was the same hunt for material that could be fashioned into everyday objects like furniture and crockery. As before, their bunks quickly became infested with bedbugs. Their clothes and shoes disintegrated equally quickly in the heat and humidity, and to save the remains of their uniforms, in hot weather they wore only a rag pulled between the legs and looped around a string belt. And what clearly grated hardest, they were forced to follow the same humiliating regulations requiring prisoners to bow to every guard, regulations that were enforced with the routine resort to face-slapping and body-punching.

Against that sort of background, the careful boxes and minute numerals by which Donald had disguised his diary seemed impossibly ordered. Suddenly Aston realized that it would have been impossible to code the entries directly into this form. There must have been at least one intermediate stage. The entries would have been written first in normal English. This was the plaintext. Presumably he would have immediately disguised this in some simple cipher. Later he would have translated it with another cipher, and then added one more layer of complexity, before the final transformation into numbers and its neat entry into the diary. Aston had uncovered two of the layers and was facing a third in the blocks of meaningless letters. Beyond that there might lie more.

Yet even as he struggled to find a key to the puzzle that Donald had set, Aston's thoughts kept returning to the circumstances in which it had been composed. From the calm and order of his small study on the third floor of Building AA, an anonymous brick rectangle on a modern university campus whose landscaped lawns and functional buildings looked down on the prosperous, ribboned streets of Guildford, it was an unimaginable distance to the prisoner-of-war camp with its gnawing hunger, its heat, and the constant threat of physical punishment. The immediate challenge was to find a solution to the code, but half-consciously he was aware of the deeper impulse to get through to that world, and to learn what it was that had happened there.

As the days lengthened and the code deepened its hold on him, he found it harder to regard it as the amusing diversion it had at first seemed. Linda began to recognize the pages of numbers and jumbled letters that he took home two or three evenings a week. In the midst of family discussions, she grew familiar with the vacant look indicating that his attention had wandered away, and whatever else he was thinking about, it was not what was happening in the Aston family. The stress began to tell on Linda. Their youngest child, Matthew, was only eighteen months old and often woke at night. When she was not listening for the baby, Linda was aware of her husband moving restlessly about in bed. "One way or the other we all spent most of our nights awake," she admitted ruefully.

After one such restless night, Aston woke with a pain beneath his ribs, and when he got out of bed, he found it hard to stretch his arms. With a wince, he recognized the symptoms. His lung had collapsed. The first time it had happened, he had been rushed to the hospital, where a tube was inserted under his left arm to remove from his chest cavity the air that was preventing the lung from expanding. Now, knowing what was involved, he decided to put up with the pain and finish some pressing work before going for treatment. He allowed himself just two days in hospital, enough time for the lung to be reinflated and sealed to his ribs so that it could not collapse again, then went back home. Reluctantly obeying orders to remain in bed for a few days, he took up some university papers to occupy him. A few minutes later Linda heard him call out, "Could you bring me up the diary?"

Yet however he examined them, the medley of letters that had taken the place of numbers—"ascg utyt ttce ashs lion tlrh mnee pfnm"—defied every attempt he made, whether in bed or in his office, to produce any sort of sense. The limitation of a computer was that it could only look for regular patterns. A cipher that rearranged the pairing "th" or "he" in the same way each time the letters appeared would produce a pattern, which a computer program could detect immediately.

What he had to accept now was that Donald had used a key which jumbled up the letters in an apparently random fashion. If there were sometimes five spaces between the "t" and the "h," and sometimes two, then seven, the machine would be defeated. In that case, only a human intelligence would be able to understand how chaos had been created out of order. Yet Aston still remained convinced that he would eventually see into Donald's secret. Chaos and complexity were Aston's speciality: his most recent paper had the apposite title "Analysis of the Control of Chaos—Rate of Convergence." And so while he convalesced, the sleepless nights in the Aston household continued.

"The great thing about Philip is that he's dogged," Linda acknowledged, and it was impossible to tell whether exasperation or appreciation dominated in her voice. "He will always keep going whatever happens. He doesn't like anything to defeat him."

Aston imagined the problem being worked on by some half-conscious part of his brain. "It's ticking over, it's on the back burner" was how he liked to put it. The process was a constant, almost visual probing at the code, as though he were mentally feeling its shape. Only when he sensed something significant would he bring it sharply into focus.

More than ever Aston was convinced that there had to be an independent key, a word or phrase that would suggest a way of rearranging the letters. What he suspected was that Donald's key depended on some specialized knowledge. It might not be related to the text, but such keys were rarely selected entirely at random. During the Reformation, both Catholic and Protestant agents would build ciphers around quotations from the Bible that suited their spiritual leanings. Later codemakers have taken a particular passage from a favorite book to indicate how letters should be re-arranged. Since Donald's key needed only to be known to him-self, it might come from anywhere. But it was a reasonable inference he would have taken it from the circumstances of his imprisonment. Time was not one of Aston's luxuries. He should have been preparing a paper for the *International Journal on Bifurcation Chaos,* but instead he snatched some hours to read more about the camps.

In some way, the encryption of his diary was almost a reflec-tion of what Donald must have been going through himself. His past would have bred in him the normal human expectations of love and hope, of personal security and predictable events. That was the plaintext, the original pattern of his life, and somewhere inside him it must still have existed. But around it he must have evolved a way of existing that concealed its fragile coherence from the madness of the prison world. To be effective, the dis-guise had to be as impenetrable as the code itself.

7

Behind the Wire

We only part to meet again.
Change as ye list, ye winds; my heart shall be
The faithful compass that still points to thee.

—JOHN GAY,

"SWEET WILLIAM'S FAREWELL"

Those who best survived life in Sham Shui Po and Argyle Street took the robust view that the camps were not too bad. In September 1942 Brigadier Cecil Templer moved to Argyle Street from the hospital after recovering from wounds received in the battle for Hong Kong, and found the contrast with the boredom of convalescence stimulating.

"There were activities of all kinds under way," he later wrote. "Lectures, courses of instruction, rehearsals for plays. There were courses in German, accounting, a debating group and a very interesting series of talks on English literature and composition every Sunday."

Other parts of the experience were, he acknowledged, less educational. Overall command of the camps was in the hands of Colonel Tokunaga, whose gross appearance gave rise to the nickname White Pig. After the war he was found guilty both of systematically looting the Red Cross parcels that were sent to the prisoners, and of being responsible for the camps' regime of random violence. In this, however, Hong Kong was no worse than other Japanese camps. David Piper, who was in Changi prison in Singapore, described a beating given to four prisoners there, catching in sharp focus both its routine nature and the curiously distanced reaction of those who had already been through it themselves.

"There they were, four lean figures lined up," he wrote. "One of the guards, about half their height, walked down the line beating their faces. He swung his arm straight from the shoulder, leaning into the blow, and each time he struck, the bayonet on the rifle in his other hand swung and caught the sunlight. At the end of the row he changed hands and worked back on the other cheek. The sound of the blows reached me late, sounding small and remote. It was as though I was watching a rather crude film that had failed to grip me."

It was not only the guards who beat the prisoners up. Every encounter with the camp authorities was made through interpreters, and the names of two in particular aroused real hatred. There was the half-Canadian Inouye Kanao, nicknamed Slap Happy for his tendency to hit the defenseless people he was talking to, or Shat in Pants for the deep hang of his trousers, and the equally sadistic Niimori Genichiro, who had spent twenty years in the American Midwest and addressed his victims as "youse guys" or "baby." Yet most prisoners also recognized that such personal violence was endemic in the Japanese army: officers punched NCOs, and NCOs slapped private soldiers. And with utter unpredictability some of those in power, like the interpreter Watanabe Kyoshi, who was a Lutheran, or another who had lived in Wales and was known as Cardiff Joe, treated them with unwavering courtesy. Like David Piper, everyone learned to wall himself off from what was being done to them.

Their diet still consisted largely of three meals of boiled rice, but even this had to be picked over to remove clumps of weevils and their eggs. Periodic issues of vegetables did provide some vitamins, occasionally supplemented in summer by chrysanthemum leaves, and once a fortnight, two ounces of grilled fish appeared with the rice. Later the prisoners were allowed to make a garden on some disused ground where tomatoes and other vegetables could be grown. Nevertheless, men lost up to eighty pounds on this regimen. Once more Donald was shielded from the worst of the food shortage by Florrie, who had eventually found out where he was.

In Sham Shui Po, she had not only brought him food but clothes, and once even a *mingtoia,* a warm, quilted Chinese blanket, and during the winter nights Donald was as grateful for that as for any of the life-saving food. Arrangements in Argyle Street were more formal. Food could be brought in and left in the guardhouse but civilians were not allowed to stand in the road outside, and prisoners were forbidden to attempt to communicate with passersby. The clandestine whispers that took place could lead to misunderstandings, and for several weeks one hungry prisoner kept receiving packets of needles from his Chinese wife. Finally, in exasperation, he ran to the wire and, defying the guards, bellowed, "I said noodles, not needles." According to witnesses, the mordant humor of this was best appreciated on an empty stomach.

The Chinese, however, were suffering just as badly from lack of food, and Florrie was visibly less healthy. Even at Sham Shui Po, Donald had repeatedly told her that she should leave the colony for mainland China, where food might be more plentiful, but she refused to abandon him. When he persisted, she told him to mind his own business. The Japanese stole her jewelry, and before long she was turned out of the comfortable flat where she lived. But she continued to bring him what she could. Her affection overwhelmed him, and he was filled with admiration for the ingenuity and persistence with which she found a way past the guards. Yet it was not an easy feeling. Her very effectiveness reminded him of his helplessness. She was spending money she desperately needed for herself to keep him alive, and he could not hope to repay her. And there was something more. What he felt for her did not balance what she so clearly felt for him. It was only Pamela that he loved. That was not a feeling that changed.

Every month he wrote to Pamela, and as time passed without word from her he began to grow anxious. Before the invasion, they had written regularly to each other. Their letters were often mundane communications about the weather and parties, but they gave him assurance that their love was a real, shared emotion, not something he had imagined. Six months without any word revived his deep-seated apprehension that whatever he most valued would again be taken from him. When the camp authorities announced in June 1942 that each prisoner would be allowed to send one letter a month, his hopes and fears soared equally.

The sharpest fear was that she might have been killed or

wounded in a bombing raid, but beneath that came a dull foreboding that her feelings for him might have changed. She loved attention, she was fun, and she was beautiful. In wartime, when life was so short it had to be lived to the limit, that was an electric mixture of qualities, and he knew how young men in uniform behaved. At times he almost clung to the hope that she had not yet heard from him.

The prisoners never knew what happened to their letters. They were collected for censoring and then supposedly for onward transmission by way of the Red Cross, but the same procedure was followed every month, and their communications simply disappeared into a void. No reply arrived, nothing happened. The letters might never have been written, except for the sense of having spent so much emotion in composing them.

In fact, many of those fervent messages never got beyond Japan. Few enough Japanese could read English, and most of those were employed in strategically important jobs. Censoring prisoners' letters could not have had a lower priority, and with ill-trained translators stumbling painfully through the mountain of post, the backlog reached such numbing proportions that frequently the letters were simply burned. When there was no response, everyone who had opened up his heart to some distant person he loved suffered his own particular torment.

Within the Argyle Street camp, there were extroverts and introverts, persnickety lawyers and diffident architects, professional soldiers and amateur musicians, cross-dressers and straight men, cardsharps, king rats, officers, gentlemen, cowards, conformists, and the courageous; and most were several of these mixed together. As Michael Wright discovered, "There was good and bad in everyone. You couldn't separate it out, the line went right down through each of us. There was good in the worst, and bad in the best. But on the whole there was more good than bad."

The absence of news from home was one of the stresses that kept the level of anxiety high. Fights broke out between prisoners over apparent trifles. The way someone talked or dressed might be enough. And all the time there was the constant, nagging inability to escape from other people. Around each crowded bed ran a boundary invisible to an outsider but as obvious as a brick wall to a prisoner, and it could not be passed without the permission of the occupant. It was possible to retreat there, but it was impossible to seal off the other forty-nine people in the hut, and the other six hundred–odd who filled the spaces around the huts.

"What we resented most during our imprisonment was not the bad food, or the cold, or the domineering attitude of the Japanese, although all these were unpleasant," wrote Major Crawford, the Canadian doctor who had refused to escape, "but what bothered most of us more than anything else was the overcrowding, the complete lack of privacy. In camp, we lived cheek by jowl with the same little group, year after year. And under such circumstances, the dearest friend can become hateful."

That was what it meant to be a prisoner. Like children, they were helpless to exercise control over their existence. All they could do was learn how to control the show of feeling. Even five decades later, that careful wall remained apparent to an outsider. It was neither hostile nor self-protective, just an instinctive piece of behavior required for survival.

As at Sham Shui Po, Donald shared his hut with other RAF officers. They were all in Hut 8, which held almost fifty people. Of the original seven, only Ginger Sullivan, Frank Hennessy,

Dolly Gray, and he remained, and they were exceptionally close. To fill the time, Donald went with them to lectures on philosophy or deer-stalking or training to be a Church of Scotland minister or any other area of expertise that someone was prepared to talk about. The most popular was one on winemaking, and when a Red Cross parcel filled with South African fruit arrived in November, Hut 8 attempted to make their own wine from the raisins. Donald went to German classes given by someone who happened to possess a German grammar. The camp had acquired a supply of books from the Hong Kong public library, which he read voraciously. With Ginger, he began to learn how to play bridge, and when volunteers were required to help dig a garden beyond the road, he gladly took part. He would do anything to fill the time.

In September the Japanese ordered an RAF officer to transfer to Sham Shui Po to be in charge of the RAF troops there. It could not have been easy to decide who should leave the circle of friends, but events were to make the selection a matter of life and death. In effect, the choice lay between just two of them. Because Ginger had to remain at Argyle Street as commanding officer, and Frank had barely got to know the men before the fighting began, it could only be Donald or Dolly Gray, the pilot with whom he had volunteered for a suicidal bombing mission in the old Vildebeestes. Donald had been an excellent commander in Sham Shui Po while the others were in Saigon prison, but in the end it was decided that he had done his stint there. Early in September, Gray was sent to Sham Shui Po. The choice was to save Donald's life.

Quite probably it was at this period that he began to devise another, safer cipher for the contents of his diary. All his classes and pastimes showed how desperate he was to keep his mind busy, and everyone understood how dangerous it was to keep any kind of record of events. One officer who took notes on camp life used to bury his journal in the ground. Another used minute scraps of paper, which he concealed in his clothes. Donald chose to bury his in the numbers he had loved in childhood. Presumably he first made a rough copy, but it was at about this time too that he acquired a stiff-backed, parchment-colored notebook. At first all he wrote in it were the rules of German grammar. Any activity helped occupy his mind and dull the growing anxiety at receiving no reply from Pamela. In November, several officers received letters from their families, and more came in December, but not for him.

Disappointment was a corrosive emotion, and it was second nature for Donald to conceal it. When he came to write his Christmas letter to Pamela, he tried not to let her guess at the suffering that loss of freedom caused.

"My darling," he wrote. "This is the sixth letter I have written to you; and so far I have received none in reply, but I am sure that it is not that you have not written."

As for me, darling, I am fighting fit, basking in the sun all day. Nearly a year as a prisoner of war, and the time just flies. Our lives our [*sic*] made up with lectures, classes and Bridge, with a spot of gardening to supply the exercise.

I wrote to my Bank some time ago instructing them to send you a hundred pounds. I hope you have received it by now.

I live for the day when I will receive my first letter from you. On that day I shall drink a toast to you in home-made raisin-wine.

All my thoughts are with you, darling. Je vous aime; Always have and always will.

Donald.

It was impossible to tell the truth, not just because the letter would have been censored, but because to acknowledge that his bones pushed through like tent-poles, that his skin itched from scabies and bedbugs and pellagra, and that time dragged by like a snail, would have been to destroy what kept him going.

Although he could not know it, the letter was to lie for two years in a Japanese censor's office. And so the silence continued and the tension of waiting banked up. It was not something he could afford to acknowledge. Like almost every other prisoner of war, he concentrated on survival, and that meant not thinking of anything more than the detail of each day's activities. German, bridge, gardening, lecture, then German, bridge, and gardening again. Early in 1943, that narrow tunnel vision was blown apart by a message from the outside world.

Lindsay Ride, one of the first men to escape from Sham Shui Po, accused the Hong Kong prisoners he left behind of not being sufficiently "escape-minded." Australian by birth and adamantly independent in temper, he later wrote of his own breakout that it had been inspired by a classic escape book of the First World War, *The Road to En-Dor* by E. H. Jones, describing his escape from a Turkish prison. One of the book's underlying themes was that simply thinking of escape had a psychological value in transforming a prisoner's outlook on his condition. Like the men of Argyle Street, Jones's fellow inmates had made an effort to occupy themselves in captivity. "But in spite of the outward cheerfulness," he wrote, "the brave attempts at industry, and the gallant struggle against the deterioration that a prison environment brings, an atmosphere of hopelessness pervaded the whole camp. At heart we were all unhappy, for we had created for ourselves an 'Inevitable.' " In other words, the prisoners had accepted that escape was impossible. From his own experience, Jones believed that whatever punishments were meted out for trying to escape, the gain in pride and self-esteem justified it. "Prisoners most of us would have remained," he argued, "but not beaten captives, the victims of misfortune, but not its slaves."

The moment he reached freedom, Ride set out to make the same opportunity available to those still in camp. To help them he set up an organization with a deliberately vague title, the British Army Aid Group (BAAG), whose purpose was to make contact with the camps and set up escape routes through occupied China to the independent city of Chungking.

Soon after Dolly Gray arrived in Sham Shui Po in September 1942, the first BAAG message reached that camp, through the work parties that were still going out to work on the extension to Kai Tak airport. Chinese labor gangs already on the site soon began talking to Cantonese-speaking prisoners, among whom was an RAF flight sergeant, Ralph Hardy. In October, one of the Chinese laborers gave him a cigarette packet, and when he opened it, he found two scraps of paper with messages on them. They contained news about the North African campaign and offered prisoners help with medicine or in organizing escapes. One was signed mysteriously, "Agent 68," but the other purported to come from a familiar figure, Douglas Clague, who had escaped from the camp in April 1942. "Keep chin up. Help in Waichow," ran the one from Agent 68. The other asked the senior British officer to send information about the camp to Major Clague.

Major Boon was the senior British officer, so the message should have been delivered to him, but his eagerness to collaborate with the Japanese made him untrustworthy. Hardy decided to show the notes to a captain in the Royal Scots, Douglas Ford. In a camp where morale was low, partly because of malnutrition, and partly because over 1,800 of the fittest men had been shipped off to Japan on board the freighter *Lisbon Maru,* everyone who met him recognized the exceptional quality of Ford's solidity and strength of purpose.

There was every chance that the messages were a trick, but Ford decided that the risk was worth taking. He consulted two other officers who shared his outlook, and with their advice formulated a measured reply to be sent to Clague. Because Hardy was in the RAF, Ford judged that his senior officer should also be told what was happening. Thus the newly returned Dolly Gray was recruited to join the tiny core making up the contact group at Sham Shui Po.

Although Ride had set up headquarters in the city of Chungking, over 150 miles away in southern China, he had sent a forward group under Clague to operate from Waichow, a scant forty miles from the camps. As a former prisoner of war himself, Clague might have been expected to sympathize with conditions in the camp, but his response to Ford's cautious message took an abrasive tone. All officers in the camps had to regard themselves as being under orders to make preparations for escape, he wrote on a scrap of silk cloth. "A much more offensive spirit must be worked up," he wrote. "To hell with this defeatist attitude. There will be risks but I am ordered by the authorities to tell you all, especially officers, that your duty is obvious."

Much of this was implicitly directed at Maltby, who discouraged all attempts at escape, but the hectoring tone took little account of conditions in either Sham Shui Po or Argyle Street. The cut in an already meager ration following the Ford group's successful breakout had shattered many inmates both physically and psychologically. The combination of less rice, no extra food from beyond the wire, and fewer vitamins had by Ford's own estimate left only 20 percent of the once fit young men with "the staying power to carry out any real job of work."

In truth, however, there was no attractive option. An escaper who was caught would certainly be executed, but the alternative was hardly better. Word was seeping into camp of the fate of the men who had been sent to Japan on the *Lisbon Maru*. A total of 1,816 prisoners had been battened down in the hold, and when the ship was torpedoed by an American submarine on October 1, 1942, just 724 survived. Further drafts were due to be sent to Japan, and even if they arrived safely the future for underfed men doing forced labor in steel mills and coal mines was not inviting.

In clear, sensible fashion Ford steered a course between the two. No escape was possible while malnutrition was so prevalent, he insisted. Their physical state would quickly improve with more Red Cross food parcels and medicine, and then they would be prepared to cooperate with any plans that BAAG put forward. By chance, a Red Cross food delivery was made that November, and BAAG's Chinese agents found ways of delivering medicine to the camp, including thousands of tablets of nicotinic acid—niacin—which was the recommended treatment for pellagra. So rapid was the physical improvement of the prisoners that by the end of 1942, Sham Shui Po's contact group was starting to plan for escape.

It was not until the spring of 1943 that BAAG's agents made contact with Argyle Street. Four times a week a ration truck came into the camp with sacks of rice and vegetables. Agent 68, a resourceful Chinese named Li Fong, bribed the Formosan driver to deliver the message either in a discarded cigarette packet or simply as a crumpled piece of paper pushed into a prisoner's hand.

Since there was always an armed guard on the truck, and guards on duty at the camp entrance a dozen yards away, with sentries patrolling the perimeter fence and others overlooking the scene from watchtowers, this operation was fraught with danger. The first unexpected note was transferred almost in open view; only the crowd of prisoners milling around as they unloaded the rice served as a distraction. The immediate priority was to devise a safer method of transmitting future messages.

The note was addressed to Colonel Newnham, Maltby's senior staff officer, since he, unlike the general, was known to be sympathetic to escape attempts. A quiet, narrow-faced man with deep-set eyes, Newnham possessed an intense and private character. Almost too readily he tried to take on his own shoulders the whole responsibility for communicating with BAAG. Initially he detailed just two officers, John Harris and Godfrey Bird, to pick up messages from the food truck. But this impulse to keep to a minimum the number who knew about the contact soon proved impractical. Camp duties, such as emptying garbage pails and peeling lily roots, were rotated among the different huts on a daily basis. In the tiny village of Argyle Street, it was quickly noticed that whichever hut was on duty for unloading food trucks, Harris and Bird were always present. Once suspicions were aroused, they would become the subject of gossip—the latrines were a favorite spot to discuss the camp's events, even though an English-speaking guard was usually lurking nearby—and the secret would soon be out. Reluctantly Newnham decided that the contact group needed to be enlarged.

The one essential quality was coolness. It was not easy to

know how the message would come, whether handed over directly or stuffed among the vegetables or left on the floor at the back of the truck. Nor could the conspirators afford to make a mistake or attract the attention of the guards. Every prisoner had seen and experienced enough of the punches and clubbings that greeted the smallest infraction of the rules to be able to imagine the punishment for communicating with British forces and Chinese guerrillas. They could expect no mercy. Godfrey Bird, whose refusal to talk under torture was to earn him the George Medal, observed wryly that just before his arrest he had been reading a book about Torquemada, the legendary examiner of the Spanish Inquisition, and that the Japanese employed every one of the many tortures listed there.

Among those that Newnham approached were Ralph Goodwin, who later broke out of camp and made his way alone to freedom. And from Hut 8, he asked Donald Hill to help. Quite typically, before letting any of them agree, Newnham went to great lengths to detail the dangers and offer each one the opportunity to think the proposition over and to withdraw if he thought the risk too high. From what is known about the contact group, it seems probable that Newnham was drawn to private, self-reliant people, not unlike himself. If so, his judgment was good, for none of them backed out.

It is doubtful whether Donald seriously considered refusing Newnham's offer. He had shown that in response to danger, he became cold and clear-minded. And the continued denial of the things he yearned for most in the world must have made the prospect of escape irresistible whatever the risk. Ride was right in estimating how much the prospect of freedom altered a prisoner's outlook. Being part of a scheme that might lead to escape blew away Donald's narrow focus on the camp's daily rituals. He still played bridge, continued to write out tedious rules for conjugating German irregular verbs, but they were no longer what they appeared to be. Now they became like Russels Mathematical Tables, an appearance of something mundane that disguised the importance of the secret within.

It was harrowing work. Each man was responsible for collecting every scrap of paper from the food truck so that no message would be overlooked, and for delivering it to Bird, who took it on to Newnham. It was also their job to see that the driver's attention was attracted so that any outgoing message could be planted either directly with him or on the truck where he could find it later. Not only were they being watched by the guards on duty around the camp, but they became aware that from elevated points outside the wire, there were other watchers studying their movements through binoculars.

If Donald ever wondered why he was running the risk, a play that the entire camp attended on March 5, 1943, would have reminded him. Written by one of the prisoners, it was called *The Golden Road,* and it played upon their deepest fears. It was set after the end of the war, a time they all looked forward to, and its story of a prisoner of war hurrying home to be reunited with his fiancée was one that most of them imagined nightly. It was the ending that came out wrong. The man discovers that the girl has married someone else. Her explanation that "two years is a long time" was greeted by the audience with the tense silence of men who recognized in it a horrible truth.

Then, amazingly, on April 10 the long silence was broken. For the first time in sixteen months a letter arrived from Pamela. In his excitement, he could hardly read it. The words jumped off the page: "My darling"; "an eternity"; "with all my love." The miracle had happened. He was still loved.

8

A Nightingale Sang

Gardenia perfume lingering on a pillow,
Wild strawberries, only seven francs a kilo,
And still my heart has wings,
These foolish things remind me of you.

— ERIC MASCHWITZ,

"THESE FOOLISH THINGS"

Writing to him had been an act of faith. Months had passed since the news of the colony's surrender, and Pamela still had no indication whether Donald was alive or dead. Although a Red Cross representative had been allowed into the camp in July 1942, no authoritative list of prisoners had been issued. Yet every week she continued to write into the silence.

The letters had become a kind of confessional, in

which she told him the things that meant most to her: how much she missed him, how slowly the time passed, and how she felt the horrible sense that her life was slipping away. "An eternity" was how she described the waiting. She had been twenty-three when she last saw him. In war, life speeded up to keep pace with death's acceleration, and in the years since she had said goodbye, her friends had seen their men off to war and welcomed them back, had fallen in love and out again, had got married and given birth, had boasted of their babies' accomplishments; some were pregnant again. In February 1943 she would be twenty-seven, and for her nothing had changed. All she had was the certainty that three years earlier she had been touched by a happiness that seemed unmatchable with any other man. So she continued to tell him what she could not properly tell anyone else, that she loved him as she had loved no one else, but that the waiting was a sacrifice. It was her choice, but a sacrifice all the same.

What made her constancy more extraordinary still was that everything else seemed to have been transformed since she had last heard from him. The relentless advance of German and Japanese forces had been halted, and after Allied successes at Midway in the Pacific and then at El Alamein and Stalingrad, the pendulum was swinging back. As eventual victory began to seem possible, the mood of the country altered dramatically from dogged duty to an aggressive optimism. The bombers still passed over Kent, but now more of them were heading in the opposite direction, toward Germany. *The Courier* allowed itself a congratulatory editorial on what the world owed to its readership: "Kent, Sussex and Surrey stood between the enemy and his objective. It was a solid bulwark of wonderful endurance, of courage and fortitude, of thrilling deeds, of daring which will never be surpassed." Even in Tunbridge Wells, where it had always seemed rather implausible that the foreigners might actually win, there was relief that the threat of invasion should have passed into history.

Surveying the town on one of his returns from military service, Richard Cobb noted that the only scars it bore were some bomb damage to a few prosperous houses in Lansdowne Road, but he acknowledged that "it would have been hard not to have hit a middle-class target in a town such as the Royal Borough." Fortunately, its only industry, a factory that made water crackers, had escaped the onslaught.

It was more complicated to reach home from Woburn Abbey than from Windsor, but Pamela continued to make the journey as often as she could. At least the train service had begun to improve in the absence of bombs and aerial gunfire, and she could still stay over the entire weekend. One Monday morning early in July 1942, she was about to step out of the door to get the London train when the phone in the hallway rang.

Automatically she picked up. "Tunbridge Wells 744."

She did not recognize the woman's voice at the other end. Her name was Beryl Sullivan, and she said her husband was Wing Commander Sullivan. The names meant nothing, but she was saying it as though they should. Then she explained that Ginger Sullivan was Donald's commanding officer, and suddenly Pamela was having to listen very hard to pick out the news that threatened to be swamped by her excitement. Mrs. Sullivan had heard from her husband, who was a prisoner of war; it was not clear how she had heard, but somehow her husband had told her that he had a friend with him in the camp called Donald Hill. He had given Miss Kirrage's name as the person to be called with the news that he was safe and well. That was all Mrs. Sullivan could tell her, that Donald was alive and well.

Pamela gabbled her thanks and hurtled out of the house. She had to race now or she would miss her train, but tears of happiness blinded her so that she could hardly see. As she rushed down the hill, her wedge heels seemed absurdly high. They caught on pavements and bumps in the road, and she kept stumbling into people who were only smudged outlines. To each of them she called out through the blur of weeping the same wonderful words, "My fiancé's safe—Donald's alive—he's alive." The train was still at the platform, and jumping aboard she shouted out her good news to everyone in the carriage. Even the normally silent commuters were moved, and out of the teary haze, complete strangers came up to her and shook her hand. When she reached Woburn, the polyglot collection of Poles and Czechs who were its inhabitants wept with her, and hugged and kissed her.

The timing of the message might almost have been fated. On July 12 it would be exactly three years since they had parted, and the anniversary had been looming grimly ahead. When she wrote to him, her letter was alight with relief and happiness. The waiting was no easier, but now at least it was for a real Donald rather than for his memory. She told him, too, that she had been to see Beryl, and that Ginger's wife had been jolly and optimistic about getting the men home soon. It was cheering talk. She had beautiful red hair, and Pamela said how much she had liked her. But she kept to herself the thought that Beryl did not really need her man as much as she, Pamela, needed Donald.

It was late in September before Donald's first letter finally arrived, and the sadness of it undid her completely. Reading that phrase "Perhaps by now you have given me up as dead, I don't know" printed in careful schoolboy capitals, she knew that compared with what he had to endure, her ordeal was nothing. She put the folded sheet of paper back in its envelope. Her clothes were strewn around the room where she had dropped them, but with great care, as though she were handling the Crown Jewels, she placed the letter in the top drawer of her dressing table. More than a year passed before a second letter joined it.

Then, borrowing a typewriter from the secretarial office, she poured out her heart, telling him how much she loved him, how she thought of him day after day, and how sure she was that one day they would be together again. Sooner or later this war had to stop, and then they could begin to build a new life and a new world. The future is ours, my darling, she wrote, and we shall spend all of it together.

For some reason, perhaps it was loneliness, she wrote to Brigit early in 1943 asking her to come and join her at Woburn. They had worked together before. In one of their periods of sibling solidarity, they had teamed up in the kitchen of Winkfield Place. Officially classified as disabled as a result of her accident, Brigit had only been able to find work too tedious for her keen intelligence. Under Pamela's guidance, she became an efficient cook and a merciless catering manager, but at the next outbreak of sisterly rivalry, she had moved off to supervise the canteen of a munitions factory. Even without the clatter of canteen trays in the background, the glamour of Woburn sounded irresistibly attractive. With the barest minimum notice, she abandoned the factory to team up again with her sister.

Neither of them was entirely sure what happened at Woburn Abbey. At first, Pamela did not even know where it was, because she had been taken there in a van with the windows blacked out. "It was a police Black Maria," she would tell her friends, "just as though I were a dangerous criminal." Security police checked all vehicles coming in or leaving the Abbey, and kept constant surveillance on the grounds. The phones were tapped, and outgoing calls were forbidden. Inside the gates they met and fed representatives of almost all the occupied countries of Europe, as well as a cross section of professors, psychologists, journalists, and broadcasters.

In fact, several secret organizations were based there, including Admiralty signals intelligence, whose work by coincidence involved codebreaking; the planning section of the Special Operations Executive; and the Political Warfare Executive. Although still nominally part of SOE, the Political Warfare Executive had acquired a new head in the abrasive Oxford don and soon-to-be Labour MP Richard Crossman, who was in the process of making it into a virtually independent body. Its goal had several definitions which changed in the course of the war—"political warfare," to describe its aggressive intent, and "information subversion" to indicate the area in which it worked, but the commonest was "black propaganda," which conveyed the sense of its illicit purpose. "White propaganda" set out to sway its audience using straightforward information and argument; the black version might use deceit, trickery, and lies, but rarely if ever the unvarnished truth. Such tactics seemed more shocking then than now. The PWE broadcast in forty different languages and published newspapers, leaflets, and cartoons, but its radio stations frequently purported to be coming from within the country they were broadcasting to, and even took on the identity and wavelength of official stations. Its newspapers were often forgeries of real ones but containing demoralizing news about diseased troops or debauched Nazi leaders.

One of the PWE's most elegant coups was to point out that the opening four notes of Beethoven's Fifth Symphony—three shorts and a long—were the Morse equivalent of the Allies' "V for victory" sign. The results were a propagandist's dream. The BBC began to use the notes to announce news broadcasts to occupied Europe; fearing that it might be thought subversive, German concert halls became increasingly reluctant to present the masterpiece of one of Germany's finest composers; and in every other part of Europe the Fifth became the unofficial anthem of resistance.

The SOE had ensured certain privileges for its agents—stately homes were requisitioned for training, the finest instructors were recruited, and the food was the best that could be obtained—and the PWE inherited their outlook. Outside the gates, the rigors of wartime rationing had made the population familiar with powdered eggs, powdered milk, whale meat, and a butter ration of two ounces a week. At Woburn, the cook had almost unlimited rations available. There was farm produce on the doorstep, as well as the results of bloody encounters between army trucks and the Père David's deer that were bred in the Duke of Bedford's park. Pamela's plain English recipe book began to bristle with beef stews and roast venison and rack of lamb in season, desserts made with fresh eggs, and newly baked cakes.

No matter how secret the place was, this was not the sort of food that could be kept to oneself. To her embarrassment, her mother would ring in on the tapped telephone. "Darling, we have some people coming to supper," she would say. "Could you possibly bring down some extra butter with you next weekend?" But however carefully the security police were listening and however much Tunbridge Wells had changed, it always remained home, and Pamela duly smuggled the butter out.

She was not the only inhabitant of Tunbridge Wells to notice the change that war had brought to what had always seemed a changeless place. Richard Cobb was struck by the lowering of the age range as military camps were set up in the area and fit young men began to populate streets that had always been the reserve of the middle-aged. But he was less prepared for another, more personal difference, and one for which Pamela was almost entirely responsible. The distant, despairing admiration he had had for her and Brigit in peacetime suddenly became more hopeful once war arrived and he appeared in the classless, patriotic garb of khaki serge.

It was Brigit, with her sharp tongue and quick intelligence, to whom he now felt most attracted. Meeting her in a tea room in the fashionable Pantiles, he let drop a hint of his acerbic amusement at the town's more bizarre social conventions, and found an instant response in her ironic commentary on the absurd exclusiveness of its bridge-playing circles and golf clubs. Whenever he had leave, he sought her out, each of them enjoying the other's shrewd humor.

He could not have known that, like her sister, she was nursing an impossible passion—in Brigit's case for a fighter pilot killed in the Battle of Britain—but he evidently understood that where romance was concerned, girls as beautiful as the Kirrages belonged to the aristocracy. Rashly he attempted to pass himself off as one. He could not be a pilot, but he could pretend to be a hero.

One moonlit night, as they walked past the town's memorial to the dead of an earlier war—it portrays in silver granite a particularly heroic infantryman with rifle and bayonet in hand—Richard let drop his desire to play a more active part in the war than his current job of teaching English to Czech soldiers. She knew that he was clever, that he spoke French fluently, and by the time he had finished she also knew, though this did not have to be spelled out directly, that he was physically brave and wanted to experience some real danger. It was a line that young men were spinning in one form or another to girls up and down the country, and few if any expected it to be acted on. Brigit, however, was different from other girls.

"I'll have a word with Eric," she said. "He'll be able to help."

Eric, it seemed, had something to do with the BBC, which did not seem entirely relevant. Nevertheless, a little later, Cobb received a vaguely official invitation to attend an interview at the Inter-Services Research Bureau in Baker Street in London. To his growing alarm, he discovered that an idle boast had been taken literally and he was being interviewed for his suitability for hazardous service in occupied territory. Colonel Jephson, who interviewed most recruits for the French service of the SOE, had a habit of switching to French halfway through the first session, and the majority of applicants were weeded out there and then. Cobb passed with flying colors, and it was a measure of his passion for Brigit that he did not confess to the misunderstanding immediately. Not until he was well into a follow-up session, which involved a slightly fuller job description about the need to learn how to set off explosives and to withstand the rigors of capture and torture, did he admit that he was not really the sort of person they were looking for.

At the end of the war, he attempted to reestablish himself in Brigit's eyes. The army and his languages landed him in Brussels, where, as he observed, one could obtain anything, and he bought her a pair of wildly expensive silk stockings. "She had not yet been demobilised," he wrote in his autobiography, "and was working as manageress of a canteen in Eastbourne. I went over there with the stockings, and we walked up and down the Front for an afternoon." But it was too late and he had fallen too far. At the end of the afternoon, he was left to find his way back to Tunbridge Wells alone. He took the rejection badly. Almost forty years later, clearly still feeling the sting, he gloated in his autobiography that since their last encounter, she had taken to bridge and lost her good looks. (Where the Kirrage girls were concerned, love's pangs and passions never seemed to fade.) But the astonishment at her having his bluff called also persisted. "She must have had influence well beyond the limits of the canteen in Eastbourne," he commented in undisguised bewilderment.

It was Eric who was responsible. And he was the only man who ever threatened Pamela's commitment to Donald.

It was hardly surprising that an attractive young cook who dressed with a sense of style and had a weakness for emotional drama should make a mark among PWE's susceptible males. She had always found it easy to make friends, and all that she asked of her boyfriends was that they should be exceptional and physically attractive. Now she was in her element. At Woburn, the men were special almost by definition.

Brigit used to remark sharply of her sister that "she always wanted to be the centre of attention," and there was some truth in the gibe. Pamela liked men and loved going to the pub outside Woburn's gates with a group of friends, or traveling up to London at weekends to see a show or better still to go dancing. But she was adamant that their feelings should not go beyond friendship. In old age, Pamela was inclined to think that the men must have behaved gallantly, recognizing that her heart was engaged elsewhere. She had no idea where Donald was or what sort of conditions he was living in. Sometimes she thought it would have been better to forget about him and concentrate on getting on with her life, but it was impossible. She thought of him the whole time, and could not help it. "He was the man I loved," she explained, "and only him."

She may have been right about the men she met. The Pole who was so impressed by the Englishwomen staffing SOE's training establishments described how they cooked or chauffeured by day, and how in the evening "in exquisite long dresses" they partnered the men in waltzes, fox-trots, and Polish *obereks* and *kujawiaks*. "Though they were young and attractive, not to say beautiful," he concluded, "we had no heart-pangs over them." But not everyone behaved with such well-bred restraint.

By the time Brigit arrived in 1943, the United States was sending over selected personnel under the aegis of William Paley, the chief of Columbia Broadcasting Services, to be trained by the PWE in the arts of black propaganda. Brigit recalled the excitement of so many unattached, intriguing men, and the need for sisters to stick together. The British and varied European males at Woburn tended to accept the boundary that governed Pamela's friendships, but the Americans, armed with nylons, lipsticks, and higher wages than other servicemen, had learned never to take no for an answer. To keep them at bay required fast repartee, faster hands, and female solidarity. But Brigit appreciated how important Donald was to her sister. Together they put up such an effective defense that they became known, not completely unadmiringly as Kelvinator and Westinghouse, the United States' two leading brands of refrigerator. What was strange, and half a century later Pamela remarked on it herself, was that with one exception, she did not find any of these men physically attractive. As she put it, "I remained awfully pure; I wasn't even tempted."

The exception was Eric, an intelligence officer who was employed as an instructor at Woburn. Had that been all there was to him, she might have remained untempted. But Pamela's description showed that for the first time since Donald, she had met a man who caught at her imagination. He was older than she, but tall, handsome, beguiling in his charm, witty, wealthy, and hardly less famous than Laurence Olivier. As if that were not enough he had just composed a song so romantic that it was entering the repertoire of every dance band and singer in the country. In short, to be wooed by Eric Maschwitz, writer of "A Nightingale Sang in Berkeley Square," was not a disagreeable experience.

There were so many mysteries in Maschwitz's life that even after his death much of it remains blurred, as though the camera had been jogged at the crucial moment. On the surface, he was constantly in the public eye. He was one of the BBC's earliest and most golden recruits, becoming editor in 1927 of the *Radio Times,* then director of variety until he resigned in 1937 to write for the theater. His hit musical *Balalaika* ran for over five hundred performances in the West End, and even before "A Nightingale Sang in Berkeley Square" came out, everyone knew songs of his like "Good Night Vienna" and "These Foolish Things." His affairs with fashionable actresses were the stuff of gossip columns, as was his short-lived marriage to the theatrical personality Hermione Gingold. In short, his life seemed to be open for all to see, and to envy.

Behind the eye-catching glitter, there lurked another career as an intelligence officer with considerable power. In 1940, when invasion by the Germans was a possibility, he was one of MI-5's recruiters, selecting what he called "local citizens likely to prove daring and close as an oyster" to be trained in sabotage should the country be occupied. Then he was recruited by the Intelligence Corps with the rank of lieutenant colonel, and transferred to the SOE. For them he did a perfect piece of black propaganda, discrediting German organizations in the United States (before it entered the war) with the help of forged information carefully leaked to newspapers and radio. This success led to a job in 1943 as an instructor at Woburn. It was there that he met Pamela, and through her Brigit, and thus fished the astonished Richard Cobb up for interview as a candidate for SOE's operations. For this sort of work, he always used his showbiz career as cover, justifying his questions and his travels as research for a new show. Nor was that merely pretense. *New Faces,* with its show-stopping song of the nightingale in Berkeley Square, was written during a mail-interception operation, and the American black propaganda coup gave rise to a successful musical play, *Waltz Without End.*

The young women at Woburn were taught not to ask questions about people's jobs and so Pamela never really understood what Eric Maschwitz was doing there. In any case, like everyone else who knew him, she found it impossible to believe that there was more to him than the easygoing charm that met the eye. He was simply too nice and too romantic to be engaged in skullduggery. He stood six feet two inches tall, had high cheekbones and dancing black eyes, and possessed one particular talent that from her point of view was irresistible: he danced beautifully.

She had waltzed and tangoed with PWE's operatives before and enjoyed it, but the experience was dimmed to invisibility by the incandescent pleasure of whirling in Eric's arms to the hiss and crackle of records played in the great hall of Woburn Abbey. The Victorians had attempted to ban the waltz because when a man held a woman close and swirled her and swayed her to that tripleting, hypnotic rhythm, it enflamed passions beyond the control of even the best-intentioned. By the 1940s, those nineteenth-century prohibitions had long since been forgotten, but the premise was not necessarily mistaken.

On the verge of the twenty-first century, the recollection of his dancing still triggered a faraway smile. "He was the only one I was attracted to physically," she mused. "And he thought he was in love with me."

This was certainly true, for it was his charm and habit always to love whatever woman he was with. Frank Muir, who knew him at the BBC, observed that he was invariably "festooned with girls" and usually in love with at least three of them at once. Nevertheless, in one entirely serious way, his love for Pamela was unlike any of the others.

When she told Eric about Donald, he reacted quite differently from other men. They regarded the distant presence of an imprisoned lover as either a challenge or a passion-killer, but Eric adored the romance of it. In his eyes, it added to her attraction. Although he had been born in England and educated at public school, his parents were Polish immigrants, and beneath the English self-deprecation and easy humor that he wore as stylishly as his cricket blazer lay a quite un-English temperament.

All his songs and musicals were about love; he himself was forever falling in love; but the real thing, the constancy of love, was something that always escaped him. In his autobiography, he offered this self-assessment in the third person: "he thinks too quickly and words come to him too easily . . . his reactions are too quick and too superficial." Now here was love, a beautiful woman unswervingly and steadfastly yearning for an airman imprisoned on the other side of the world, and he was bowled over. Everything he did showed that he must have wanted the emotion for himself, and everything he did made her feel that he was someone who understood her fully. It was a dangerous combination.

She learned that he liked Carol Gibbons, her favorite bandleader, who played at the Savoy, and the next time they danced it was beneath the chandelier in the Savoy ballroom. She had been taken there before, by her father, but then she had been anonymous. Now she was in the company of the king of romantic lyrics, and when they walked on to the dance floor the band struck up his hit "These Foolish Things."

A cigarette that bears a lipstick's traces,
An airline ticket to romantic places,
And still my heart has wings,
These foolish things remind me of you.

The next letter to Donald was unusually sunny in tone. She could not help herself. Everything was going so well, she told him; it was undeniable, the war, the work, her whole feeling about the world, but it was impossible to explain why. Censorship rules prevented her mentioning the war or her work, and good sense censored any mention of Eric, so she restricted herself to writing about the fine weather and their bright future, and even added that she and Brigit were getting along together very well.

At Woburn the sisters had to share a bedroom, and the simmering rivalry that marked their relationship frequently boiled over into argument. Yet despite the quarrels, the similarities in their demanding and beguiling temperaments went deeper. Pamela might be the more emotional and more intuitive, Brigit the better read and less conventional in outlook, but they were utterly alike in manner, alternately imperious and seductive, slow to tolerate fools, and as quick to freeze with annoyance as to smile when amused.

When Eric was away on clandestine missions, he would let the girls stay in his Mayfair flat. It had white walls, white carpets, and white furniture and, slightly to their alarm, black satin sheets on the bed. The sheets looked better than they slept. Staying overnight on their way to Tunbridge Wells, they found them so hot and slithery that they lay awake for hours. Still, as they told each other, this was Mayfair and these were Eric Maschwitz's sheets.

When he returned, he took Pamela to West End shows and to glamorous parties enlivened by Noël Coward's dangerous wit and spring-heeled consonants, and Judy Campbell's spectacular beauty and husky voice. They went dancing; one night he took her to the Mirabelle nightclub, and later, in Berkeley Square, he sang his song just for her:

> *That certain night, the night we met,*
> *There was magic abroad in the air.*
> *There were angels dining at the Ritz,*
> *And a nightingale sang in Berkeley Square.*

> *I may be right, I may be wrong,*
> *But I'm perfectly willing to swear*
> *That when you turned and smiled at me,*
> *A nightingale sang in Berkeley Square.*

She never forgot the moment. It was a warm night and she was wearing a dress made from delicate prewar silk. To have succumbed in such circumstances might almost have been forgivable. But had she done so, they would both have lost what they loved most. At the last moment, he drew back and, as she gratefully acknowledged, "He was decent enough to realize how much I loved Donald, and that I would not want to be unfaithful to him."

Curiously, once the prospect of his slippery satin sheets

faded, a genuinely warm friendship emerged. Each met a need of the other's: she gave him proof of the reality of romantic love; he gave her glamour and a dancing partner. She took him down to Tunbridge Wells to meet her parents. Her mother was immediately won over, but then she often gave the impression that she was grateful to find any man interested in one of her daughters. When Sheila rang before dawn one morning to say that the farmer she worked for had just asked her to marry him, Marjorie offered her a distinctly backhanded blessing. "Far be it from me," she sighed down the phone, "to interfere in any way in a romance that takes place in a cowshed at six o'clock in the morning."

Pamela's father, on the other hand, was far more suspicious of Eric, a man of such overpowering charm. However, his brusque behavior and pointed references to the impropriety of his daughter associating with a man twice her age failed in any way to deter Eric. "Dear Krusty Kirrage," he purred, "how deliciously traditional you are."

Brigit once asked him where the inspiration for the Berkeley Square nightingale had sprung from.

"Oh, I was in love with such a beautiful girl," he began.

"No, no, Eric," she interrupted briskly, "that's what you always say about all your songs. I want a proper answer this time."

But that was the only one he would give, so perhaps it was true. No such song appears to have come from his time with Pamela, but the example of her constancy clearly had its influence. He decided to marry Phyllis Gordon, who had fallen in love with him before the war and remained faithful to him through all his wartime affairs. The marriage was not a great success. As he acknowledged in his autobiography, "he has had great happiness from women, and made several good women unhappy."

When Pamela next wrote to Donald, she dropped in a reference to Eric, but only as the family friend he had become. It would have been impossible to explain how close she had come to betraying the man she loved.

In any case, very few of her letters got through the maze of different channels that had to be negotiated. The quickest took nine months to reach him, and his almost as long to come back. The appearance in early 1944 of a strange typewritten envelope with the red stamp "Service des Prisonniers de Guerre" and a little block of Japanese characters was the first indication she had that any of her hundreds of letters had got through at all, but when she opened it the emotion leaped off the page. It was dated April 17, 1943.

"My Darling One," he had written,

> Last week a miracle happened. I received a letter from you, dated 11/7/42. My first letter Darling and what a difference it made. I was so excited that I started reading it upside down. To know after all these months that you are safe and well. Darling what more could I ask.

It had taken a year and a half, but finally they were in communication. Each of them knew what the other was feeling. Yet when he should have gone on, he suddenly resorted to banality, as though he had let his guard down.

> Ginger and I were delighted to hear that you had met Beryl. We have started to plan the reunion party when this is all over. Incidentally it's the first time I knew you had a passion for red heads darling. He's in great form and has been absolutely grand.

From the safety of Britain, she could not guess how in-grained the habit of concealing feelings had become. But it was only a momentary lapse. Again he wrote of what concerned them both.

Nearly four years of separation darling and I love you as much, if not more, than ever. I remember so well how the prospect of three years away from you seemed a lifetime. It has been an eternity Darling. But having stood that test we can be sure of the future. I just live for the day when I shall see you again my darling. I shall probably be struck completely dumb.

I have just about used up my 200 words. I would need another 200 to tell you how much I love you my darling. You are for ever in my thoughts.

Take great care of yourself my Darling.

I love you,

Always have and always will.

Don.

She read it through over and over again, as though she could hear his excited voice in the typed words. The letter moved her more deeply than the most seductive of Eric Maschwitz's enchanting lines. "Nearly four years of separation," he had written, and now as she read the words, it was nearly five. The endless waiting made sense only if he felt as she did, that when the future came they would always be together. And here was the proof: "having stood that test we can be sure of the future."

For a few moments, she could almost drink the happiness created by those words. She put the letter with the other two, then took them all out to read again, trying to catch more of him. Those three sheets were all she had to stretch across the empty years. They contained barely six hundred words, less than a word for each day in all that time. However hard she tried to squeeze him from every mark on the page, there was less of him than before. Suddenly the happiness went and she began to weep from the emptiness of it.

Throughout the rest of 1944, the PWE's activities accelerated as broadcasts to occupied countries were stepped up and radio stations were established in newly liberated areas. Then Allied armies crossed into Germany and all at once the purpose for which the PWE had been brought into being was more or less achieved. Very quickly its operations were wound down, the staff at Woburn dispersed, and Pamela moved on to cook at a hospital in Nottingham. She did not mind. For her, the smallest cog in the PWE's engine, the advance meant only one thing, the restoration of her whole purpose in life. A mighty gulf existed between love and grand strategy, but the least emotional planner could see that once Germany fell, the focus would turn on Japan. Then the most important battle of the war, at least as seen from Queen's Street, Tunbridge Wells, would be fought.

As the end of the war in Europe approached, people's thoughts turned from war's grand objectives to the smaller, more insistent goals of peace—education, employment, and the welfare state promised in the 1942 Beveridge Report. Divorce rates soared as men and women who had married in the expectation that life was too short to wait discovered the prospects lengthening and repented. "Heaven knows it's going to be a crazy world when this war is over," Donald wrote in a letter that Pamela received in 1945, "families broken up and everyone seeking new ideals."

The envelope, forwarded from Winkfield, bore a new address: Epperstone Manor Convalescent Home, near Nottingham. It was there that Pamela moved from Woburn in the last months of the European war. Everything was ending—PWE, the war, and eventually their separation. His letter emerged from the prisoner-of-war camp like an archaeological specimen from an earlier age. It was dated June 9, 1943.

My Darling One,
I wrote to you last month saying I had received my first letter from you. I must have read it well over a hundred times and every time it thrills me. I have your ring, your photograph and your letter as my inspiration darling.

Donald's tone swung from the passionate to the oddly banal. "This kind of life makes one frightfully domesticated," he wrote in one paragraph. "I am rapidly becoming a master of the needle and thread as well as being adept at the arts of culinary. I've even learnt how to bake bread. I hope to be a distinct asset around the house darling when we are married." He made her smile. It was almost like a parody of normal life. "Time passes fairly quickly. I'm learning German, Japanese and polishing up my French. Ginger and I play bridge most nights and I think I've learnt just about all the card games in existence. We spend many pleasant hours planning our reunion parties when this is all over."

Then abruptly the tone changed. "I can endure anything darling with the thought of seeing you again," he burst out, "holding you in my arms and being able to tell you all that is in my heart, things that have been stored up all these years." Those were the phrases that made her loneliness bearable.

Yet the contrast in tone offered a clue that something was

wrong. She could hardly have guessed, but the letter had been written at a moment of crisis. The petty rituals of the camp continued, but behind them loomed a monstrous fear. On June 9, at the very moment he was writing, everyone involved in communicating with BAAG and the Chinese guerrillas had just become aware that the organization had been penetrated by the Japanese police. A few days earlier Agent 68 had sent in a terse signal on the food truck: "71 detained by gendarmerie. Suspend operations." After that single message there was silence. The terrified Chinese drivers who had acted as their go-betweens would no longer even look at them, far less pass messages. The civilian Japanese gendarmerie was backed by the dreaded Kempeitai, or military police, who had a ferocious reputation for their use of torture. If Agent 71 passed into their hands, it could only be a matter of time before his mind and body and all resistance were destroyed. The trail would lead from him into the camp, and to the contact group. A dozen or so prisoners were part of it, and Donald was one of them.

All Pamela could detect was that he still loved her, and like her yearned for the freedom to be together again. "And so my Darling our reward is not so very far away," he ended, "until then I can take anything that comes along." He meant more than she could possibly have known.

9

Entering Darkness

There had been evil omens. Agent 71's carelessness had seemed to be tempting fate. Then, toward the end of May 1943, the guards became more aggressive. Day after day they would march into huts to conduct searches. With deliberate violence, they turned over the beds that were the prisoners' homes, ripped open carefully sewn-up mattresses, tore apart patched cushions, and broke into neatly made boxes. The destruction caused so much anger that Maltby had to warn the prisoners against the danger of being provoked into retaliation.

When Agent 68 sent his emergency message into both Argyle Street and Sham Shui Po, informing them of 71's arrest and ordering the operation to cease at once, there was a chill realization in both camps that they had allowed themselves to become overconfident. What had started simply as an attempt to help people escape had changed direction to become an intelligence-gathering ring. Its ramifications had spread far beyond the prison wire. Agents had recruited other agents, and not all of them could be relied upon. In Argyle Street, Newnham told his contact group of the message. It was possible, he suggested, that 71 had been arrested at random and that there was no direct connection with what was happening in camp. There was a strong risk, however, that the arrest was as a result of 71's work for BAAG. They would just have to wait and see.

That threat was still hanging over Donald when he wrote to Pamela four days later. It was in this letter that he started to count over the incidents of the golden summer in which they first fell in love. There was the dance at Gosport where they met; he reminded her that he had gone back later to photograph the secluded place behind the officers' mess where they had first kissed. The picture of that sacred spot was one of his talismans. He recalled the accident with the Whitlock, the highballs, the early-morning coffee at a snack bar, the loss of his hat in a tea room, and their last poignant days together. "These are just a few of the things about you that I remember so well," he concluded. "They are all for ever coming back to me and reminding me that the future holds so much in store for us darling."

For the few minutes it took to write, he must have been able to hold at bay the unthinkable present, but his emotions were those of a man on the lip of the abyss. When he assured her that "I can take anything that may come along," the phrase included every apprehension of the brutality that might await him. If the worst happened, the letter would serve as a testament to what had meant most to him in his short life.

In retrospect the conspirators knew they should have taken more precautions, but even with the omens gathering, they were more aware of the value of what they were doing. In the course of three months, their fragile contact with the outside world had developed into a successful information-gathering operation, and the groundwork was being laid for a mass breakout from all Hong Kong's prison camps. To have stopped all that simply out of suspicion that they were going too fast would have been to admit another defeat.

The connection with BAAG had been prickly from the start, with Clague on the outside accusing the inmates of being too supine to escape, and Newnham angrily retorting that "you are in ignorance of the greatly worsened conditions" imposed as retribution for his escape. The details of this correspondence did not go beyond Bird and Newnham, but the gist of it seeped out to the contact group. To them, it was plain that the escape of a single group of prisoners would condemn the rest to starvation rations again, meaning death for all but the fittest. Thus the escape of perhaps six men might result in over a hundred of their companions dying. Under pressure from BAAG, they agreed to consider a plan for escape but with the condition that it comprised everyone in camp.

Whenever there was an air raid, the Japanese called out all reinforcements to guard the camp, and Ride proposed that it would be possible to coordinate a bombing raid with an ambush by a guerrilla army. With the Japanese garrison wiped out, the occupants of all three military camps—Argyle Street, Sham Shui Po, and Ma Tau Chung, where the Indian troops were held—and the civilian camp at Stanley would be free, and could be rescued by a shuttle of aircraft flying into Kai Tak. The size of the operation would have presented formidable problems even if all the prisoners had been healthy. One competent military historian has described the plan flatly as "suicidal." Nevertheless, for some prisoners the risk was worthwhile. Ralph Goodwin, who later got away by himself, pointed out the basic flaw that all it needed was some artillery on the hills or a naval vessel offshore to prevent a single aircraft landing at Kai Tak. Yet compared to the possible gain of freeing several thousand prisoners, he decided the mass escape was a danger worth facing.

Donald, too, was prepared to take the gamble. In his next letter to Pamela, written almost as retribution was being dealt out, he revealed how much he missed flying, and how deeply he yearned to be with her. There would have been casualties in a mass escape, but in any military operation casualties were inevitable, and so long as there was a reasonable chance of success they were acceptable. He ended the letter, "I live for only two things to be free and to hold you in my arms again."

In the event Newnham took the same decision as Ford in Sham Shui Po, deferring plans for escape until the prisoners' health had improved. As at the other camp, BAAG's agent began smuggling in medicines and the vitamins needed to supplement their diet. What was different about Argyle Street was its proximity to the Indian soldiers' prison camp at Ma Tau Chung, and Newnham's realization that those prisoners had links with civilians in Hong Kong which could be exploited. He decided that it was worth collating all the information they could gather about

Japanese activities so that it could be passed on to Allied forces. In the short term the operation was infinitely more realistic than escape, but in the long run it proved no less dangerous.

The information was gathered initially by Indian civilians and soldiers employed by the Japanese on guard duty at docks and depots. Their reports on shipping and troop movements went to Indian officers in Ma Tau Chung before being relayed across the garden separating the two camps to Argyle Street. There the information was written down in an invisible ink made from rice water, and then sent out of the camp by way of the contact group and the food truck. Its eventual destination was British military headquarters in Delhi, for distribution to the U.S. Army Air Forces in China. In an assessment of BAAG's operations toward the end of 1943, American intelligence rated as "excellent" its information on shipping and transport movements. The report did not reveal, and the unwitting prisoners would never know, that American intelligence also believed BAAG to be a political nuisance, which aimed to serve British colonial interests at the expense of the Americans' client Chiang Kai-shek. That judgment meant that no American planes would be available for BAAG's escape plan, and without U.S. resources the project could never take place.

Nevertheless, for over three months after the first prickly exchange with BAAG, medicine and news were smuggled into Argyle Street and information flowed out. The contact group found that the medicines were too bulky to be transferred by hand or left in the rubbish at the bottom of the food truck. Instead, they devised a scheme to attach them to the underside of the truck's chassis with rubber bands, which could be quickly twisted off. Donald and the other members of the contact group practiced feeling blindly under the floor of the truck until they could find and remove a message or package and slip it into a pocket in seconds. The timing had to be perfect, and the operator's nerves cool enough to allow him to do the job without attracting attention from onlookers watching the food being taken out or even from the rest of the hut party milling around the truck. Their nerves would often be stretched more tightly because the agents outside had been too ambitious about the size of the object that could be fitted into a space. Donald or whichever operator was on duty would find himself desperately attempting to tug free a package jammed into a corner of the chassis, and hoping that his efforts would not arouse the onlookers' attention or be spotted by a suspicious guard through the scrum of prisoners.

The improvement in the prisoners' health and morale must have been very noticeable, although the guards did not usually pay much attention to such matters. By June, BAAG had recruited a network of civilian informants outside the camps from among sympathetic Chinese, Indians, and Portuguese, and in the Indian camp the exceptionally courageous Captain Mateen Ahmed Ansari had begun supplying information directly to BAAG. The very success of the operation had bred a dangerous overconfidence, and the sheer number of agents increased the chance that one would fall into Japanese hands. When news about the arrest of Agent 71 came in, the danger was suddenly obvious, but by then it was too late.

At first nothing happened. The morning parade took place with no one called out. At eleven o'clock the ration truck came in, with the drivers staring rigidly ahead, obviously frightened. Yet no arrests were made. As the days passed, the strain on Newnham was plain to those around him. Even among the skeletal features of the prisoners, his face appeared gaunt, the dark eyes sunk deep in their sockets. When Michael Wright walked unexpectedly into his hut one day, Newnham's outburst of anger was that of a man living on his nerves. The continuing appearance of normality forced them toward the same secret calculation: somewhere outside the camp, the Kempeitai had found out what they needed to know. Either the danger was receding or it was about to burst upon them.

For Donald, as for the others involved, this was a peculiarly solitary ordeal. Officially his work had to be kept secret so that if he were arrested no one else would be involved. He could say nothing even to Ginger Sullivan, who must have known what he had been doing. Even with other members of the group, contact had to be kept to the minimum in case the now ever-present guards were watching. He had never known Bird and Harris, the original pair, especially well, but there were two members of the Hong Kong Volunteers whom he liked: a young naval officer whose name, Haddock, gave rise to bad jokes and worse nicknames (of which "Kipper" was the kindest), and a middle-aged schoolmaster in his forties called Gordon Ferguson, known as Fergie, who had been commissioned into the artillery and liked to boast that he was the oldest lieutenant in the British army. Yet it was no more possible to discuss with them than with strangers the one topic of overwhelming concern: what would happen next?

Almost three weeks after Agent 68's warning, Newnham decided to break the silence. The resourceful Goodwin devised a hollow bolt that could be substituted for the real one in the truck's chassis, and a message was rolled up in it and sent out. There was no reply.

Then, on the morning of July 1, the ration truck appeared unexpectedly. The moment its two guards got out, the driver stretched his hand through the open window waving a piece of paper. The duty operator for the day was not in sight, but by chance Haddock was nearby and took the paper. Immediately he felt that it was a setup, and instead of taking it to Bird, left the scrap of paper in a lavatory. The safety measure was useless. Guards arrested him as he returned to his hut, and took him away. On the same day in Sham Shui Po, the two airmen, Dolly Gray and Ralph Hardy, together with Sergeant Routledge, a Canadian member of the contact group, were arrested. A week earlier Captain Ansari had been taken from Ma Tau Chung camp, and from Stanley civilian camp and elsewhere in Hong Kong, almost fifty others—Indian, Chinese, and European—were detained. Finally, on July 10, Newnham and Ford were taken away.

In camp the anxiety was palpable. Outside the circle of the contact group, prisoners suddenly realized that a conspiracy had been going on of which most were utterly unaware. Any who had not heard of the arrests learned through the irritation of the guards. As before, rations were cut and food supplies, which had become almost dependable, arrived irregularly or often not at all. New rules were introduced, which became apparent only when a nearby guard abruptly halted a prisoner and punched him in the face or slammed a rifle butt into his unprotected ribs or kidneys. It might be because he was walking too close to the wire or because he was smoking where he should not be, but it was mostly because the evidence of communication with people beyond the wire reflected badly on the guards and they were taking out their irritation on the prisoners.

"One thing all we prisoners have learned during our captivity," Goodwin wrote in his diary during that period, "and that is how to hate."

The intelligence gathering remained a secret, but news of the escape plans leaked out, and prisoners like Cecil Templer directed their fury less at the guards than at BAAG. "The British Mission at Chung King hatched up a *crazy* plot for a mass escape from our camps under cover of a bombing raid," he commented in a note added later to his journal.

The arrest of Newnham and Haddock brought the threat of the Kempeitai very close, but in Donald the reality of danger induced a clarity of mind that was a long way from the venom Goodwin expressed or the confused anger and apprehension in the camp. Since there was nothing he could do to change the situation, he had to handle it as competently as possible. He must assume that under torture Newnham would reveal the full extent of what they had been doing in camp. Once the Kempeitai had the names of the contact group, he would be taken in for questioning. What was important, then, was to separate the safe knowledge from the dangerous. He could say what he knew about the passing of messages, since the Japanese would know about it anyway. But what the messages contained, who else was involved, all that had to be pushed to some deep irretrievable pocket of his mind.

In the midst of this, on July 11, Donald received another letter from Pamela, and for a brief moment it swept all other considerations aside. "My Darling it was like water to a man dying of thirst," he exclaimed. What made it especially welcome was that it came as a reply to the very first letter he had written her, thirteen months earlier. She told him of her delight at hearing from him at last, but also of the slowness of the long empty years without him. What sort of world would it be, she asked, when they were finally reunited? He had been about to write to her in any case, because July 12 would be the fourth anniversary of their parting. Now the dislocation between his present danger and the spontaneous joy of hearing from her produced some strange leaps in his reply.

> My own sweet Darling to know that you are well and still love me after four years of waiting is almost too much to believe. Often at night I lie awake thinking of you, wondering when I shall see you again. I know fully all the sacrifices you have made because of me, and I'm overwhelmed with love for you. Heaven knows it's going to be a crazy world when this war is over; families broken up and everyone seeking new ideals. But you are all my ideals rolled into one sweetheart, to work and to live for, and to try to make up to you everything that you have sacrificed for me. I live for two things; to be free, and to hold you in my arms again. Four years ago today we were together for the last time. Those few days and nights we spent together have been with me all these years darling.

As with her first letter, his deepest feelings came to the surface in response, but at such a moment they were a weakness. Thoughts of Pamela and of freedom could only be a distraction from the threat he might shortly have to face. Abruptly he turned to the safety of concealment.

"I'm very fit," he said with unconvincing briskness. "Haven't had a days's [*sic*] illness since I left England." He was reading a lot, he added, and took plenty of exercise. But there was one other distraction that caught at his mind. "I miss my flying terribly," he confessed, "and when I'm not thinking of you, my thoughts turn skywards. I'm very proud of the Service and regret deeply not being an active member of it." Then once more he drew down the blind: "My allotted space is up darling. Your letter has given me added strength to face things cheerfully. Please give my love to the Family."

The cloud hanging over him lent poignancy to his farewell:

Here's to our future my darling and until then I shall just have to dream about you. I love you so much that it hurts.

All my love my darling one. I love you now and always,
DON

Although she knew nothing of the particular circumstances in which it was written, Pamela herself recognized that it was a letter designed to keep her from worrying. But the quandary Donald faced went beyond the usual prisoner's problem of finding something to say without mentioning the terrible reality in which he lived. If he was to withstand whatever lay ahead, his mind needed to be utterly clear, and the delight and optimism and dreams that Pamela's letter aroused diverted his attention. They were as dangerous as his knowledge of the messages. Everything about life in camp drove a man to conceal his vulnerability, but at this moment survival must have seemed to depend upon it.

It was probably during these tense, empty days that the final transformation of his coded diary took place. The searches were growing more frequent, and the diary might be used against him. In its rough form it would have appeared as blocks of numbers, but any guard who saw it would want to know what they signified. Donald might have destroyed it, but that would have given a victory to his captors. Instead, he chose to hide it in a guise that appeared utterly innocent. Like every schoolchild in the days before computers, he was familiar with the long columns of figures that appeared in multiplication and logarithm's tables. So many educational classes were taking place in camp that one more mathematical aid would not seem out of place.

On the back cover of the parchment-colored notebook used for his German lessons, he wrote out the words "Russels Mathematical Tables." Then, on the inside back page, he ruled a grid of tiny boxes, but before he entered the numbers in this new form, he added one final twist to his code. Using a secret key word, he jumbled up the order in which they appeared. It was an intricate, time-consuming process to translate the order in which the numbers were to be read and then to enter them on the page. But that must have been a great part of its attraction. While his attention was focused on the code, he had no opportunity to brood on what might be coming.

The blow never fell.

With a degree of courage that defies imagination, Newnham and his fellow principals from Sham Shui Po, Ford and Gray, resisted every attempt to break them. For seven weeks they were kept in solitary confinement without bed or blankets. They were taken out only for interrogation, and the sound of their screams and the blows as they were beaten with leather whips and clubbed with bats penetrated through to the cells where the others were kept. Their wrists were lashed behind their back, and with the other end of the rope looped around a beam they were hoisted off the floor. Bird, who later fell into the hands of the same torturers and survived, told of the horror of the water torture. Strapped in a coffin so that he could not move, he saw a silk cloth draped over his face, then felt the coffin slid beneath a dripping tap. As the cloth became saturated, the air was gradually blocked off so that he had to draw in larger breaths. The tap was turned on harder, and each breath sucked in water which filled his mouth and nostrils. With the next gasp his lungs were flooded. Choking and struggling for air, he pulled in more water, so that he was suffocating and drowning with each breath. His body convulsed uncontrollably inside his bonds until he fell unconscious or the cloth was removed. If he did not speak, the procedure was repeated.

Captain Ansari, arrested at the same time, endured similar treatment. Forty-eight civilians had also been seized. Several died in the course of their torture, and of the remainder, thirty-three were sentenced to death at a brief trial. Ansari was beheaded on October 20, and the others were executed in the same way nine days later. Newnham, Ford, and Gray, together with their subordinates, Haddock, Hardy, and Routledge, appeared before a military court on December 1. Despite beatings and torture that had crippled them so severely that only Ford could walk unaided, the three senior officers refused to admit anything other than that they alone bore responsibility for what had happened. The others, they insisted, were acting under orders. Not one of the six gave the name of any other member of the contact group at either camp. As Goodwin commented in his account of what happened, *Passport to Eternity*, "Theirs was an almost incredible feat of fortitude."

The three senior officers were sentenced to death, while their subordinates received prison sentences of fifteen years. In the midst of the brutality occurred a moment of almost unbearable pathos. Overcome by pity for what had happened, the Japanese soldier in charge of the escort party taking them back to their cells burst into tears. To comfort him Newnham mumbled through swollen lips, "Cheer up, we aren't dead yet." On December 19, he and Ford and Gray were taken down to the beach and shot.

Their fate was not known until after the war, although it was assumed in camp that the worst had happened. But prison life dislocated feelings from experience. Beatings happened to other people, or if they happened to you, they were endured until they were in the past and could be moved away from. The problem was to survive mentally and physically, and that daily struggle kept attention concentrated on the immediate present. In August every officer over the rank of lieutenant colonel was transferred to Taiwan, and some weeks later a series of spectacular air raids, culminating in the destruction of the oil tanks in a blaze that lasted for three days and nights, began to build hopes that victory might be in sight. For most prisoners, the breakup of BAAG's information-gathering system soon passed out of mind.

Even members of the contact group moved on to other concerns. Bird tried to reestablish contact with Agent 68, but was soon arrested. Attempting to find another way of getting news into the camp, a new group was set up and successfully operated a clandestine radio for months until its hiding-place in a flower bed was discovered. Donald continued to write to Pamela, telling her of his love and of the small distractions that hid the reality of camp life. But the lure of escape had gone.

Given the inmates' enfeebled physical state and the Americans' hostility to BAAG, the mass breakout envisioned by Ride was never feasible, but Donald had believed the risk worthwhile and had been ready to support it. Years later in the early 1970s, when he heard of the Israelis' airborne raid to free hostages held captive in Entebbe, he took an almost personal pride in their success, as though they had achieved what he had set out to do himself. Without that lure he relapsed into the easier, narrower pastimes of prison life.

From his early days of mending clogs in Sham Shui Po, he had become a self-taught cobbler, and like several others occupied much of his morning making and heeling prisoners' clogs, when his hut was not on garden duty. During the afternoon, he plowed through the camp's supply of books, or took part in marathon card games: a bridge competition that lasted for months; a piquet challenge over 150 games; and a rolling poker game involving Ginger and his friend from the contact group, Fergie Ferguson, which continued into the spring of 1944. The scores and amounts of money owed were meticulously entered in the journal. Next to them was a list of the 285 books which he had read, together with his judgment on each. His favorites were romantic sagas like Hugh Walpole's *Herries Chronicle* and John Galsworthy's *Forsyte Saga,* and it is easy to understand why such tales of family rivalries and triumphant love in a green and distant land each received five stars of approval.

In May 1944 the Argyle Street camp was moved back to Sham Shui Po, where numbers had been hugely reduced by levies of men to Japan. A few weeks later, Ralph Goodwin, taking advantage of a torrential downpour, climbed over the electrified fence topped with barbed wire and made the most audacious escape achieved from Hong Kong. He had deliberately chosen to go by himself so that no one would be punished by association with him, but the response was serious enough. The prisoners were paraded and told that in future each hut would be held responsible for ensuring that its inhabitants did not break out. If one person escaped all the others would be executed. At the same time, their rations were severely reduced. This might have been intended as punishment, but it was also true that Allied attacks on Japanese shipping were beginning to have their effect. Japanese soldiers also had their food supplies cut. The effect on the prisoners, always hovering near the brink of starvation, was far more dramatic.

Until then Donald had survived better than at any period of his imprisonment. A breakfast of boiled rice supplemented by some bran and beans, would be followed at midday by a soup of rice and boiled vegetables with a pinch of salt fish and soy sauce. An evening meal consisting of a pint of boiled rice with two or three shallots from the garden completed the basic nutrition. But approximately twice a year, Red Cross deliveries of bully beef, peanut oil, and milk powder provided essential protein and fats. BAAG had also sent in vitamin tablets. The last food parcel arrived in November 1943, but it had been severely depleted by the prison guards, and there were no more illicit supplies of vitamins. When the supplements of fish and soy sauce were cut, it quickly pushed Donald over the edge. And this time Florrie was not there to save him. Almost certainly she herself died that year, probably as a result of the hardships she had suffered under the Japanese occupation.

By the summer of 1944, Donald was suffering from pellagra as a result of vitamin deficiency. It produced not only its most characteristic symptom, a rough, intolerably itchy kind of eczema, but more disturbingly a deterioration in his eyesight, which became so dim and blurred that he could no longer read or play cards. His friends tried to help by scrounging fresh food and vitamin supplements through the guards, but there was too little to make any real difference. At this literally darkest moment, he always remembered with gratitude Fergie Ferguson offering to read to him. Ginger Sullivan had no taste for books, but the middle-aged schoolteacher was happy to sit by him in the camp hospital working his way through Arnold Bennett and J. B. Priestley.

The prisoners' state had grown so desperate by August that when the Red Cross representative made his hurried round of the camp, one prisoner, Captain Barnett, ran up to him crying, "We are dying of hunger." The beating he received for this infraction of the rules put him in hospital for weeks, but the protest evidently had some effect on the guards, because some days later they distributed two hundred gamebirds apparently discovered in a cold store. Later in the year a few bulk supplies of corned beef and dried milk eked out over the months helped meet their basic nutritional needs. Gradually Donald's vision recovered, and by the end of 1944 he had returned to the life of the camp.

What he focused on now was surviving. He had boasted of his good health in his letters, and if that had been partly to spare Pamela, it was at least true that he had never been in hospital. This time he had suffered severely, and was slow to recover. And accustomed as he was to being a dependable rock for others, he must have been shaken by the helplessness of being blind. Physical weakness and the real fear that he might not see again narrowed his ambition down to making it through to the end. And the news that filtered into camp through whispers from sympathetic Chinese made the end increasingly certain.

The Allies were advancing through France, the Americans island-hopping across the Pacific; even in Burma the Japanese invasion was at last being turned back. Everywhere the tide was flowing one way. Through the spring and summer of 1945, once dominating landmarks crumbled and were submerged by the flood—Mussolini was executed, Hitler killed himself, and Germany surrendered. Even the pro-Japanese newspapers that were sometimes allowed into camp could not conceal such events from their readers. The news that Russia had entered the war against Japan made the outcome certain, but the inmates knew only too well how their enemy regarded the ignominy of surrender, and rumors began to circulate that there would be a slaughter of the prisoners before that point was reached.

It was not until August 12 that the first rumor of a Japanese surrender came through the wire. Through alternating delight and gloom they tried to read the truth of it in the behavior of the guards, but nothing changed until the evening of the fifteenth, when Lieutenant Wada, the camp commandant, placed a large wireless on a table ceremonially covered with a white cloth. The guards came down from their watchtowers and filed in from the gate to line up in front of the table. A strange thin voice emerged from the loudspeaker, and they all bowed. To the watching prisoners, it was utterly incomprehensible; then someone guessed, and the word raced around the camp: Emperor Hirohito had announced his country's surrender. The war was over.

The next morning no change was apparent, and two prisoners received the customary full-armed slap in the face for not saluting their guards. That, however, was the last of the humiliation. On the same afternoon, a week after the second atom bomb had dropped on Nagasaki, the camp commandant acknowledged that the Emperor had "granted peace to the world." On August 17 a service of thanksgiving was held, and for the first time since Christmas 1941 the British national anthem was sung. "It was the most impressive ceremony I have ever attended," Captain White, a Canadian prisoner, wrote in his journal. "Hell of a feeling in one's chest, we kind of choked up. Hearts were too full for much singing, many tears in evidence, I couldn't keep them back. We all realized more than ever before the meaning of Freedom. Some wives with their children arrived from Stanley to meet their husbands. It was so moving I couldn't watch."

Yet for another agonizing ten days, the prisoners had to remain in camp. The delay was partly for their own safety—Hong Kong was full of Japanese troops and armed Chinese guerrillas eager for battle—but mostly because no one knew whether the colony would return to the British or be handed over by the Americans to Chiang Kai-shek and his Nationalist Chinese. Behind the scenes, American, British, and Chinese politicians negotiated for advantage while the prisoners fumed. "Complete amazement and fury among all here," Templer wrote, "why no British troops have come or even dropped messages let alone supplies on us—quite incredible."

It was Franklin Gimson, the colonial secretary who in 1941 had called Donald to warn him that war was coming, who broke the deadlock. Although interned in Stanley civilian camp, he arbitrarily set up a provisional government representing Britain on August 20, and thus cut short the international card-shuffling. Recognizing the changed situation, the Americans released the nearest British naval squadron, and on August 29 it sailed into the colony's harbor, formally reestablishing British control.

One day later, Royal Marine commandos hoisted the Union Jack over the regained airfield of Kai Tak. There were hardly any RAF representatives available, but to their credit the Royal Navy had ferried over to the airfield two cadaverous figures. They walked on sticklike legs, their eyes were dull and sunken, and their skull-like heads seemed too large for their narrow bony shoulders. They wore their own RAF caps, but their borrowed shirts and shorts had been made for better-filled bodies than theirs. They were there because they symbolized continuity with what had gone before. Now the British were back, and what had happened in between would be wiped away. Normal service was being restored. The flag rose, the band played and Flight Lieutenant Donald Hill and Pilot Officer Frank Hennessy saluted. Perhaps just for that moment it was possible to imagine that the events between December 8, 1941, and August 30, 1945, could indeed be erased.

PART III

10

Together at Last

Every farthing of the cost,
All the dreaded cards foretell,
Shall be paid, but from this night
Not a whisper, not a thought,
Not a kiss nor look be lost.

— W. H. AUDEN,
"LAY YOUR SLEEPING HEAD, MY LOVE"

Infuriating though the last days of prison were for inmates, for at least one outsider the added delay was almost unendurable. After the news of Japan's surrender, Pamela expected to hear from Donald at any moment. Even if she had known how to reach him, communication from Britain to Hong Kong was almost impossible for a civilian. Most telephones were out of order, most cable offices closed, and military and government calls had top priority on the few long-distance lines still working. She would have to wait for Donald to call her. With an intensity of yearning that recalled the long silence after she first met Donald, she waited by the telephone in her parents' house, willing it to ring. Only after two p.m., when it was ten p.m. in Hong Kong, would she give up hope for the day and allow herself to go out.

It was not until the day he shuffled out of the gates of the Sham Shui Po camp to attend the flag-raising ceremony in Kai Tak that Donald was able to arrange a call to the United Kingdom. The ceremony almost overtaxed his feeble strength, but he was determined to tell her he had survived. Using a line from the airport, he booked his call to Tunbridge Wells 744 through the operator and waited to be connected. The call came through late in the morning, and the phone had barely rung twice before Pamela snatched it off the receiver. Hearing the slow, hoarse voice on the other end, she could not recognize it for a few seconds. Then she knew who it was, and the sense of relief was so overwhelming she could hardly answer.

"I can't believe it's you," she said at last. "When will I see you?"

There was a little pause. "I don't think you'd want to see me as I am," he answered carefully. "But we'll get married the moment I get back. It's been long enough."

Many years later, after his death, she did see him as he had been then. A TV documentary about the victims of Japanese prisoner-of-war camps showed some film taken of the Hong Kong survivors as they left the camp. Among the emaciated men, Pamela immediately spotted the tall figure of Donald Hill. Far from being "fighting fit" or "very fit" or any of the other comforting labels he had used in his letters, the reality was that he had been reduced to a skeleton whose sharp bones were almost pushing through his skin. His head, thrust forward, seemed too big for the emaciated torso beneath, and the hollow-cheeked face was drawn and wide-eyed with the experience he had been through.

As a result of their treatment, barely 60 percent of the prisoners taken by the Japanese survived the war. The majority of these were shipped first to the Philippines and then on through the United States and Canada to Britain, but those who had suffered most severely were sent to recuperate in Australia and New Zealand. Donald was among them. It meant that he and Pamela were to remain apart for another six months until he had recovered physically. However desperately she wanted him back, Pamela knew that he needed treatment for what had been done to him. But after a separation of over six years, this last delay was almost unbearable. She could hardly keep herself from tears.

Apart from one raid on Darwin, Australia and New Zealand had escaped being bombed, and their farms had developed into a cornucopia by definition providing for consumption at home and for much of the war-ravaged northern hemisphere. Physically, what the former prisoners needed was a good diet, and in convalescent homes near Sydney and Christchurch, they quickly put on weight. In appearance at least, before Christmas Donald had returned to a semblance of the man he had been. But prolonged malnutrition produced other effects than thinness.

By a painful irony, during the last months of the war while the inmates of POW camps in Japan and Germany were experiencing unavoidable hunger, thirty-two well-fed volunteers at the University of Minnesota became guinea pigs in an experiment to discover what these effects might be. For six months they were fed just 1,570 calories a day, exactly half of their normal daily requirements, while a battery of medical and psychological tests monitored their response. All necessary vitamins and mineral trace elements were provided, and it was only in its lack of calories that the diet was comparable with what Donald and his fellow prisoners had had to eat. Equally important, the experimental subjects had space, clean clothes, and washing facilities. Even so, the consequences were marked.

"How does it feel to starve?" one of the volunteers wrote afterward. "It is something like this. I'm hungry, always hungry—not like the hunger that comes when you miss lunch, but a continual cry from the body for food. At times I can almost forget about it but there is nothing that can hold my interest for long. . . . I'm cold. In July I walk downtown on a sunny day with a shirt and sweater on to keep me warm. At night my well-fed roommate who is not in the experiment sleeps on top of his sheets but I crawl under two blankets wondering why [he] isn't freezing to death. . . . I'm weak. I can walk miles at my own pace in order to satisfy laboratory requirements but often I trip on cracks in the sidewalk. To open a heavy door it is necessary to brace myself and push or pull with all my might. . . . Social graces, interests, spontaneous activity and responsibility take second place to concerns of food. I lick my plate unashamedly at each meal even when guests are present."

He went to see films, but was only interested in "scenes where people are eating. I couldn't laugh at the funniest picture in the world, and love scenes are completely dull." He could talk and think normally, but had no wish to do so. "My talk is of food and past memories, or future ambitions mostly in the cooking or eating line."

That an intelligent, independent-minded student living in a stimulating environment with every comfort available except sufficient food could so quickly be reduced to that ineffectual state gives a useful yardstick to measure Donald's achievements in camp, the long list of books, the painstaking attempt to teach himself German, and the prolonged concentration required to encode his diary. Evidently he possessed enormous self-discipline, well beyond the norm, if he was capable of pushing his energy-depleted mind into completing such mentally demanding projects.

But the chief interest of the Minnesota experiment lay less in the actual period of starvation than in the after-effects. Three months after returning to a normal diet the subjects' gauntness had disappeared, and their weight was climbing to its original level although muscle tone remained flabby. They still felt hungry even after a huge meal, and were subject to food bingeing, consuming over six thousand calories in some cases. "The men continued to want more than they received," the report ran with just an undercurrent of alarm, "their appetites were insatiable. The men continued to be concerned with food and their rations above all else." Nevertheless, in physical terms most subjects had returned to something close to normality six months after the experiment ended. Psychologically, however, they were still affected by the experience. They were prone to depression. They found it difficult to concentrate. They were moody and listless and irritable. One monitor concluded from their behavior that they showed all the symptoms of having suffered "an experimental neurosis."

Consideration of the brevity of the experiment and the cosseting that the Minnesota volunteers received suggests the extent of the invisible damage that the Hong Kong prisoners took home with them after what Donald scornfully called "our so-called recuperation." Perhaps he could have stayed longer in New Zealand and recovered further, but he had told Pamela that he lived for just two things, and so long as he remained in a Christchurch nursing home, the purpose of surviving prison was only half-achieved.

In December he seized the chance of a seat in a cargo-carrying C-47 that eventually took him to Sydney. After waiting a week, he hitched a lift in an American troop plane to Colombo in Ceylon. Several abortive efforts at onward flights left him stranded over Christmas near Allahabad. Eventually he picked up a flight in the tail gunner's seat of a Lancaster bomber; it carried him as far as Aden, where he caught a civilian flight on to Britain. He arrived there on January 7, 1946. It had taken him almost six weeks and over 120 hours of flying.

The details of every flight, its duration, the points of departure and arrival, and the make of aircraft, were entered meticulously into a fresh page of his pilot's logbook. The previous entry had been made on December 8, 1941. "War with Japan. Aircraft destroyed by enemy fighters." On this new page, all the running totals were carried forward. He remained a pilot with 884 hours' flying time, and the expectation of adding to them.

When the war in Europe ended, Pamela continued to work for the Red Cross until she fell ill with appendicitis and was sent home to recover. Even if Donald had not minded, she could not have returned to modeling. She was approaching her thirties now, too old for that sort of work. It was not just the passage of years; the experience of war had changed her too. At Woburn there had been an intensity of emotion that suited her. The prewar attentions of lounge lizards and eager curates might have been welcome enough to a teenager, but they could not compare to those of a young man about to risk his life to blow up a bridge or join a guerrilla gang, still less to those of a sophisticated, successful songwriter. But while other twenty-year-olds grew so addicted to the storms of passion and intrigue in the SOE that they found it difficult to adapt to the mild weather of peace, she had sailed through dreaming of the day when hostilities would cease and she could be reunited with Donald.

On the threshold of her thirties, there was an extraordinary certainty about her. It was a matter of being with one man. And he was coming home. That was all that counted. Seen from the wrong end of the century, she acknowledged that her outlook might no longer appear so obvious.

"I know today it must seem so silly being in love like that," she said as she tried to push his letters back into a large brown envelope. "People have lovers all over the place. People find it so easy to fall in love. But that wasn't how I felt." She had her head down so that her face could not be seen. "There was just this one person. He was the only one who made me feel complete." The letters refused to go back in. She put them down on the table. "I don't know why I was so sure. Seven years is such a long time to wait, and when you love someone, being apart is such a *waste* of time. Time you could have spent together."

There was a brief silence while she gathered herself. Then she took up the letters again. This time they slid neatly into the envelope. She laid her thin hand on it gently. "At least we knew that we both felt the same way about each other. But it was still a long, long time." Her sigh was barely audible.

On January 8, 1946, she received the telephone call that brought the waiting to an end.

After the first delighted greeting, the conversation became awkward. Caught between the sense of being lovers and strangers, they stiltedly made arrangements over the telephone for their meeting the next day. He was staying in his mother's flat in Swiss Cottage in north London. It was more convenient because he had to report to RAF Hendon, which was not far away. Could they meet at the flat? They could. The address was 36 College Crescent. And would tomorrow evening be convenient? In that case she was to ring the bell in the hall, and he would come down. It was the top flat. He had to come down three flights of stairs, so she was not to go away before he arrived.

He spoke with the careful precision of an invalid.

When she put down the phone, she realized she had nothing to wear. Her prewar clothes were out-of-date, and her postwar clothes were made of ugly, coarse utility material he would hate to see her in. She had been waiting almost seven years for this moment and when it came she had nothing to wear for it. Frantically she burrowed through her cupboards and found some prewar material in navy blue. She raced around with it to her dressmaker. An artist to her fingertips, the dressmaker recognized the supreme urgency of the situation, and dropped all other work. For the best part of twenty-four hours she cut and sewed and tacked and hemmed. The next evening, when Pamela stood in the hallway of the block of flats where Donald was staying, she was dressed in an exquisite navy suit with a flared skirt, and a great big navy hat. She thought that she must at least look better than she felt.

A fearful happiness gripped her so tightly she could hardly breathe deeply enough to feed air to her pounding heart. She pressed the top bell, and moments later heard his footsteps running down the stairs, leather on stone, around and around the stairwell. She was struck by sudden panic. What will he be like? she wondered. Will I even recognize him? Then suddenly her fiancé was before her at the foot of the stairs. He was Donald and not Donald. Older, strained, and tense, but otherwise the man she had loved for all those empty years. She tried to speak but could only cling to him, too overcome to do anything but weep. She had waited 2,435 days to hold him again.

Of all that they talked about, she recalled nothing except the memory of feeling and hearing and seeing him. Fifty years later that had lost none of its intensity.

They must, however, have discussed the wedding, for that weekend he came down to discuss it with her parents. In a formal, old-fashioned way, Donald explained that he and Pamela were finally going to get married and that he hoped they both still approved of him as a potential son-in-law. Her parents, having had to postpone their approval for so long, gave it with spontaneous affection, but Brigit who was there also remembered their reservation when he said they wanted the wedding as soon as possible. Pamela had found out they could get married by special license in ten days' time. The wedding could take place as early as January 23.

Brigit could see from Donald's drawn face what sort of ordeal he had been through, and sensed that her father wanted them to put the wedding off until he was better. It was not something that could easily be put into words to a couple who had waited through the entire war. Discreetly her parents voiced their doubts: perhaps Donald had changed; certainly their daughter had; were they sure they still felt the same way about each other?

It was a reasonable reservation, but one that missed the point. They had both undeniably changed. The war had shattered them, just as it had the country at large. Everything about them was different, just as it was in the country. But whatever its form, life imposed certain constants. Men and women had to eat and drink, and they had to love. What Auden had written in "September 1, 1939," on the eve of war was still true in the dawn of peace:

> *There is no such thing as the State*
> *And no one ever exists alone;*
> *Hunger allows no choice*
> *To the citizen or the police;*
> *We must love one another or die.*

And if there was only one other person to love, then all else was swept aside.

"How could we have waited any longer?" Pamela demanded. "We only wanted each other. That was everything we wanted. And we had wanted it for all those years."

Among the casualties of war was Donald's younger brother, Ralph. A slighter version of Donald, he had joined the army in 1939 and been sent to India. Having spent his entire life under his mother's thumb, except for five years at public school, he was singularly unfit to deal with the world, still less the atmosphere of the remote garrison town on the Burmese border to which he was posted. Early in 1942 he had shot himself. It was not clear why. His mother believed it might have been because he was depressed by a rumor that his adored elder brother had been killed in the battle for Hong Kong, but it was also said that there had been a love affair that went wrong, and he had not been able to handle being rejected.

"He had been domineered and overshadowed by mother," Donald told his own son. "It was a very sad thing. He had never been brought up to the rough side of life—she completely protected him—and I think the life out there undermined him until he couldn't stand any more."

Whatever the circumstances, Ralph reacted as his father had when he lost what he loved. For Donald, the connection was too close to be ignored. Where his family was concerned, at the foot of despair lay death. It was one more reason for loving the woman who had helped him survive the humiliations of the camp.

Almost equally poignant was the loss of Derry McConnell. He had made it through the war, having been awarded not one but two Distinguished Flying Crosses for his gallantry in Coastal Command. The flying that he loved had claimed him in the end. When a new version of the Meteor jet was being developed in the months after the war, he had grabbed the chance to act as test pilot, but on an early proving flight the plane had suddenly plunged into the ground, killing him instantly. As Donald and Pamela walked and talked together, and ran through the little roll of honor of their friends, it was not difficult to feel that they were survivors, the ones who had come through. Small wonder that they felt destined for each other.

For his best man, Donald chose Frank Hennessy, who had shared the burden of carrying their kit to Sham Shui Po, but events conspired against the choice, and by the time the wedding day arrived the man standing beside him with the ring turned out to be another of the little RAF group, Fergie Ferguson, who had helped him in what had been literally his darkest hour. It was the romance of the occasion that was to blame. The news quickly spread among their friends, that Pamela who had waited through all those years of war and Donald who had suffered so badly as a prisoner were getting married after being kept apart for so long. Even the least susceptible were touched by the evidence that love could indeed conquer all. Now in his late forties and so shy he was almost in the confirmed bachelor class, Fergie was one who succumbed to the power of love, and Brigit, whose acid wit might in other circumstances have dissolved Cupid to pink mush, was another. She was in bed recovering from jaundice when Fergie came to discuss details of the wedding arrangements. He saw her in her jaundice and her nightdress, and was instantly smitten. As Brigit herself admitted, it was quite a color scheme. The nightdress was green and her skin was, in her words, "the color of a banana." The fact that Fergie never blinked an eye instantly won her heart.

One person who steadfastly resisted romance was Maud Hill. Pamela had always found it difficult to fit Donald's mother within the circle of adoration that enclosed Donald. It would have been hard for any mother to live up to her expectations, but Maud failed spectacularly. Years of widowhood had taught her to follow her own road, and she had developed a particular style that was the reverse of romantic. Having grown up in the last years of Victoria's reign when the old queen had been in perpetual mourning for Prince Albert, she had a clear idea of how a widow should appear. Layers of black bombazine were piled up in skirts and bodices and blouses and jackets and bonnets until they shimmered shapelessly around her. Her manner, by contrast, was definite. What she wanted she got, partly because she was shameless in asking for it, and partly because there was an undeniable force about her, which had bent her husband and both her sons to her will. When her deep-set eyes started to flicker acquisitively around the room, it made people uneasy, as though they might not be able to resist if she arbitrarily demanded one of their possessions.

Her eyes and her hair were her most noticeable features. She was proud of her hair, which was thick and lustrous and was sometimes allowed to fall about her shoulders when it was not piled up under her black bonnet. But Pamela preferred not to think too much about her hair.

"I'll tell you the secret of keeping your hair looking nice, my dear," Maud said to her at one of their early meetings. "You should wash it in your own urine. That's what I do with mine. Have done for years. And just you look at it."

It was difficult to know which image was the more revolting—the one of a black bombazine mountain squatting over a chamber pot, or that of the contents being poured over the mountain's head. Eager to win fresh converts, Maud confided her secret to Brigit and to anyone else she could find. Soon all Pamela's friends knew of her about-to-be mother-in-law's peculiarity.

As the wedding approached, Pamela found it easier to think of Fergie and Brigit. They were spending enough time together to make her parents feel that the most dangerous and vulnerable of their daughters might have found her own match. At the last moment they announced their engagement. It was too late for a double wedding, but Frank stepped aside so that at least Fergie went up the aisle as best man. Amid the mounting anxiety of preparing for the wedding, it was one arrangement that was easy to make. With only ten days to go, there was a rush to get everything in place, the decisions about announcements and invitations, fittings for the wedding dress, flowers for the bouquet, discussions with the vicar, and a reception to prepare—with all the complications of ration cards and austerity restrictions on light and heat. Everything was in short supply, especially the luxuries of food and drink that a wedding demands, and the reception had to be held in the doctor's house, which had a particularly large drawing room. Postwar reality took no account of romance.

The twenty-third was a Wednesday, a holiday in Tunbridge Wells, and despite the short notice, the number of acceptances made it clear that Holy Trinity Church would be full. By this stage there was only the bride's last and most demanding test to be taken. The greatest day of her life demanded only that she wear the sort of dress that made her as beautiful as she had ever dreamed, and the morning was devoted to putting it on. It was white taffeta, a classic 1930s style, cut square in front with a neat waist and full-length skirt, but with its simplicity offset by clouds of white veil drifting from head to ankle. The top of the veil was the problem, for it had to be pinned in place with a garland of flowers. At just that moment when the bride and her best friend and her mother were staring tremulously into the mirror, where three pairs of hands were holding hair and veil and garland in place, they heard the unmistakable rustle of black bombazine coming into the room behind them.

"I've been told you can get wonderful vegetables in Tunbridge Wells," Maud announced in her most definite voice, "so I've come early to buy some potatoes. Now, can someone show me the best place for really good potatoes?"

It was a wonder, Pamela thought, that such a creature could have produced Donald. Someone was hastily deputed to shepherd Maud to market before it closed, and only then could they finally pin the veil as it should be. The mirror told her it had been worth the trouble. The dress was exquisite, and wearing it she felt as beautiful as a bride should.

The photographs of the wedding were some of the few that she always kept with her. They helped bring back the details of the day. Of the ceremony she recalled most clearly the emotion of it, the smiling faces turned toward her as she came down the aisle as though each of them had been hoping for this moment as long as she had, and the sense of peace when she said, "I do"; it felt as if she had at last reached harbor. Looking at the picture of them taken afterward on the steps of Holy Trinity reminded her of the details—the prettiness of the winter bouquet of maidenhair fern, lilies, and white carnations; and the veil, which threatened to catch on every car door and flower stem. They reminded her, too, of the look in Donald's eyes, tender and quizzical and strained. For him, too, this was an arrival, but the journey had been infinitely harder.

The hardship was brought closer by the presence of others who had come through it. "Four Ex-POWs at Wedding," ran the headline in *The Courier*'s report of the occasion. In addition to Donald and Fergie, Frank Hennessy and Ginger Sullivan had turned up, and for them in particular the marriage must have seemed a small miracle, an unmistakable sign that the horror was over.

The bouquet went to Brigit, and the magic worked: she and Fergie were married within the year. Then Donald and Pamela got the train to Charing Cross. There might have been more romantic means of departure, but it was only a step from the London station to the Savoy Hotel, where they had promised each other so long ago that they would spend the first night of their honeymoon.

As they waited for the train, the sight of a black tent-shaped dress on the platform made Pamela bury her face in Donald's shoulder for fear that Maud might want to share a compartment with them. Fortunately she walked past, but it was not until after the train had pulled out that Pamela realized that somehow her going-away suitcase had been left behind in Queen's Road. As a result she learned that one immediate advantage of having a husband was that he could be left to deal with the crisis. At Charing Cross he telephoned her home to have the case put on the next train so that it could be delivered to the Savoy. To her mortification, however, while he was still on the telephone at Charing Cross asking her parents to make the arrangements, Maud appeared once more.

"Will you ask them to send on my potatoes too?" she said. "I must have left them behind in all the excitement." And with Maud-like obstinacy she insisted that her wretched potatoes be sent to the Savoy Hotel as well. Imagining the hotel porter's thoughts as he collected one suitcase and a sack of potatoes in the name of Flight Lieutenant and Mrs. Hill in the Bridal Suite made Pamela so embarrassed she could not bring herself to utter another word to her new mother-in-law.

Nevertheless the ration-free, black-market luxury of the Savoy was designed to soothe the most savage breast, and soon Maud and her potatoes took their proper place as low comedy. Being with Donald reduced everything else to its true proportion. They had come through. That was the only thing that mattered.

In the dining room, she noticed him looking around at all the luxury with an incredulous lift of his black eyebrows.

"Was it very hard in the camp?" she asked.

"Oh, it wasn't bad," he said offhandedly. "Other people had it much worse." Then he added, "I kept a diary for some of the time. I'll show it to you one day. That'll tell you."

She could feel that there were secrets that had to be told, and more than that, that she was the only one he could tell them to. But at this moment she did not want to know more. It was enough that he himself did not feel scarred by it. When the time was right, she would ask him more, and the diary would be there to answer her questions. That evening, the past and with it all the accumulated tension of waiting were finished. They could plan their future together. Donald had three months' leave due to him. They had so much time they could squander it like millionaires.

They spent their honeymoon beside the sea, in a flat she had taken in the little town of Bexhill. The only reminder of the past came in March, with the arrival of a letter from Buckingham Palace to tell Donald that he had been awarded a military M.B.E., making him a Member of the Order of the British Empire, for his services in Hong Kong. Unlike gallantry awards such as the Distinguished Flying Cross, which were awarded for specific actions, the M.B.E. recognized service over a period of time. The citation's turgid language effectively muffled the high pitch of endeavor demanded by battle and prison, but it was wording that the service understood:

> This short service officer displayed before, during and after the operations all those qualities associated with the best traditions of the R.A.F. He was at all times ready to carry out any duty alloted to him with calmness, efficiency and determination. His powers of leadership were outstanding and his invariable cheerfulness was of particular value when he and his party were holding a part of the line, a task that was utterly foreign to them. As a prisoner of war, his conduct was exemplary, and at a time when he was left in charge of the R.A.F. unit, he was largely responsible for the high morale and good behavior of the Unit.

Donald was pleased, because he hoped that the award might persuade the RAF to put him back on flying duties when his leave was over, and because he knew it must have come at Ginger Sullivan's recommendation. Otherwise, it was not an honor that he made much of.

Donald's was one of a batch of decorations for service in the Far East, and among them was a remarkable quartet of George Crosses, the highest recognition for courage outside battle. These were awarded to the four prisoners executed for their roles in the collaboration with BAAG: Colonel Newnham, Captain Ansari, Captain Ford, and Flight Lieutenant Gray. From Donald's present happiness, the agony they had all endured must already have begun to retreat into the infinite distance. It simply had no part in the present day. The gap that had opened up made it impossible for him to put into words what he felt on seeing the newspaper picture of Dolly Gray with his cap on the side of his head, and his luxuriant winged mustache. They might both have done something worthwhile had Maltby not forbidden their bombing raid. Donald might have gone in Gray's place to Sham Shui Po. Instead he had lived, and his friend had suffered unimaginable torture and execution. It was pointless to speculate; it was pointless, too, to bring back memories.

That summer he and Ginger held the great reunion they had planned in camp. Familiar faces, once skeletal but now half-hidden by the return of muscle and fat, appeared, and they talked so glancingly of the camp that to their wives and girlfriends it sounded more like an eccentric boarding school than a prison. The future was what they discussed in detail. Most were out of the services and back in civvy street, and loudly complaining of the Labour government's penal rates of tax. Donald was the rarity.

The RAF might be discarding personnel as quickly as possible, but for him the future could hardly have been brighter. In March he had been given a permanent commission. Two months later he had been appointed station commander at RAF Hendon, one of the largest training and administrative establishments in the service, and in July he was promoted to squadron leader with seniority dating back to December 1, 1941, a week before the outbreak of war. He more than anyone, with the possible exception of Fergie, had cause to look forward to the postwar years with confidence. Fergie could be optimistic for another reason: he was about to take his new wife back with him to Hong Kong, where he had a job in the Education Department.

Altogether the reunion was a curious event. They were noisily pleased to see each other, but then it seemed that no one was quite sure why he had come. They could say nothing to one another about the great event that bound them all together.

Between themselves, Donald and Pamela behaved in the same way. He told her what the camps looked like and gave a thumbnail sketch of a typical day, and the boredom of it. Sometime in the future they would talk in detail about what had happened to him in the war, he promised, but now was never quite the right moment. When they were settled, they would go through it all, and Donald would decode the diary. Meanwhile, Pamela told stories about her cooking, and about London in the Blitz, and about meeting Eric Maschwitz who was such a good friend. That was as much of the war as either of them wanted to discuss. They went dancing wherever there was music being played, even if Benny Goodman was no longer the dance bands' favorite. She discovered how much he loved her, and how little she knew about him, on the day she went up to London to meet him wearing her latest sauciest little hat, a boater tilted to one side with a flower in front. Donald kissed her and said, "Darling, I love everything about you, but would it be dreadful to say I don't like your hat? In fact, I don't like hats at all."

In May he took up his job at Hendon as station administration officer, a plum job that demonstrated the value that the RAF placed upon the qualities listed in his MBE citation. The one drawback was that for some intolerable weeks, until she could find a place of her own, Pamela had to share Maud's flat in Swiss Cottage. The saga of the potatoes had permanently soured their relations, for it had not ended with their delivery to the Savoy. With what seemed like positive malice, Maud had telephoned at seven on the first morning of their married life to ask whether the sack had actually arrived. Except for breakfast, Pamela succeeded in avoiding her almost completely during their weeks as flatmates, but it was the one area of married life that was, she felt, less than perfect.

In the bitterly cold spring of 1947, Donald was posted to Nottinghamshire, but later that year Pamela found a flat for them back in Tunbridge Wells. It overlooked the Common, a wild expanse of parkland decorated with tall trees and unexpected rock escarpments. Here she felt they could be utterly happy, and by then she was pregnant. Part of her knew that he was not as he had been before he went to war. The camp had damaged him deeply. He was less certain of himself, and more irritable. He complained that he could not concentrate, and the huge competence that she had been accustomed to would often break down into petulance. Yet he was still the man she loved. She felt sure that she could repair the damage. It would take time and it would take love, but there was enough of those to heal anyone.

11

Breakup and Reconciliation

I hate and love. You may ask why I do so,
I do not know, but I feel it and am in torment

CATULLUS,

"CARMINA LXXXV"

Donald and Pamela's first child, Joanna, was born on October 21, 1947. The arrival of a beautiful child with blue eyes and dark hair should have been the completion of what they had waited so long for, life together and the beginnings of a family. Instead, she came just as her parents were made brutally aware of the legacy left by Donald's years in the prison camps.

In the months immediately after their wedding, Donald and Pamela might have found a way of approaching the problem. However hard doing so would have been for him, he was prepared to try to tell her about what had happened to him, and the very act of talking would have countered the prisoner's instinct to conceal whatever meant most to him. The diary, deeply coded, camouflaged and unreadable to an outsider, was the perfect representation of his psychological state, and his offer to decipher it for her showed that he was willing to let her read him as well. But the last time he mentioned reading it was during the preparations for the reunion party with Ginger. After that the impulse seemed to fade.

There was every good reason why Donald and Pamela failed to find the key. The most obvious was that it did not seem important at the time. Neither they nor the experts believed that there was anything to be gained by bringing back painful memories.

When the prisoners returned to Britain, the few who were offered any help discovered that "help" amounted to little more than a medical examination and the occasional issue of extra leave. The official attitude was expressed in a directive from the Ministry of War which was issued in 1945 to everyone dealing with servicemen returning from Japanese prisoner-of-war camps. They were told to advise the ex-prisoners not to say anything of their experiences since it would only upset their family and friends and could do nothing to put right what was done to them. At the time most accepted this as sound advice, and for Donald and Pamela in particular the feeling that they had arrived in their safe haven after a long voyage made them even less anxious to return to the past.

The first evidence of any long-lasting damage appeared while Donald was at Hendon. In part it was simply a matter of having been away for so long. The old, prewar RAF he had known in Britain was still imbued with the stiff discipline of its founder,

Lord Trenchard. But since then the service had been transformed by the arrival of the teenagers and youths in their twenties who had won the Battle of Britain, then by the incursion of egalitarian-minded Australians and South Africans, and finally by the more tolerant attitudes required to cope with the high tension of repeated bombing tours. To the new station officer, these modern standards of behavior were shocking. With the end of the war, morale and discipline seemed to have gone. He could not conceal his dismay. "Everyone was drinking too much, and looked pretty scruffy," he complained. "My proudest and happiest moments had been in the Air Force before the war and now quite frankly I was almost ashamed of being in the Air Force."

His outlook belonged to another era, and to the young flying crew on the station hauled up before him for being improperly dressed or behaving in a disorderly fashion, he must have seemed impossibly remote and severe. There would have been rumors that he had been a prisoner of war of the Japanese, and presumably at first allowances were made for him. But it was more than a matter of being out of touch. The RAF was one of the two poles of his existence, and it had thrown up a barrier which shook his fragile confidence to its foundations.

He had always thought of himself as a pilot. It was not just for the prestige of the wings on his chest but because, as he said, "the happiest time of my life was flying." Before the war, flying had released him from the drudgery of accountancy, and from the dark weight of his mother's influence. His pilot's logbook was among the few possessions that he kept with him through prison camp, and when he returned, he imagined that flying would again be part of his freedom. But in March 1946 a medical examination showed that although he was physically fit, he suffered from color blindness. He suggested that this must be a result of his blindness at Sham Shui Po and would in time disappear. But the medical board banned him from nighttime and combat flying, and, rubbing salt into the wound, entered on his record their conclusion that the defect was "unknown on entry as pilot." In other words, he must always have been color-blind, and the implication was that perhaps he had not really been fit to be a pilot in the first place.

"That's a load of old rubbish," he raged. "It's the effect of malnutrition." But he was not believed, and it seemed to him that a slur had been cast on what he prized most. Years later it still stung. "They had no idea about the effects of malnutrition," he expostulated on the tape he made for his son, "they hadn't a clue at all, no clue at all."

Instead of being returned to flying duties, he was made station commander, a ground-based job, and despite the prestige of being at Hendon, he felt it as a rebuff. Quite soon, the stress of the position began to mount, and as it did so he found it increasingly difficult to cope with unexpected memories of the camp that broke his concentration. The sense that he was losing control made him anxious and bad-tempered. For the moment he could still hold things together, and in September 1946, when further reductions in the force were made, his superiors recommended that he be retained for a further eighteen months. That was the high-tide mark of his RAF career, and thereafter the tide began to ebb.

By the end of the year, it was clear that he could not cope with the strain of Hendon's busy schedule, and in April 1947 he was transferred to Wymeswold, a much smaller station in Nottinghamshire. With lighter responsibilities, the job should have been easier, but in the narrow confines of a provincial station he was thrust more into the life of the base, and there was less to shield him from the high spirits of his young successors in the cockpit. He was still clinging to his sanity, but only just. With a fog of anxiety clouding his mind, his adherence to rules and regulations was as rigid as the grip of a drowning man. He could see that he was getting it wrong, that he was losing touch, but he could do nothing about it.

"I was completely antisocial. I was an officer on the station, yet in the evening I did not mix with the other officers at all," he admitted. "I felt almost as if I were unclean. There were parties going on in the mess with a hell of a lot of drinking, and it was all foreign to me. I'm sure there wasn't the slightest interest in me, they were more concerned with boozing it up."

His worst anxiety was that he could not understand what was happening to him. He had no self-confidence, he could not concentrate, and his temper would erupt uncontrollably. He and Pamela were living in a flat near the base, and she did her best to look after him. This was not the kind of love she had expected to give to a man who had been so competent and high-spirited when he left, but she believed that she could rescue him from the pit into which he was sliding. There were times when the strained look left his face. She would take him dancing, and if the band played some of the old Benny Goodman music they had danced to before the war, they could still recapture the past. Sometimes in the evening, when they sat alone in the flat, he clung to her as though she were his only hope and she could soothe the fear from his eyes.

At other times, a trivial incident might provoke an outburst of rage. In a pub one evening, she recognized a wartime friend and introduced him as someone she had danced with. When the man left, Donald's calmness dissolved into fury and he accused Pamela of having arranged the meeting behind his back. The quarrel lasted for three days. They made up as passionately as they had fallen out, but both were frightened by the violence of his reaction.

Eventually the RAF recognized that he was no longer capable of doing his job. In September 1947, he was relieved of his duties, following an adverse report from his commanding officer, and ordered before a medical board. Having heard the evidence of his reclusive habits and unpredictable, explosive behavior, they made a preliminary diagnosis that he was suffering from "affective disorder" and recommended that he receive treatment at Woodside, a psychiatric hospital near Woking. For Donald, it was a shattering experience, but he was forced to acknowledge that his symptoms had grown too serious for him to continue: "I wasn't functioning at all. My morale had gone completely. My concentration seemed to have gone to hell—I could not concentrate."

While they waited for his admission to hospital, Pamela took him back to Tunbridge Wells, where she found the flat overlooking the Common. She was in the last weeks of pregnancy, but she had her parents and friends at hand and she recalled it as a happy period. Without the strain of his RAF duties, Donald became calmer and more rational, and in October Joanna was born. They revisited old haunts and pretended that normality went deeper than the surface. In February 1948 he was admitted to Woodside, and Pamela rented accommodation nearby so that she and the baby would be able to visit him.

For a man who had survived over three years in a Japanese prison camp, Woodside presented a particularly terrifying aspect. No one was tortured there and food was plentiful, but doors were locked and the men in white coats had as much power over their patients as guards did over prisoners. Under the pressure of war they had evolved an interventionist approach designed to return patients to active duty as quickly as possible. Early forms of amphetamines were administered to combat depression, and hyperactivity or mania was treated by inducing deep, comalike sleep with large doses of insulin. In the nearby mental hospital of Belmont, Dr. William Sargent had popularized the use of electroconvulsive treatment in cases of depression when drugs failed to work. At that time, ECT employed huge voltages with so little preparation that bones sometimes broke as bodies arched under the impact of the current, and blood spattered the walls from bitten tongues and lips.

The ultimate weapon in psychiatric treatment was brain surgery. In the 1930s the usual operation was frontal lobotomy, in which the entire frontal lobe of the brain was removed with an instrument rather like a giant corkscrew, but in the aftermath of the war, this was superseded by the more delicate leucotomy, in which major neural connections between the lobe and the rest of the brain were snipped away. In Woodside a number of strangely placid patients with bandages around their heads illustrated what the outcome might be. The spectacle was enough to jolt Donald out of his incapacitated state and into the cold clarity that he felt in the presence of danger. Suspecting that he was being prepared for surgery, he decided to resist every attempt to treat him, including the ECT prescribed by the doctors.

"It was my fight, and I was bloody well going to win it," he explained angrily. "I wouldn't allow them to touch me in any way."

The hospital took his refusal to accept ECT as evidence of paranoia. Instead of offering him any other treatment or attempting to understand the cause of his fears, they sent his case back to the RAF medical board, which accepted the psychiatrists' judgment that he was suffering from "affective disorder para-noiac state." It was the end of his career. In April he was ordered to "proceed home and await instructions." There he was in-formed that he was to be invalided out of the service. He had four months' leave owing to him, and when this finished on October 6, 1948, he ceased to be an officer in the RAF.

It seems clear that Donald was suffering from post-traumatic stress disorder, a condition first so called in the aftermath of the Vietnam War. Its commonest symptoms are flashbacks, loss of concentration, sleeplessness, high anxiety, and aggression. In the standard definition offered by the fourth edition of the *Diagnostic and Statistical Manual of Mental Disorders,* used by American psychi-atrists, these are precipitated by the sort of stress that would evoke symptoms of distress in most people and is generally out-side the range of such common experiences as simple bereave-ment, chronic illness, business losses or marital conflict. As examples, *DSM–IV* lists earthquakes, car accidents, physical in-jury, and such deliberate man-made disasters as bombing and death camps. "The disorder may be especially severe or long last-ing when the [cause of stress] is of human design."

Treatment today is based on bringing to the surface the fear and shock that were first experienced, often in group-centered therapy sessions and sometimes simply by listening to the pa-tient's account. In 1983, the realization that former prisoners of the Japanese were still suffering from their treatment persuaded the British government to offer them free health assessments. During the next fifteen years, over a hundred consulted Dr. Keron Fletcher, an RAF psychiatrist. Interviewed for a television documentary in 1998, he recalled his findings: "It was amazing—forty-five years after the war, I'd ask a question like, 'What was the worst part of your wartime experience?,' and they'd break down and cry. They were still getting sleepless nights. I reckon that over half had significant symptoms."

Neither diagnosis nor treatment was available in 1948, and when Pamela took Donald and the baby back to Tunbridge Wells that summer, he had sunk as low as he could. There were periods of normality, but increasingly they were broken by bizarre behavior. As though looking after Joanna were not enough, Pamela had to deal with Donald's agitated and mad advice about how to do it. In the immediate postwar years, all baby food had to be home-made, and some of the first solid food she made for Joanna was mashed potato and milk.

"You can't feed her that poison!" Donald shouted in a rage. "Don't you know potatoes give you cancer? You'll kill the child."

She tried to appease him, explaining that potato was on the list of recommended baby food, but he would not be convinced. Potatoes were killers. It was the first of his remarks which bore no relation to reality, but over the ensuing weeks such statements became more frequent. Terrified by the growing signs of mental instability, she turned to her mother for help, but Donald stonewalled her enquiries putting on a show of normal behavior. The only form of counseling available was provided by the minister of her local church, who offered cold comfort. A lot of men back from the war were behaving oddly, he told Pamela; their wives just had to put up with it. Yet Donald felt equally tormented by the knowledge that he was out of control.

One evening his condition reached some sort of crisis. He was aware of being tensed up and nervous, when suddenly tears started running down his face. He couldn't explain what was happening, only that his whole body and mind became clear. A thought struck him so clearly he heard it like a voice—"There's no point to all this worrying"—and it felt as if an enormous weight had been lifted off his shoulders. "And from that moment," he would say, "I got back faith in myself."

This seemingly spontaneous recovery produced such a sense of relief that neither questioned how it came about. Donald at least was convinced that his problems were solved, and the past was over. Clearly the attempt to return to the career that once had made him supremely happy, and now made him supremely unhappy, had created a degree of stress he could not cope with. Sometimes madness is the only reasonable response to an utterly intolerable situation. When the tears came, they must have signaled that at some emotional level he felt able to let that bit of his past drop away. With it went the stress that he found so unbearable. Tentatively, in the calm that followed, he and Pamela began to rediscover their happiness in each other.

Yet even then, she sensed that what had happened in the camp might represent unfinished business. Although she was reluctant to test his newfound lucidity, she tried to ask him about the war, but this time it was he who deflected her. "I can think of more interesting things to talk about," he would say defensively when she raised the topic. Her tentative efforts to return to the diary were pushed aside in the same way.

Perhaps by then it was too late. The tears after his breakdown were the result of some deep psychological shift. Donald wanted to leave his past behind, and that included the festering anger and fear and humiliation that prison camp conditions had created. "There's no point in going back," he always insisted. "The past is over." In *The Railway Man,* Eric Lomax wrote of his similar determination in 1945 to leave behind the memories of his torture and humiliation in a Japanese prison camp. "I didn't understand yet that there are experiences you can't walk away from," Lomax commented, "and that there is no statute of limitation on the effects of torture."

Donald was now thirty-six, with a wife and child to support and no job. Long before—almost, it must have seemed, in another existence—he had been an accountant. It was the only salable skill he had, and he scoured the employment columns while Joanna crawled around the floor beneath his feet. But in 1948, the war boom was over. Manufacturing industry was contracting nearly as fast as the armed forces had done, and laying off skilled and unskilled employees alike. The classified columns, which still bulged with advertisements from former middle-ranking officers seeking an opening in sales or administration, now carried almost as many from production and administration managers seeking any sort of job at all. Nobody was advertising for an accountant, let alone for a part-qualified accountant who had not practiced for over a decade.

On his return from the Far East, Donald had three years' accumulated pay, but by the summer that had practically all gone. Before the war they had lived extravagantly on nothing, but being married was more expensive. Pamela required a certain standard of living, and a baby's needs devoured bank notes faster than mother's milk.

"I can always get work as a cook," Pamela volunteered once, but Donald could not bear the idea of living off his wife's income. Then just as they were growing desperate, an advertisement appeared for what seemed like an ideal job with the Iraq Petroleum Company. He was called for an interview. To his immense relief, a glowing reference from his former commanding officer and his experience of life in a hot climate counted for as much as his qualifications, and he was offered the post. It sounded ideal. The accommodation was free; the salary was generous and it came tax-free; but when he got back to the flat that evening he gave Pamela the news with a somber face. When she heard what he had to say, she screamed.

His job was in the Middle East, and because he was on probation for the first two years, he would not be allowed to take his wife out with him. Pamela hardly took it in. All she could think was "What have we done to deserve this? We've had barely two years together, and now we're to be separated again." It did not seem bearable.

In an emergency, he had always responded with icy clarity, not letting fear or anguish deflect him from doing what had to be done. This was the only way he could find of supporting his family, and he had to take it. In the last few weeks before leaving, she clung fiercely to him and he did his best to comfort her. In September 1948 he left for northern Iraq, leaving her to a loneliness she thought had gone for good.

Aspects of it were different. There was not the fear that he might be dead. They could speak every night on the telephone. She had Joanna to look after, and she soon learned that she was pregnant again. Her parents lived nearby, and with three generations on hand her days were filled with family matters. She was in the town she had grown up in, and she had never found it difficult to make friends. But at the heart of it all, there was a space. No one to share the shape of her life, and at night no body in the bed beside her.

His absence left her devastated. She cried a lot and, if asked what the matter was, said simply, "I miss him all the time, every minute, but most of all at the end of the day." Yet for that generation who had come through the war, stoicism was second nature, and the response never varied: "There's nothing to be done about it; you'll just have to put up with it."

The center of Iraq's fabulously rich oil-producing region was the town of Kirkuk. Almost 150 miles north of Baghdad and far from the irrigated valley of the Tigris-Euphrates, the area would have remained an empty desert were it not for the discovery of oil in the 1920s, which had spawned storage tanks, extraction pumps, several settlements for expatriate oil workers outside Kirkuk itself, and the perpetual smell of gas. All this was owned by the Iraq Petroleum Company, itself a subsidiary of Standard Oil, then the largest petroleum company in the world. IPC's massive profits were split with the government of Iraq, and its influence on political affairs was enormous. Until the overthrow of King Faisal II in 1958, a major plank of Britain's foreign policy was to sustain the king in power in order to safeguard its access to Iraqi oil and to protect IPC from nationalization.

Within this petroleum empire, Donald's job could hardly have been less demanding. Initially it consisted of supervising the ledgers and accounts kept by the company's Iraqi bookkeepers. He lived in one of the company's expatriate settlements, known clinically as K-3. Over time his responsibilities increased but a job he did not love never evoked the sort of dedication he had given the RAF. Nevertheless, he was widely liked. He played tennis well, and there was something about his large, calm presence that was immediately reassuring. The crises that are endemic in oil production did not upset him. He himself felt more relaxed than ever. He did not look for responsibility and never pushed for promotion. Almost, it seemed, he was without ambition. But in the middle of the desert and far from the nearest town, K-3 had the atmosphere of a frontier settlement, and it was more important to be a good man than to be a hotshot thruster. Donald lived in the bachelors' block, where the parties were riotous, the cocktails were mixed in dustbins, and practical jokes were constant. Beds were apple-pied, doors were booby-trapped so often that the sound of falling metal buckets was one of the block's trademark sounds, and one hung-over bachelor woke after a party to find a donkey in bed beside him.

One month in twelve he was allowed home on leave, and after the second leave he brought out Pamela and his two daughters, Joanna aged four and Carolyn aged two, to live with him in K-3.

Coming out of the BOAC airliner into the searing heat of Baghdad with two children in tow and the prospect of a six-hour car journey ahead, much of it across tracks and dried-up wadis, Pamela's first instinct was to hate the place, but the profits of IPC were so enormous that it could afford to cushion its expatriate employees against the worst discomforts of desert life. They lived in a bungalow but it offered a way of living which seemed the height of luxury after the penny-pinching restrictions of postwar Britain. They had an amah to look after the children and a houseboy to take care of the housework. The company supplied a gardener and a free taxi service to take them shopping and to the club and to the Olympic-sized swimming-pool. A free primary school provided an excellent education for their children. There was, it seemed, no material want unsatisfied, and better than all of that the two of them were reunited once more.

In her happiness, Pamela took it all at face value. It was the first time she had lived so far away from her parents that she could not visit them, and she felt homesick, but it counted for nothing beside the security of sharing her life again with the man she loved. There was a dance at the club most weekends, and on each occasion the purely physical sensation of being in his arms restored an old pleasure.

It did not take long to discover the reality below the surface. The summers were blindingly hot; the average daytime temperature was 110 degrees, and the air-conditioning units in the bedrooms were noisy and inefficient. The days began at five-thirty, when the men went to work, and the women occupied themselves with coffee mornings and dressmaking until two P.M., when work on the oil fields ceased. A siesta occupied the afternoon, and then there was tennis and the club. Sometimes there were weekend expeditions up into the hills, or an occasional week's holiday in Tripoli on the North African coast could be arranged, but otherwise its few hundred inhabitants did not leave K-3.

The Hills made an attractive couple, good-looking and sociable, with her vivacity and flair allied to the charm of his quiet solidity. Joanna went to the company's school, and an amah helped look after Carolyn. When Pamela became pregnant with their third child, it seemed to her like the seal on their rediscovered intimacy.

She was older now, however, and more aware of the shadows beneath the surface. The parchment-covered notebook was among the possessions that she had brought out with her; one evening after she had put the children to bed she asked him whether he would let her read it at last.

"Why?" he asked in surprise. "Why would you want to read about that awful time?"

He made it sound like an intrusion, and a little uncertainly she answered, "I think it's important; we've never really talked about what happened to us in the war."

Suddenly he flared up. "What happened in the war was that you went dancing at the Savoy with Eric Maschwitz while I was locked up in a prisoner-of-war camp."

The attack was so unexpected, she stared at him appalled. "But that's unfair. You mean I was never supposed to go out at all?"

Seeing her outrage, his mood abruptly changed once more. "I don't think either of us need rake up those memories again," he said calmly. "The war's over and forgotten. Besides, there are more amusing things to read than my old diary."

It was easier to let the moment pass than to provoke another outbreak of anger. The diary's contents, she recognized sadly, had sunk a little deeper from view. Soon they would become inaccessible. She went to pour them both a drink.

Like many couples, they tended to accept the roles that their friends made for them—in the Hills' case, that she was the outgoing one and he the reserved. In K-3 the distinction was cruder than at home, where old school friends knew the shyness behind her showing-off, and fellow pilots who shared his deep love of flying instinctively understood some of the passion beneath his self-control. Here the difference came closer to caricature, and imperceptibly Donald found himself thrust into the background. Eventually it triggered a scene she never forgot.

She so obviously loved dancing that she was never short of partners at the club dances. There were more men than women, and the bachelors queued up to dance with her. One evening she came smiling off the floor and with a mock elaboration of courtesy asked him for the pleasure of the next dance. It should have been an unnecessary request. Dancing, after all, was what had first drawn them together, and they always enjoyed it. This time he dourly shook his head. She was hurt by the refusal.

"Why not?" she asked.

"I don't feel like it," he answered.

She could not understand the sudden coldness. "But what's happened?" she demanded.

"Nothing has happened," he insisted shortly. "I just don't want to dance."

At last she concluded that she was being punished. "What have I done wrong?" she wailed, but the only answer was a stony silence. The reason for his refusal was simple jealousy, she decided.

But, as was to become clear, there were more complex causes for the abrupt changes of mood. What had happened in prison left Donald peculiarly ill-equipped to deal with frustration. It touched the deep reserve of anger built up by years of helplessness, and provoked quite unreasonable spasms of rage. While he was in the RAF, his mounting frustration had sent him spinning out of control. What enabled him to regain command of himself was the tearful moment when he removed himself emotionally from the cause of the frustration. This need to walk away from upsetting situations dictated the pattern of his behavior. When he was by himself it was quite easy to avoid frustrating circumstances, but when he was with Pamela her behavior was liable to trigger feelings too powerful and spontaneous to be held under.

In a revealing passage in his taped life story, he remarked how well he had played tennis before she came out. "I've never felt so relaxed in my life," he said. "My reflexes were lightning fast—in fact, in my volleying and service I was a top-class tennis player."

That ease began to go when Pamela came out to join him, and some of the old symptoms triggered by his beloved RAF reappeared. "My concentration started to slip back," he noted. "Suddenly the antisocial thing was back. My confidence started going." The anxiety affected his tennis, among other things, and he imagined that people were laughing at him because he was playing so badly. "I think this was the most humiliating thing that ever happened," he said, "because I think Pamela was probably watching, and here was I who had been a good tennis player making a complete fool of myself. That was a very very shattering experience."

Where she was concerned he had no defenses. His behavior when she came off the dance floor was triggered by more than simple jealousy; it was an emotion that threatened the edifice of his sanity.

The birth of Christopher in 1952 introduced another facet to their relationship. Donald liked the idea of having a son, and the boy always intuitively understood that his father's affection could be counted on whatever happened. Nevertheless, with children the controlled expression of feeling that was becoming his habit did not provide enough stimulus. Pamela was inevitably the center of their emotional life, while he was perceived as a distant, regulating force. Soon after his birth, they moved from the desert to the relative sophistication of Kirkuk. The expatriate life allowed the children such freedom that all of them grew up thinking of Iraq as a kind of paradise in which the sun shone all day, where their friends would be waiting by the enormous swimming pool, and where there were parties every week.

To Carolyn their life seemed extraordinarily privileged. "It must have been like that in the British Raj," she said, "all those servants to look after us, and the sense of wonderful liberty."

The liberty had strict limits. From the age of six or seven the girls were sent home to be educated. For them summer holidays took on the quality of a return to the promised land. They would turn up in school uniform under gray skies at London's Heathrow Airport, and emerge into the dazzling light and heat of Baghdad, and the prospect of parties and sunshine and poolside friend-ships.

The outcome for their parents was less joyful. When the girls departed, the bungalow was left empty, with nothing to buffer the growing disparity of need between the two adults. On the one side there was a man who needed to maintain his remoteness to keep control of his sanity, on the other a woman who yearned for overt affection. Each made the other's love treacherous—she was the person who aroused his deepest feelings, and he was the only man she wanted.

Alcohol has always played a prominent role in expatriate communities, and in Kirkuk gin was cheap. To dull the sharpness of unexpressed feeling, they began to drink, and the alcohol ex-aggerated their differences. The emotion that then surfaced most frequently was anger. As the years passed, the returning children became aware of the frozen atmosphere and of sudden argu-ments that ended in tears. But while Donald could restrain his feelings—*had* to restrain them—Pamela's emotions and drinking easily flew out of control.

She knew she provoked him, but didn't know why; it was too difficult to disentangle one feeling from another. One moment they would be very close and somehow end up a moment later shouting at each other. But it was the closeness that bred the shouting, and the closeness was still there when the shouting stopped.

She was in her early forties when she became pregnant again. It was a baby she desperately wanted in order to bridge the widen-ing rift, but news of her father's illness forced her to fly back to Britain in the summer of 1960. He rallied, and she decided to re-turn to Iraq with Carolyn, now aged eleven, whose holidays were just beginning. Worrying about her father, and anxious about her marriage, she caught the flight back, but while they were still in the air, she felt an agonizing pain in her womb. The four-month pregnancy had ended in a miscarriage. The anguish of her loss found expression in a record that she had brought back with her from London. It was the soundtrack of *South Pacific,* and Carolyn used to hear her playing one song in particular time after time: "This Nearly Was Mine." The eleven-year-old heard it so often she almost knew it by heart, but only when she was a woman did she realize that her mother had been playing it for the child she had lost.

From then on everything seemed to go bad for them. To dull the grief, Pamela drank more, and the arguments became more high-pitched. Then, in 1961, they lost their privileged position in the sun when the republican regime that had overthrown the king three years earlier nationalized IPC's assets. The expatriate community quickly dispersed, and at Pamela's urging Donald decided to buy a house in Tunbridge Wells. She had missed being close to her parents, and looked forward to visiting them again, but soon after they moved in, her father died. The loss was made worse when a quarrel over Mr. Kirrage's belongings pushed her always prickly relationship with Brigit into outright estrangement.

Donald's experience with an oil firm had helped him get another job quickly, this time with a subsidiary of the conglomerate Trafalgar House, which was drilling for water in Libya. Soon after his arrival, he saved the company from a large loss by uncovering a network of fraud in its overseas operation. In recognition he was quickly promoted, and, finding himself appreciated, he gave his work a degree of attention it had never commanded in Iraq. He commuted into London, and the entire family found themselves together again for the first time in ten years. In this renewed proximity the sudden alterations of mood that had crippled his love for Pamela began to corrode his relationship with his daughters as well.

It was Joanna who was most prepared to confront him. In what was almost a stereotype of the 1960s rebellion against the older generation, her whole outlook represented a challenge to her father's tightly controlled nature. Impassioned and idealistic, she espoused causes like banning nuclear weapons, played pop music, and wore sweaters so tight and skirts so short they seemed a direct affront to good taste. With no less commitment, she also confronted him over his treatment of her mother, and indeed any other member of the family who aroused his anger.

Christopher's memory of these years had a significantly different emphasis. Between him and his father there existed a warm though unspoken bond, which was typified by Donald's response to his son's request to read the diary. The boy was only about twelve years old, but the event had made an impression because within the family the diary was regarded as a forbidden topic, and at first his father had tried to discourage him.

"There's nothing important in it," he said, "and translating it would be a very laborious process."

For once in his dealings with his father, Christopher had persisted, and surprisingly Donald agreed to show him how the code worked. The parchment-colored notebook had been taken out, but in the end his father had been forced to put it aside. The reason, as Philip Aston would eventually discover, was that by then Donald himself had forgotten how the code worked. The key to unraveling the past had been lost.

Nevertheless, the boy understood the significance of the gesture: he and his father were on the same side. In later life, when Christopher talked of the same quarrels as his sisters, his memory was not of Donald bullying the others, but of the mother and daughter allying against him. For Christopher, it was his father who was the victim. "There was almost a conspiracy against him," he insisted. "All he wanted was a quiet life." Specifically, he pointed out that although there were explosions of temper, his father did not respond to attack, but instead retreated into himself. That, too, was something his daughters remembered: he would not argue or try to defend himself.

Among traumatized prisoners of war, this withdrawal is so marked that it is almost a symptom of their condition. With terrible lucidity, Eric Lomax described a pattern of behavior that might have been Donald's: "withdrawals into cold and blank anger in the face of hostility, pulling my shell around me and locking it tight.... Confrontation threatened my whole being, triggering flashes of memory that I could not articulate to anyone, and most tragically of all, not even to my wife."

Donald betrayed one other unmistakable legacy of the camp—he ate prodigiously, even greedily, finishing up other people's leftovers. It was a habit that he was to retain to the end of his life, and one typical of those who have suffered starvation. Perhaps he could have functioned well enough, keeping the memories at bay, had he not felt so deeply about Pamela, but the very intensity of his feelings ensured that any wayward act or word of hers would trigger the explosion of all the locked-in anger. Carolyn recalled that as the destructive spiral grew worse she would be awakened by the sound of raised voices, and would sit huddled at the top of the stairs wishing with every fiber of her body that they would stop.

At the end of the 1960s they decided bitterly that they could no longer live together. Pamela rented a flat on Mount Ephraim, a hill in Tunbridge Wells, and tried to build an independent life, helped by visits from her daughters and a wide circle of friends in the town. Donald seemed to become entirely solitary. It was almost a commonplace that she was so sociable and he so remote, but now the contrast became extreme. He kept to his regular schedule of driving up to London every day and returning at night, but he saw no one on his return, while she could scarcely bear to spend a moment by herself. In each it was a measure of their unhappiness at being separated. As Christopher observed, "They might not have been able to live together, but they certainly couldn't live apart."

At the first opportunity, they came back together again. In 1971 Joanna got married, and the need to plan the wedding gave them the excuse they needed to talk, and the talk led to the renewal of their old intimacy. Nothing had changed, however, and their relationship quickly returned to its tempestuous, destructive form. Its shape was becoming blurred now. They made a habit of blaming the place they were living in for any shortcomings in their marriage, and in the attempt to find a solution, they kept moving house, but always within Tunbridge Wells and its environs. Alcohol, which had begun as a palliative for Pamela, was rapidly becoming an addiction, and it made her loud and demanding. His behavior at home grew more violent, not to her but to objects that she loved. Letters and photographs were burned, china ornaments she valued were given away, mementos of her past were destroyed.

Again they flew apart. This time Pamela went to stay with Joanna who, with her new husband, Richard Wilkinson, had immigrated to Australia. It was a more terrible repetition of their first separation. She was drinking more, and despite Australia's greater tolerance her behavior was becoming embarrassing. Yet even that handicap did not obliterate Pamela's continuing appeal. Joanna was struck by her talent for relating to people. "She lightened up a room the moment she walked in," she said appreciatively. "She was a very stylish woman, but also very funny, with a dry, ironic, almost camp sense of humor. It was a winning combination."

And she could not live without Donald. On her return, they tried yet again to live together. They were in their late fifties now, old enough to understand what was happening, and to give each other room.

For all his tightness toward his own family, Donald's attractiveness was immediately apparent to an outsider. In 1974 he acquired another son-in-law when Carolyn married Stuart Morris, "a long-haired, bearded leftie" by his own description, who should have been anathema to him. Instead the young man found in the older what he called "an ideal father-figure."

The quality in Donald that most impressed Stuart was "an undeniable dash. In some ways he behaved like a typical pilot, always drove too fast and had that outlook which is ultra-conservative, but doesn't much care for the rules." At the same time, he noted that Donald tended to be happiest by himself and liked going for long solitary walks in the country. He summed him up as "very much a loner, but a natural leader, the sort of officer you would follow anywhere."

Yet when they came together again, the elegant amusing woman and the dashing natural leader were as emotionally destructive as ever. There could be no rational explanation for how they felt about each other. Perhaps it was the key to his remoteness that she hungered for, and he wanted the secret of her ease with people, for they dug into each other as though to excavate whatever lay within. Neither could really pretend to be in control in the other's company any longer.

Talking about that period in her life, Pamela lost all her animation. "He would ring me up, and I would go to him," she said dully. "I loved him, what else could I do?"

What Donald remembered of those days was the strain of coping with the vastly more complex work that Trafalgar House demanded of him, then coming home to a marriage that was blowing itself to pieces. But even when they were living apart, he would respond to her pleas for help as automatically as she did to his. "She used to ring me up," he told Christopher, "and I used to go across to her flat and stay with her in that flat all night, comforting her and trying to keep her off the drink. Then I had to get up in the morning and drive forty miles to London and do a responsible job."

When Pamela finally recognized that she needed professional help, it was Donald who drove her down to the respectable-sounding treatment center in Sussex. To his consternation, she was put in a bare unfurnished room which to his experienced eye looked like prison. Both the doctor and Pamela's brother who had come with them assured him that there was nothing to worry about, but later that night Donald received an anguished call from Pamela pleading to be taken away. He raced down to the center, and when the nurse asked what he was doing there, replied, "I've come to take my wife home." Even when he recounted the story on tape several years later, a note of hair-trigger aggression came into his voice, as he told how the nurse answered flatly, "You can't." "Oh, can't I?" he replied. "You try to stop me." The menace conveyed by his voice is unmistakable, and the nurse evidently appreciated the danger, for a doctor was hastily summoned and responsibility for Pamela was signed over to Donald. At the level of hero and heroine, knight and maiden, they still functioned. It was ordinary living that defeated them. Carolyn eventually found her mother a more suitable place for treatment, and there she gradually recovered.

The strain had told on Donald to such an extent that mistakes crept into his normally meticulous figures, and in the effort to catch them he worked later and later at the office. Sometimes he stayed up all night because he was not confident about his calculations. He would check and recheck, and suddenly find an elementary mistake. Then he would start to panic because the document had to be presented the next morning.

Sensing that he was beginning to slip, and that too many people had found errors in his work, he asked for early retirement. Professionally it made sense, but it removed the last solid structure in his life. Recognizing the danger that their relationship presented to her fragile sobriety, Pamela had gone out to stay with Joanna in Australia, and he was left living alone in the large house they had shared in Mayfield in Sussex. Donald had taken to gardening in a rather wild way, growing quantities of kale, which he would leave as a present heaped up outside Carolyn and Stuart's door. There were long solitary walks with his dogs, but apparently nothing else. When Carolyn went to see him, she was shocked to find him living like a hermit in one room.

"He had everything there, his bed and clothes and a place to cook," she said. "It was all very neat but rather fusty, as though he didn't wash much. It almost looked as if he had gone back to the prison camp."

His loneliness must have been intolerable, otherwise he would not taken to reading the lonelyhearts advertisements, nor have replied to one from a comfortably-off widow in her fifties. Soon afterward, in 1978, he telephoned Pamela in Australia.

"He said he wanted a divorce." She cried as though the pain of it was still fresh twenty years later. "I couldn't believe my ears, and when he said it again I couldn't believe he meant it."

What prompted the call was Donald's meeting with Cynthia, a wealthy widow who had advertised for a partner. They had started an intense physical affair. Pamela flew back from Australia immediately, but it was too late. Three days after her return he announced that he intended to marry Cynthia.

It must have seemed to him like an escape from the past, from memories of the camp, from the love of Pamela, from emotions he could not control. He never pretended that he loved Cynthia, but for just that reason she seemed to present no threat to his mental stability. With her he could relax, and to Stuart, accustomed to his officerlike reserve, there was something shocking about the sudden coarseness of Donald's conversation when he talked about their life together. More ominously, he who had been so restrained in his drinking now ordered in whisky by the case.

At first it seemed that Pamela would fall apart completely. Rather than oppose the divorce, she drowned her days in a blur of alcohol and misery. It is not a time from which much has stayed with her except the pain, until again she decided to get help. What she recovered to was a life of grinding poverty, mitigated by one unexpected act of generosity—for years Donald continued to pay the rent on her flat. On her birthday another came in the form of flowers from him, with a brief, tender note. On several occasions he telephoned to find out how she was, and she fancied that in their talk there was more than a trace of the old warmth. Jealously she hoped that Cynthia was aware of it, too. But just as she pulled herself back from the brink, Donald was plunging toward it.

243

He and Cynthia lived in a cottage near Yeovil in Somerset, not far from the Devon countryside in which he grew up. Soon the outline of catastrophe began to emerge. His new wife drank with a heavy persistence and, released from his self-imposed control, Donald joined her. To Carolyn and Stuart, who kept in touch with them, the signs of mental deterioration were obvious: his temper grew more wayward, he cared less about his appearance, and memory lapses became more common.

When he went out to Australia in 1981, Joanna immediately noticed how unfocused his mind had grown, and how old he appeared. It occurred to her that he had come to put things right with his children. The visit seemed to be like a pilgrimage, as though he had a sense he was not going to live much longer. She decided that he had come "to sort things out."

With Christopher, that was easy. His son had gone to Australia to stay with Joanna and Richard in 1974, and after a succession of jobs in catering and publishing, had at last found something that fulfilled him. At the age of twenty-eight, he had just earned his pilot's license. In the clear Australian sunlight, he took his father up in a little Tomahawk trainer. It was flying as Donald had experienced it, with the ground below visible from the cockpit, and the whole expanse of sky offering freedom in every direction. Briefly he let himself enjoy an almost forgotten taste; then, abruptly, anxiety flooded in and he begged Christopher to take him down.

On the ground, he recovered himself and, turning to Christopher, said "One day you'll fly me from England to Australia." His son was astonished. Flying was just a hobby, and he had no thought of making a living from it.

It took Donald's financial and moral support to help Christopher cross the vast gulf between a private and a commercial pilot's license, but he had clearly inherited the flair for flying that Donald had discovered in himself. Once qualified as a commercial pilot, he was taken on by British Airways and was quickly promoted to become a senior officer, flying jumbo jets on long-haul routes.

"I've never forgotten what Dad said," he acknowledged, "and when I'm flying the London–Sydney route, I always feel as though I'm flying with him."

It was harder to make things right with Joanna, and Donald's first attempt to do so ended disastrously. He adopted his familiar prescriptive style, telling her how she should lead her life, and with a directness learned in childhood and developed by Australian manners Joanna let him know she did not need any lessons from a father who had so spectacularly failed her. She told him of the impact of his years of emotional coldness, the harshness of his rules and prohibitions as she was growing up, and the way he had belittled her achievements so that she had always had to fight for self-respect. Before she finished it had become a shouting match, and they parted with a fury that on Joanna's side left her so upset she could not eat all day. But when she returned home that evening, she found a shaken Donald waiting for her. In gingerly fashion they talked through what had gone on between them. It was a cathartic experience, and in the end they reached a level of understanding that brought an end to their old quarrel.

Reconciliation had come very late. When her father left for home the next day, she knew that she would not see him again. Later that year, he made a tape for Christopher recounting his life's story. The voice is controlled and coherent, and studiously free of emotion. It is hard to quarrel with the reasonableness of his conclusion. "It was nobody's fault. When your mother last saw me [before the war], I was a fit, active man. Seven years passed, and when she met me again I was a shadow of my former self. It's quite understandable that she began to drink. No one was to blame. But there's no point in going back." It was reasonable, but only half-true.

The last acts in Donald's tragedy took place very rapidly. By October 1983 his outbursts of wild behavior had become so marked that his doctor recommended him for treatment in Yeovil's psychiatric hospital, but when he went there no permanent bed was available, and he was sent home. On November 2, 1983, he was examined at his own request by a psychiatrist who concluded that he needed help urgently, but even with that diagnosis, no place could be found. Two days later, neighbors in the village of Chiselborough heard screams coming from their cottage and called the police. When they arrived, they found Cynthia bruised and bleeding, and an incoherent Donald shouting violently. It was clear that he had attacked her in the course of a drunken quarrel, though what it was that finally pushed him over the edge of self-control was never explained. He was arrested and charged with intentionally causing grievous bodily harm. Carolyn received a call from the Somerset police to tell her that he was being held in custody, and immediately went to visit him.

"Seeing him in a police cell was the most distressing sight," she said. "He was a broken man. He didn't know where he was or why he was there. I think at times he believed he was back in Sham Shui Po."

He was charged the next morning, and on police advice was denied bail. By a bitter irony, his size, which had led the Japanese guards to make him a particular target in prison camp, was also the reason why the police feared that he would be a danger to his wife if released. But when Stuart and Carolyn went to say good-bye to him after the hearing, they found Cynthia in the cell, kissing him. Pamela, who wrote to him giving her support, received a card back from Exeter prison, where he had been taken. In its attempt to reassure her, it had a flavor of his wartime letters, and it was written in scrawled capitals as though he were still subject to Japanese prison camp regulations. But now his writing also had the wild incoherence of a mental breakdown:

Was touched by your card—full [of] warmth and affection. Never felt so well. Vacate your flat and move to the croft [the cottage where he and Cynthia lived] your new permanent home w[h]ere we all and admire love you. Burn *all* hot water bottles we have super log fires roll on January. I love you but care for Cynthia.

He appeared in court a week later. Cynthia made it clear that she did not want him punished, and he was so obviously confused that he was taken away while the magistrates decided what should be done with him. The reality was that the mental health services had failed him as spectacularly in 1983 as they had in 1948. Realizing that his father could not survive the experience of prison, the family decided that whatever the cost he had to be given psychiatric help. Christopher had found a private hospital, Ticehurst in Sussex, which would look after him, and the court agreed to remand Donald to their care for twelve months. Once he was receiving proper treatment, it was not long before the staff agreed that he presented no danger to visitors.

The hospital was only half an hour from Tunbridge Wells, and one afternoon, an elegantly dressed lady in her sixties approached the reception desk. Her name, she said, was Pamela Hill and she had come to visit Squadron Leader Donald Hill.

"Of course I had to go to see him, I couldn't not have gone to see him," she said indignantly.

What she said to him no longer exists in memory, but perhaps it can be imagined. Soon afterward she returned to Australia to visit Joanna, and while she was away a crisis occurred. Ticehurst was expensive, and in less than a year the fees had eaten up all Donald's savings. Rather than let him be returned to the custody of the court, Christopher decided that cheaper care had to be found for him. It was complicated to change the court order and so, to save time and money, he simply kidnapped his father, flying him first to Scotland, where he was working, then south again to a hospital near Milton Keynes, close to Carolyn and Stuart. At last the health system that had failed Donald so badly worked for him. Retrospectively the paperwork for his transfer was completed, and once the twelve months' supervision required by the custody order was up, the family were free to take him anywhere. It does not seem to have been a hard choice.

When Pamela came back from Australia, she found that Donald was in a nursing home in Tunbridge Wells, within walking distance of her flat. It was natural to drop in to see him when she passed by. Soon it was no less natural to direct her walk toward the nursing home, which had a fine situation on Mount Ephraim looking over the town. And not much more time had elapsed before it was her daily habit to visit the man she had first loved so long ago. Sometimes the matron would call her saying that he was upset. At times like that, it was always Pamela he wanted to see, and her arrival made him happy again.

Day by day, their old intimacy returned. In the autumn of 1984 he insisted on taking her to the Spa Hotel. As they walked slowly along the road he stopped to buy her some flowers. "Darling," he said awkwardly, "you know you're the only one I have ever loved."

It was not 1939, not even 1946. "It's a bit late for that now," she answered sadly.

"No, no," he said, "it's not too late. I want to marry you."

"Darling," she exclaimed, "it's impossible, you're already married." Then she saw his anguished expression, and relented. "We could always say we're married."

A look of pure relief came into his face. "We will *always* be married," he declared exuberantly.

In the prosaic surroundings of the Spa Hotel's lobby, they sat facing each other, and he whispered to her that he took Pamela Hill to be his wife, to love and to cherish in sickness and in health, till death parted them. From his little finger, he took the gold ring she had given him forty-five years before, at their engagement. "With this ring," he said softly, "I thee wed," and he slipped it on her finger.

It is doubtful if anyone who saw the elderly, slightly battered-looking couple exchanging kisses in the corner of the lobby would have realized that they were bride and groom, but it would be nice to imagine that someone did notice the look on their faces.

In the cold of winter, Donald's strength faded. He looked healthy and still possessed a prisoner's appetite, absent-mindedly eating his granddaughter Lauren's sandwich and her peppermint creams when she and her parents paid him a visit, and then devouring lunch. But his heart was gradually failing. Christopher came down from Scotland to see him, and found him sitting in an armchair but desperately weak. He told his father of his progress as a pilot, and saw his look of pleasure. As he was leaving, he turned at the door to say good-bye, and found his father looking at him. There was a terrible sadness in Donald's eyes, as though he knew they would not see one another again.

The next day, February 25, 1985, the head nurse took Pamela aside and told her that Donald's heart had begun to give up, and he was on his way out. The doctor came, but could only confirm the nurse's opinion. While Carolyn took Lauren to be cared for by friends, Pamela sat with her arm around Donald in the chair. Before her eyes his life began to fade away.

"I told him that all the things I had said to him in the bad times, I wished I hadn't said, and I told him that I loved him, and that we would always be married, and I told him that I had never stopped loving him since the first time we danced together all that time ago." She blinked rapidly. "They say that the dying can hear right to the end, that hearing is the last thing that goes. I'm sure he heard what I was saying and that he took it with him."

Carolyn returned, and they took the dying man's hands, talking to him so that he who had been so solitary in life would know at the very end the comfort of being loved. Then very peacefully, so that they were aware of it only by a slight relaxation in his body, Donald died.

1 2

The Diary Decoded

My love, my love, no, there is no waking
From that long bed or that sleep.
My love, my love, the heart is here for the taking,
And we can take, but not keep.

—GEORGE BARKER,
"WILD DREAMS OF SUMMER WHAT IS YOUR GRIEF"

The parchment-colored notebook was in the pitifully small parcel of Donald's possessions that Pamela took home after his funeral. Apart from his pilot's logbook, there was almost no other documentary evidence to bear witness to his life. Each crisis had swept away more of his belongings, so that instead of the steady accumulation of possessions that most people make, the record of his days had been reduced to this single notebook. He had saved it from Japanese guards, from the restless house-moving, and from the repeated urge to destroy everything inessential to existence. Whatever was in it had meant that much to him.

The notebook's cardboard cover was beginning to poke out at the corners through the brown manila paper cover, but holding it in her hands Pamela was determined that the diary must be read. It contained something that had cast a shadow across her husband's life and as a result had darkened hers. Yet the contents held less significance for her than the secrecy. That was what had really haunted their marriage. She needed to drive out that ghost.

In material terms, the years following Donald's death were the hardest Pamela had to endure. His pensions from the RAF and his employers had gone to Cynthia. But for a discretionary RAF pension and help from her children, she would have found it difficult to survive. Distracted by illness and poverty, she struggled to find someone who could unravel the mystery Donald had left behind. The problem was simply that his disguise for the diary had been too good. When she sent the notebook to the Imperial War Museum, the staff there concluded that it was no more than a mathematical aid. Like them, the RAF Museum at Hendon concluded that it was simply an interesting artefact from the prison camp, and saw no reason to devote resources to examining it further.

When Colonel Quayle of SSAFFA found Dr. Aston, Pamela did not let her hopes rise too high at first, but with Aston's discovery that it was indeed a diary, she had difficulty keeping her excitement in check. Then, as the summer of 1996 arrived and nothing further emerged, she began to grow anxious. In February she had reached her eightieth birthday, and there could not be many more attempts if this one failed. Had she known Aston's state of mind, her anxiety might have come close to desperation.

He was not the sort of person to abandon a project, but the end of July now loomed as a deadline. After that date, preparations for the new semester, the extra work generated by a fresh generation of students, and the sheer mass of research and publication that he had put on hold meant that he would not be able to return to the diary for six months or longer.

"If I can't solve it by the end of the month," he said to his wife, Linda bleakly, "I'll have to send it back."

What he had come up against was the one part of the code that was not susceptible to purely logical analysis. Here the computer had proved itself helpless. It generated huge quantities of mathematically analyzed patterns, but the pattern that Donald had created came out of his own heart and mind, and no software existed to follow human hopes and inhibitions. In its entry under "Cryptology," the *Encyclopaedia Britannica* notes that "cryptanalysis is as much an art as it is a science. The reason is that success in cryptanalyzing a cipher is as often as not a product of flashes of inspiration, gamelike intuition and most importantly, the recognition by the cryptanalyst of pattern and structure at almost the subliminal level in the cipher."

For months Aston had methodically picked away the layers of Donald Hill's encryption. Now he had reached a point where logic could go no further, and his cryptanalyst's mind had to sense rather than deduce the key. At first the frustration of dealing with fuzzy intuition rather than the clear-cut certainties of math prevented him making the final leap.

"When you decipher a code, you don't get it half-right," he

pointed out. "It's either completely right or completely wrong. There were a number of possible solutions to this problem, but there was just one answer, and that's what I had to find." In fact, it was staring him in the face, but to recognize it he had to make an unconscious shift that finally brought his dogged, problem-solving mind into line with Donald's vulnerable, disguise-making personality.

One morning in June, Aston suddenly awoke with a picture in his mind of the inside cover of the notebook. At the foot of the page, Donald had written his name out in full, DONALD SAMUEL HILL, and beside it, his fiancée's name, PAMELA SEELY KIRRAGE. Idly Aston began to count the number of letters in the names; there were thirty-four, the same number of jumbled letters in each line. Immediately he saw that putting the names together might create a keyword for rearranging them.

The purpose of a keyword is to define the order in which variable parts of a code should be read. When he was trying to explain the code to Christopher, Donald had written a number under some letters in the names. Beneath the first A, in "Donald," was the figure 1, beneath the second A, in "Samuel," a 2, and so on until the fifth in "Kirrage," beneath which was the figure 5. There were no B's or C's, but under the two D's in "Donald" were the figures 6 and 7. Suddenly Aston had it. He did not care that the secret had been there for him to see all the time; he was simply delighted that he had got the keyword and could finally work out the order in which the confusing mixture of letters should be read. The fourth letter in the row should be taken first, then the eighth. When he put the full solution on the screen it looked like this:

1 21 31 4 5 6 7 8 9 10 11 12 13 14 15 16 17 18 19 20 21 22 23 24 25 26 27 28 29 30 31 32 33 34

D O N A L D S A M U E L H I L L P A M E L A S E E L Y K I R R A G E

6 27 26 1 18 7 31 2 24 33 8 19 14 15 20 21 28 3 25 9 22 4 32 10 11 23 34 17 16 29 30 5 13 12

The top row was the existing order of the letters, the bottom was the order they *should* be in. He wrote a program to rearrange the columns so that the first letter was put in sixth place, the second in twenty-seventh place, and so on. When he ran it, he saw to his despair that the block of letters had simply been scrambled into a different order. Then the intuitive part of cryptography came to his aid. There was an aptness to this romantic combination which, he was utterly convinced, made sense. So far, each step of the code had been coldly rational, a conscious mental disguise. But the key to it had to be something that sprang from the inexplicable heart.

So strong was his conviction that for the first time he dared to suppose that Donald had made a mistake when attempting to show Christopher how the code worked. Each block was made up of thirty-three rows and thirty-four columns. Instead of arranging the letters from left to right along each row, it was possible that they should have run from top to bottom. Laboriously Aston retyped the letters, this time arranging them so that they ran down each column rather than along each row. Then he applied the keyword once more.

To his amazement, coherent words like "Japan" and "war" began to appear on the screen. He stared at it scarcely daring to believe what he saw; then came a tremendous sense of achievement. "I've cracked it!" he thought. "After all this time we can at last read Donald's story." Reluctantly, he tore himself away to concentrate on the day's teaching, but that evening, unable to wait any longer, he downloaded the diary and the program for decoding it onto a laptop computer so that he could continue reading it at home.

"I've done it!" he shouted to Linda as he came into the house. "The words are jumping off the page, I've got it, at last I've got it."

The next morning he continued the work, typing in every digit on every page and unpicking each step of Donald's code until the original plaintext was uncovered and available for reading. He had to put spaces in between words, and except for periods, which were marked as X's, the text had to be punctuated. A final block was incomplete, and the missing letters had to be guessed, but eventually he had just over thirteen pages of text.

The diary covered the period from December 7, 1941, to March 31, 1942, beginning with the last day of peace, followed by the confusion of the battle for Hong Kong and the demoralizing impact of defeat. The style was clear and detailed, and it did not alter when it described the disease, malnutrition, and brutal beatings that the defeated men experienced in Sham Shui Po camp. What struck Aston as extraordinary was the resilience of character that emerged as Donald and his fellow captives set about rebuilding a sense of purpose and order. For the first time, he understood fully the sort of circumstances under which Donald had devised the code, and still more the phenomenal strength of mind needed to apply it.

The translated diary was presented by Philip Aston to Pamela on a sunny autumn day in 1994 at the university, but it was not until she was back in the privacy of her own home that she dared read it through. At first its matter-of-fact tone surprised her. There was nothing here to be concealed. The existence of Florrie did not shock her. She had learned about her from Donald after the war. It would have been strange if he had not found a girlfriend, and she was glad that that girlfriend had proved so generous with food and clothing. It was only as she read about the punishing conditions in Sham Shui Po camp, and learned about the hunger and the brutality he had endured, that she recognized how the experience came to be locked away.

Whatever happened, his spirit must not be broken. "We are determined to bear our humiliation without a murmur," he had declared, and the phrase told her what she had never before understood. All through those terrible years it was not the enemy he had feared, but himself. No one must guess at the shame and degradation he felt. His self-control was the one thing he could still take pride in. If that went, he would break utterly.

Then she came to the entry barely a week before St. Valentine's Day: "Spend hours these days thinking of home and family especially Pam. Thank God for you Pammy darling your memory is ever with me." Reading these words, which he had hidden so carefully, she began to cry.

"If only he could have talked about those feelings," she said later. "We might have found a way through all the secrecy. We might have found a way of sharing the burden."

Yet as she wept, she finally realized why he had found it impossible to tell her. Even after he returned home he could not escape the prisoner's instinctive secrecy. To reveal feelings so profound was still to risk being broken.

Long after she had finished reading, an unexpected but profound sense of peace took hold of her. The diary had revealed to her something quite different from what she had imagined. The code had hidden not dark secrets, but his vulnerability. Reading his actual words seemed to remove a mask that had distorted his character. It felt as though the man she had first loved had been restored to her.

Above all, she could not forget the significance of Philip Aston's discovery. The key to the code came from the two names, Donald and Pamela, locked together. That alone made sense of the jumbled letters, and that alone made sense of the tangle of their lives.

Appendix

DONALD HILL'S DIARY

Sunday 7/12/41. Much talk about war with Japan but no one seems to think anything will happen. We, the RAF in Hong Kong, are a very small crowd: seven officers and sixty men with five aircraft, two Walrus and three Vildebeeste. Group Captain Horry sails for Singapore on the *Ulysses* leaving Wing Commander Sullivan as our CO. I have the doubtful honour of being i[n] c[ommand] of our one and only flight and have three other pilots F[lying] O[fficer] Gray or Dolly, who is also signals officer, FO Baugh, or Whimpey, equipment officer, [and] P[ilot] O[fficer] Crossley, or Junior, a New Zealander just arrived from Singapore and with very little flying experience. PO Thomson, the colonel, our adjutant, is a V[olunteer] R[eserve] who came to Kai Tak with me from Singapore last June. Finally we have an Australian, PO Hennessy, just arrived from

Singapore to start a fighter operations room. The joke is that everything is being prepared for the arrival of fighters but they are not expected for a month. With only five obsolete aircraft and one aerodrome our prospects are not rosy, and it looks as if we might finish up in the army if war comes to Hong Kong. During the day the news gets worse and all precautions are taken, everyone being confined to camp. I take a Vildebeeste with full bomb load on a test climb during which I try to imagine where would be the best place to drop them and what would be my chances if attacked by fighters. But everything is peaceful, and Hong Kong looks quite beautiful beneath.

We park the Walrus on the water and disperse the Beests, but what beautiful targets they make. The 2nd Battalion Royal Scots and two battalions of Rahjputs [*sic*] are in their positions in the New Territories, and the island is being defended by two battalions of Canadian raw recruits and, only just arrived, the Middlesex battalion man the coast defences. Finally, the [Hong Kong] Volunteers, four thousand Europeans, Chinese, Portuguese, etc. Our navy has one destroyer, ten M[otor] T[orpedo] B[oat]s, and a few gunboats. Not a very formidable force, especially as we shall be completely cut off from outside help and our food and ammunition supply is only sufficient for a hundred days. Still, everyone seems cheerful. I am duty officer and wonder if I shall get any sleep.

Monday 8th. I am disturbed early as the Colonial Secretary rings up to say that war with Japan is imminent. Hell, there goes my sleep, and I wake the other officers. Over breakfast we are told that we are at war with Japan. We dash down to flights just in time to hear an ominous roar of planes and nine bombers escorted by over thirty fighters appear heading our way. There's no time to do anything except to man our defence posts. The bombers pass overhead but the fighters swoop down on us and pour a concentrated fire into our planes. We give them all we've got, which is precious little. Some Indian troops get panicky and rush into a shelter; in their excitement they fire their Lewis gun. There is a mad rush for safety and by a miracle no one is hit. After twenty minutes of concentrated attack by the fighters, the Beeste with bombs goes up in smoke and the two Walrus are left blazing and sink. Finally they make off, not unscarred we hope, and we inspect the damage. Both Walrus are gone; one Beeste is ablaze, another badly damaged, leaving one plane intact. We attempt to put out the fire, praying that the bombs won't explode. The blaze is too fierce and she is completely burned, with two red hot heavy bombs among the ruins. One aircraft left but no casualties to personnel. Eight civil machines are burnt out, including the American Clipper. In the afternoon, bombers come over again bombing the docks and Kowloon, one stick dropping on the aerodrome. Heavy fighting reported on the frontier; the Japs said to be using one division with another in reserve.

Tuesday 9th. After a quiet but sleepless night comes a hectic morn with rumour and counter rumour. Heavy bombing of docks and shipping and a big blaze is started in Kowloon. The Japs make a breakthrough on the Castle Peak Road. Chiang Kai-shek's army reported to be coming up behind the Japs and we realize it is our only chance of holding the mainland with two brigades against two divisions. Oil dump at Lai Chi Kok set ablaze by bombs.

Wednesday tenth. News of fighting on mainland bad and we are ordered by the G[eneral] O[fficer] C[ommanding], Major General Maltby, to evacuate the island. We smash up all valuable equipment and burn all secret papers. All arms and ammunition to be carried with us, parties taken off by lighters proceed to Aberdeen and thence to the A[berdeen] I[ndustrial] S[chool]. I left late in the afternoon on the last lighter with twenty men and all the arms and ammunition. Aerodrome strewn with all kinds of obstacles to prevent use by the enemy. Chinese loot our mess as the lighter leaves. When just off the waterfront, bombers appear and our skipper takes fright; have to use force before he will proceed. Heavy shelling and bombing of Stonecutters [Island] which is bombarding the Japs advancing down Castle Peak Road. We are fired on by our coastal defences after rounding Davis [Point] but we run up a Union Jack and all is well. Arrive Aberdeen and get everything off just before dark. The AIS is full of naval personnel, all trying to find accommodation and food. After a mad scramble, manage to find a bed and retire early, tired and hungry.

Thursday eleventh. Commander Millet, O[fficer] C[ommanding] AIS, asks me to form anti-aircraft and defence posts for Aberdeen as RAF [are the] only people with machine guns. I fix up four posts on the roof with tommy [Thompson sub-machine] gun posts on the verandahs. The AIS makes a wonderful target being half a mile from the naval dockyard. A hospital has been set up next door to the armoury. For breakfast we get one slice of bread and a little butter, and tiffin [midday meal] is the same. For supper, if we're lucky, we get hot stew. Intensive bombing of Aberdeen harbour causing heavy casualties. How we curse the bombers and wish we had a few Gladiators which would make short work of them. Jap fighters are quite slow.

Friday twelfth. Up early and drive into H[ong] K[ong].[1] Buy food, cash a cheque, and have a steak at Jimmies [restaurant].

[1] The town of Victoria, the colony's capital, on the east side of the island of Hong Kong.

Send cables to Pam and Mother. HK shelled from Kowloon. All our troops evacuated from mainland. Hear that Walter Rosa, Dick Stanton, Houston Boswall and Bell, who messed with us at Kai Tak, have all been killed.[2] Small party of Indians still fighting on Devil's Peak. Royal Scots fired on in Nathan Road[3] by Chinese fifth columnists using automatic weapons, but Scots wipe the whole lot out. Chinese reported assisting Japs on large scale. Amazed at sinking of *Prince of Wales* and *Repulse*,[4] also Jap successes against Americans. No one, however, doubts the final outcome, and we realize that HK is only small fry in a tremendous issue.

Saturday thirteenth. I set up anti-aircraft positions on Bennetts [*sic*] Hill and Reservoir Hill w[ith] RAF personnel. C[ommanding] O[fficer Sullivan] goes to battle hqrs leaving me in charge. Dolly goes to Little Saiwan and the colonel to Stanley. After much sweated labour, get guns etc. in position. Whimpey is in charge of Reservoir Hill and I of Bennetts Hill. I return to AIS for the night and at midnight there's a hell of a commotion and everyone is roused as the Japs are supposed to have landed on Aberdeen Island. Whole thing is a farce and return to bed.

Sunday fourteenth. Set up positions on Bennetts and start digging holes in side of hill for billets. Junior and I dig like mad but, owing to rocks, make little progress. Quiet day except for a few air raids. Bed extremely hard and rain comes in.

Monday fifteenth. Contact Canadians who have positions at foot of Bennetts. They are very helpful bringing us hot tea and helping us in our digging. Am now in the army without a doubt and under the orders of Major Baillee [*sic*] of E Battalion, Win-

[2] All the men named belonged to the 2nd Battalion Royal Scots.
[3] Main street in Kowloon.
[4] British battleship and battle-cruiser sunk by Japanese air attack.

nepeg [*sic*] Grenadiers with hqrs at Wanchai Gap. More heavy bombing of Aberdeen harbour, heavy casualties to naval personnel caused by explosions of torpedoes and depth charges.

Tuesday. Japs attempt landing at Lye Mun but party wiped out by six-inch gun. Heavy shelling by Japs of Wanchai Gap and Stanley bombed. Driving the staff car into HK, I have a lucky escape as a stick of bombs meant for the *Thracian*[5] in Deep Water Bay drops on the road just behind me.

Wednesday. Hennessy goes to Canadian hqrs on Col. Sutcliffe's staff. Intense bombing and shelling of island defences. One stick aimed at us misses. Another day of hard work and very little food. During the night enemy warships shell the island and shrapnel shells burst right over our heads giving us an uncomfortable time. Two cruisers and one destroyer had been seen the previous night. One six-inch shell of British make struck the AIS and knocked a large hole in the wall of MTB repair shop, also completely writing off my car.

Thursday. Enemy succeeded in landing on island last night and forced their way into Happy Valley despite heavy casualties. Scots and Canadians fail in attempt to drive them out. Japs in large numbers assisted by fifth columnists. Landing covered by intense artillery and naval bombardment. News muddled and rumours of all kinds rife.

Friday nineteenth. News still confusing but Japs push into Wong Nei Chong Gap. My positions were designed against attack from the West, not East, and we have to improvise a new line. Lt. Campbell takes a party of men to go to the assistance of Canadians trapped in Wong Nei Chong, their place being filled by Chinese Volunteers. Major Giles R[oyal] M[arines] arrives with a small

[5] World War I destroyer.

party. Eventually the Chinese go, much to our relief, as they are much too jumpy. Junior is now in charge of Bennetts with Giles and myself commanding a sector running from the foot of Bennetts to Mt. Nicolson. Situation very tense and we spend a sleepless night. Pours with rain all night and bitterly cold. Everyone soaked through and half-dead by the morning as we had no protection against the weather. Spend half the night pouring rum into semiconscious men who are dead tired after sleepless nights with very little food. We have no reserves and everyone has had a gruelling time. A Canadian sergeant returns to our pillbox at midnight in a state of mental and physical collapse and reports that all his party have been killed. A few hours later another Canadian arrives in a similar condition and with the same story. Worst night I can ever remember, and never was dawn more welcome.

Sunday twenty-first. Naval personnel recalled by the commodore for defence of the dockyard, leaving us seventy Canadians. We all carry a good supply of grenades as the Japs are very skilled at getting to close quarters without being spotted. The Jap soldiers wear rubber shoes and are as stealthy as cats. They carry a bag of grenades, automatic weapons, and light rifle of quarter-inch calibre. They always attack at night and from all directions. Their snipers seem to be everywhere. Japs now using their mortars and artillery much more, being firmly entrenched on Shu Shun Hill. Our artillery do some excellent shooting at Shu Shun and Japs run in all directions. No one seems to know where the Japs are or how many there are. The High Command, whose daily communiques reveal nothing, seem to know less than anyone else. Chiang Kai-shek's army reported attacking Japs in the rear and we are told to hang on as they will be with us in a few days.

Monday. Japs break through Middle Gap and now very close to us. Scots take a heavy toll and retake some positions but Japs always come back in strength. There is no doubt now that the Japs have a very large force on the island, well equipped and experts in this guerilla warfare. Spend the night on continuous watch. The men very jumpy as every sound has to be investigated. If only one could see them instead of this hide-and-seek. In several cases Japs have crept up to pillboxes and dropped grenades down the airshaft, killing everyone.

Tuesday twenty-third. Several Canadians who had been given up as lost return with amazing stories. Many wounded Indians come through our lines kitless but not broken. Heavy shelling of Bennetts. Just before dark enemy starts terrific bombardment of our positions. Hundreds of shells whistle just over our heads. Major Baillee rings up constantly and seems very jumpy about our positions. At two A.M. he orders us to evacuate our positions and retire to Aberdeen. We are amazed at such an order but apparently the Japs have broken through over Mt. Nicolson turning our left flank. We collect our small force and start our retirement. Heavy firing coming from Wanchai Gap where fierce fighting is going on. What a forlorn sight we make groping our way back through the hills in the dark. Finally reach Aberdeen, the Canadians going up Mount Gough and I take my men to the AIS. Atmosphere depressing and everyone falls to sleep through exhaustion. Up early, lucky for me, as a bomb lands on my bed as I leave the room wrecking everything including my kit. AIS heavily shelled causing many fires and casualties.

Wed twenty-fourth and Thursday Xmas Day. The retirement order was a mistake and back we go to Bennetts with guns and equipment. Just as we reach the top the Japs open up on us with mortars. We have no protection and lie flat. The shells land right amongst us. Man next to me hit, also several others. Piece of shrapnel glances off my helmet and am half buried in flying debris. If we stay we shall all be killed so order the men to disperse and dash for cover, and miraculously we make it. During the barrage I had noticed that one of our previous posts was still manned by Canadians who obviously had not received the order to withdraw. Cpl [Corporal] Blueman A.C., Canadian, volunteers to go with [me] to try and get them out. We climb on our bellies through the thickest undergrowth but are fired on several times. Finally we get within hailing distance and get them all into a pillbox. We collect all the arms and equipment which we can't carry, pile them in the pillbox, and throw a couple of grenades into the pillbox. As we start back, everything goes off at once and we have to duck flying bullets. Eventually we arrive intact at the AIS. No one seems to know where the Japs are, so back we go to a new position guarding the bridge over Aberdeen reservoir.

My party consists of twelve Canadians and ten RAF. Up to midnight all is quiet, although every sound indicates Japs to the men. Soon after midnight heavy firing starts just across the bridge. The Japs' weird war-cry is plainly heard, and soon a small party of Canadians retire over the bridge. They report heavy attack by Japs who crept up on them and broke through. We open up with everything we have across the bridge. The Canadians are badly rattled, even their officer seems to have lost control of his men. The Japs start shelling us and confusion sets in, and the men start leaving their posts. A scene I never wish to see again, I am in an awkward position as I have no command over the Canadians.

Just as they start moving back [up] the road, Major Baillee advances down the road waving a revolver and shouting to his men to get back to their posts. Some obey and some don't. The major is highly excited and his voice rings through the night calling his men all the names he can think of. The Japs must have a good idea of our positions. He calls his officers and men all the names under the sun and shouts for volunteers to cross the bridge. The Canadians refuse to budge so I, more [out] of a desire to back the major than [out] of any thought of heroics, go across with him. We reach the other side safely, whereupon he is violently sick, and I realize he is drunk. Through overwork he worked himself into a state of complete collapse, and should have been releaved [*sic*] of his command earlier.

We retire still intact. We can hear the Japs' wild animal calls and they appear to have gone another way. Most of the Canadians have disappeared and with the few left we set up a mortar which fires its first shell into a nearby tree, explodes, blowing the operator's right arm off, and another man nearly loses a leg. Get the wounded into a dugout where there are some others badly wounded and try to stop their bleeding. We only have bandages and several of them are in danger of bleeding to death. Their moans are terrible and although I keep ringing up for an ambulance, none arrives. What a horrible mess, and I try to restore some kind of order. After a good talking-to, the men pull themselves together and go back to their posts. Thank God the ambulance arrives at last, Lts. Campbell and Park. Campbell threatens to put the major under arrest, and Baillee threatens to put every Canadian under arrest.

Comes the dawn and most of the Canadians have disappeared. What a Xmas Day, empty stomachs, tired out and heaven knows what is going on. At ten A.M. a message arrives saying their [*sic*] is a truce until midday. This news is immediately followed by a terrific bombardment of our positions. Not my idea of a truce. More Canadians melt away leaving our line practically undefended. I gather the few remaining men together and proceed to climb Mt. Gough hoping to join up with our main forces. When we reach the top and strike the main road, we run into several hundred Canadians in retreat from Wanchai Gap. Wanchai Gap is the most vital sector of all and this means the end. We are told that is land surrendered at three-thirty, over an hour ago. The troops have no arms and are completely worn out. A scene I will never forget with ammunition dumps going up everywhere and the Japs pouring hundreds of shells just over our heads into blocks of houses across the road. Finally the barrage stops and white flags appear from all the houses. The troops have got hold of quantities of beer and are singing to releave [*sic*] their shattered nerves.

I am too stunned to describe my own feelings but decide to try and escape. The Japs are reputed never to take prisoners. With Junior and three of my men we grab an Austin Seven and decide to make a dash for Aberdeen to try to get a boat. The engine won't start but it's all downhill. By now it's dark and the road is very narrow and tricky. We throw away our arms and get aboard. What a ride, crashing through barbed wire and roadblocks in the dark, but the old Austin showed her worth and we finally coasted into Aberdeen without seeing any Japs. We go straight to the AIS and get hold of a Chinese boy who says he will try to get us a boat with food and water. Then, to our horror, we discovered that the building had been locked and we could not get out as the Japs were outside. What a disappointment, and we had nothing to do except find somewhere to sleep not having had a real one for ten days. My old room was a complete shambles, so slept on the floor.

Friday twenty-sixth. Woke to a beautiful morning, being unnaturally quiet and peaceful so that the last few weeks seemed as nightmare. We were all under orders for the dockyard. Spent most of the morning smashing up thousands of bottles of beer and spirits for fear the Japs would get drunk and run amuk [*sic*]. Got a car and set off for the dockyard, passing hundreds of Chinese laden down with loot. On arrival at the dockyard, we're told to go to the detention barracks, the men being locked up in the cells, and we went to China Command.[6] Had a real wash and shaved off my fortnight's growth of beard. The Colonel [Thomson] was in hospital having received a bullet through the neck, eight of our men were dead and several missing.

We had no kit, so I decided to try and get back to the AIS. The only transport I could find was an old dairy farm lorry. Whimpey and Frank came with me. Soon we ran into several thousand Japs marching along the road, looking tired and ragged. An officer signalled us to stop, made me turn the lorry while troops climbed in the back. He indicated by signs that I was to drive them to HK. The troops seemed baffled by our blue uniforms but were quite friendly. Dropped our load and once more set off for the AIS. Passed hundreds more Japs, but after some nasty moments finally reached our destination. Found most of our kit, and got safely back. Just as I was congratulating myself on a good day's work, a Jap officer came up and ordered me back into the lorry. Whimpey and Frank got off. He directed me by hand signs to drive to Courtland's Hotel which had been taken over by the Japs. The few remaining residents looked pretty scared. More troops piled in and after a very trying drive through Kennedy Town, we finally reached the St. Louis Industrial School where they all got out. We had passed hundreds of troops and the streets were littered with dead Chinese.

I was beginning to think my work was done when several of-

[6] Headquarters in Victoria of the defense force.

ficers started arguing and kept pointing at me and looking aggressive. Suddenly one of the officers whipped out his sword, and I thought they had decided to bump me off, but to my amazement he produced a bottle of beer, nipped the top off with his sword, and handed me the bottle. I was then given a loaf of bread. Apart from one or two soldiers, they had treated me very well. My wings seemed to fascinate them. By now I wanted to call it a day, but another officer got in the lorry and off we went back to the hotel. He had some beer with him and handed me the bottles to open. I stopped the van and wedged the tops off on the mudguard. This seemed to amuse him and he tried to do the same on the dashboard with drastic results.

Once more the van is loaded up with troops. Another officer takes over who is not so pleasant and I get half an inch of bayonet in my bottom for being too slow. Back to the School, where another terrific argument starts. I want to go back with the van, but two officers decide to drive me back in a Ford Ten. They don't use any lights and we have several narrow escapes from hitting lampposts. Suddenly I see we are heading for one of the islands in [the] middle of the road, and shout a warning. Too late, and there's a terrific crash and we finish up on our backs. By now I am fed up, so bowing politely I leave them and walk the two miles to China Command.

Saturday. Five of us sleep in a small office. All our water has to be drawn from a stream nearby. No one knows what is going to become of us and everyone tries to guess at our future destination. Some Jap officers inspect us.

Sunday twenty-eighth. More troops arrive from Stanley and report that Japs raped and bayonetted nurses in St Stephen's Hospital, also killed the wounded. Colonel Smith, whose wife was one of those killed, goes nearly mad and tries to get at the nearest Jap.

Several atrocity stories come to light and atmosphere becomes very tense. Two destroyers and one cruiser anchor off the dockyard, followed by a victory parade including a flypast of sixty bombers and fighters. All very galling.

Monday twenty-ninth. News is that we are to be moved to the mainland at dawn tomorrow, and that we will be given no transport and can only take kit that we can carry. The GOC and commodore are treated the same as everybody else. Obviously we are going to be humiliated. For dinner we open all the tins in store and eat royally, washed down with beer and champagne. Pack what little kit I have, also any tinned food left over.

Tuesday. At dawn we prepare to move off. Frank and I sling our kitbags on a pole coollie [*sic*] style. We sling blankets round our neck[s]. We are determined to bear our humiliation without a murmur—our day will surely come. We form into units and after two hours waiting move off, over six thousand strong. Arrive at the ferry and, after another long wait, are ferried across to Kowloon where we form into units again. Off again but where no one knows. After a mile or so, we come back into Nathan Road. By this time we begin to feel the strain and have to rest frequently. Each unit has its own guard. Thousands of Chinese line the streets, a few jeering but mostly quiet and some are in tears.

It would appear that we are going to Sham Shui Po, several miles away. Our guard is a decent fellow and seeing we are having a rough time allows coollies to carry our kit. Eventually we reach SSP barracks, eight hours after leaving China Command. A battle for billets commences. The whole camp has been stripped of every useful article by looters, and had also been bombed. All doors, windows, furniture, and fittings had been taken, leaving just hulks of buildings. Even in peacetime it was an awful dump, but now it looked as if a typhoon had hit it. We found a small hut, and then a tremendous hunt started for anything resembling a bed. Found some horsehair and wrapped [it] into one of my blankets. Several men had been here for days, being captured earlier on. Two W[arrant] O[fficers] had been tied up with wire, stripped of everything, and left for three days without food or water after having seen several of their comrades bayonetted. We get rice twice a day which tastes foul and does not alleviate our hunger.

Wednesday thirty-first. Moved to a slightly bigger hut, the Wing [Commander Sullivan] moving in with us; the men are in another hut close by. There are over six thousand men in the camp with no sanitation and rotten food. We have no lights and go to bed soon after dark. We have one meal at nine and another at five consisting of soggy rice, and are permanently hungry. And so ended nineteen forty-one.

Jan. first. A new year which we hoped would see the end of the war. We hear no news, only wild rumours, and we all wonder what our people at home are thinking as we are unable to tell them of our safety. Soon adapted ourselves to our surroundings and began fixing our rude quarters into some sort of shape. Bits of wood and attap[7] made windows, and no kind of scrap was wasted. Had no eating utensils; any old tin had to suffice. Cigarettes very scarce, but luckily we had brought some with us.

Second. Our camp adjoins the main road, and the Chinese sell us food stuff at exorbitent [sic] prices. We have three hundred dollars and add considerably to our stock of food. My boy, Ah Cheung, brings a basket of food and I slip him some money to get some more.

Third. Take it in turns to go [to] the wire. Often the Chinese, usually boys, grab the money and run away without giving any-

[7] Burlap or sacking.

thing in return. Junior put in charge of messing, and we open a tin a day.

Fourth. Our chief danger is flies, which swarm everywhere spreading dysentery, and the added menace of cholera. We have practically no medical supplies as the Japs have taken them all for their own wounded, which run into thousands. Just as we get to bed, a lorry arrives and we are disturbed by the squealing pigs. Thirty for six thousand men. We all assist in chasing them, and put them in a hut.

Fifth. Each receive a small lump of fat with our rice, very unappetising.

Sixth. My batman, Cpl Moulton, who was my fitter,[8] is a great little scrounger and handyman. Manage to buy a camp bed for ten dollars at the fence. Sheer luxury but the canvas is rotten, and during the night it collapses and lands me on the floor.

Seventh. Moulton fixes my bed but breaks my rice bowl. Buy a tin of coffee and some vegetables. We make a stew in a bucket and do we enjoy it. Many of the troops have Chinese wives and girlfriends who bring them food. Japs get very strict about buying food at the wire, and many Chinese get beaten up, women being stripped naked in full view of everyone. Indians are getting unruly. Several deaths from dysentry [*sic*].

Eighth. Florrie and her amah arrive with more food. She tries to cross the road but I signal her back. No parcels get through as a general is expected to visit us. My boy also arrives. What a disappointment.

Ninth. Jap general arrives with an escort of twelve cars, and troops manning machine guns in lorries. He drives to the guards'

---

[8] Aircraft engineer.

hut, steps out, has his photograph taken, and drives off without a word. What a farce. Many wild rumours but as usual no truth in them.

Tenth. Bed collapses again during night. Our roof leaks from the effects of a bomb, but so far the weather has been perfect. The flies swarm everywhere due to the filthy condition of the camp. All buying at the fence stopped, the Japs torturing any Chinese who come near the fence.

Eleventh. Florrie arrives again and I receive a parcel of bread, butter, milk, and tomatoes. What a treat, and the six of us make short work of it. Rumours even wilder: Tokyo reported bombed, Japs suffer severe naval defeat, Hitler committed suicide, and Japs evacuate Malaya. Have grand supper of coffee, bread, butter, and jam.

Twelfth. All buying definitely stopped, many Chinese beaten up.

Thirteenth. Many sick with tummy trouble. One feels fairly fit but completely lacking in energy. Twenty Scots arrive from Fan Ling, amongst them being Potato Jones who commanded the company at the Shing Mun Redoubt, and Lieut. Thompson who was hit by a grenade and is practically blind. Japs refuse to take him to hospital, which will probably cost him his sight. Florrie brings another parcel. I throw a message to her across the road screwed up in a cigarette holder.

Fourteenth. Everyone's stock of food running low. Rumours still wild, but always good news and we think things are going well.

Fifteenth. Florrie comes again, but Japs won't allow parcels through. Get some soya beans which help the rice down. Junior falls down and nearly breaks his leg.

Sixteenth. Start Japanese lessons. Florrie arrives again, and this time I'm lucky. Whimpey gets a blue mood and refuses to talk to anyone.

Seventeenth. Florrie's amah arrives with more food.

Eighteenth. Sentries wire up streets facing camp and shoot a man and a woman for trying to sell food. Florrie turns up again but can't get her parcel through. What a girl. Two Chinese bodies washed up near fence. Everyone feeling weaker due to lack of proper food. Rumours and counter-rumours so contradictory that I don't believe anything. Some real news would make such a difference.

Nineteenth. Now get three meals of rice a day but quantity the same. Rice by itself is awful muck, but we save our small stock of milk and sugar for our evening tea. Over hundred men arrive from Queen Mary's Hospital.

Twentieth. More men arrive in lorries, some unable to walk and dressed only in pyjamas and socks. Troops give a concert including a dance band. Cigarettes very scarce.

Twenty-first. Fight between Middlesex and Indians. Rice ration very short.

Twenty-second. All Indians moved out of camp. Canadians being moved tomorrow, destination unknown.

Twenty-third. Disturbed early by troops detailed for work at Kai Tak, a three-mile walk. Wonder how they'll make out on the diet.

Twenty-fourth. Navy are moved from the camp, and we are going into Jubilee Buildings.[9] Usual mad scramble for accommodation. Wing gets peeved with Brigadier McCleod and tells him a few things. News is that we have withdrawn in Malaya and that

[9] Married men's quarters when Sham Shui Po was a barracks.

there's a rumpus at home about HK and Malaya, and quite rightly too as both places were very weak in defences, especially aircraft, and men have had to fight against overwhelming odds. We all hope these blunders will soon be rectified.

Twenty-fifth. Move into Jubilee, which is much more comfortable and on the waterfront. The six of us have three rooms and even a bathroom. What a relief after our squalid hut. Junior has planned to escape with several others. They hope to get to Mirs Bay in a junk, and then fifty miles overland to Wai Chow, which is still in Chinese hands.

Twenty-sixth. Junior gets up at five to contact the Chinese who is escaping and is going to arrange for the junk to pick the rest of the party up tomorrow.

Twenty-seventh. Junior up at five and contacts the junk but doesn't get away. Frank and I up at six and go down to the jetty which is now the only place one can buy food. We get seven lbs of sugar. It is pitch dark and we have to wade some distance to the junk. The Chinese are very cunning at avoiding sentries, but several have been shot.

Twenty-eighth. GOC talks to all officers and NCOs about morale, which is very low, and warns us against disease. We are all staying up late tonight and are having a late meal to feed the escapists: Junior, Capt. Scriven, and Capt. Hewitt. Whimpey is also due to go but one of their party backs out and upsets their plans, which is to swim to the mainland then walk to Wai Chow. A perfect night with a bright moon and as still and quiet as a graveyard. We sit up until two o'clock playing cards by the light of the moon. Finally they go and we get some sleep.

Up to thirty-first. Junior and Whimpey's escape[s] don't come off due to the junk not turning up and Whimpey's raft collapsing.

Many Chinese escape, and some Europeans, many being captured and brought back. Japs machine[-gun] all junks moving by day. Many cases of dysentry and typhoid.

Feb first. Japs stop all food coming into the camp. Whimpey and Junior due to try again tonight. Four of us get up at two to wait for the trading junks. Several hundred in queue. Sampan arrives at four and we buy sugar, milk, and sardines. Whimpey goes just before midnight, it being very light. Shortly after, we hear rifle fire and we pray that he made it.[10] Bullets fly past our verandah. Junior gets off at two A.M. in one of the trading junks.

Second. We feed well today as we get rations for six. We are all a bit on edge wondering how they got on.

Third. Frank and I up at four and go down to the jetty. The Japs have locked the gates, but we make a hole and get through. Japs hold a parade to count us, as they caught three gunners last night. On parade the Japs spot that we are two short and ask the Wing why. He says he has no idea but they were with us last night. They seem perturbed about escapes.

Fourth. Up at three and down to the jetty, but the sentries are awake and shots start whistling nearby. This happens every half-hour and we take shelter. After two hours and no sampan turns up and bullets getting too close, we retire to bed.

Fifth. Japs now wise to escapes and we have to parade again at eight for two hours. Another parade at one, which takes over four hours. All very annoying and they don't seem very clever at counting us. They don't take precautions to prevent escapes, but seem very surprised when it happens. In the Jap army to escape is to desert.

Sixth. Wake up to find the others busy dressing and packing.

---

[10] Both men succeeded in escaping and returned to active service as pilots, but Baugh was later killed.

They have been ordered to be ready to move at short notice, but I am not included. No one knows what it's all about. Just time for brief farewells and they are gone, driven off in a car, and what luggage they have follows in a lorry. I am now the only RAF officer left. A sad day for me to lose such grand companions in distress, especially the Wing. Someone brings me a parcel which Florrie had brought me. The Japs have started to allow a limited number through. A large tin of cocoa, milk, butter, soap, and biscuits. How the others would have enjoyed it. I go down to the fence and see Florrie and have quite a long chat with her. She has been interned at Stanley for a fortnight. She seems very cheerful and is coming again tomorrow. What a girl. Sentry offers me ten cigarettes for my gold wristwatch, a twenty-first-birthday present from Billie.[11] When I refuse, he indicates my gold signet ring given to me by Pam. I would not part with either for the world, so no business is done. Roy Haywood and Ken Glasgow come and have evening cocoa with me. Spend hours these days thinking of home and family, especially Pam. Thank God for you, Pammy darling, your memory is ever with me. I still have your photograph, signet ring, and cigarette case. I will never lose them.

Seventh. Eight officers move into the flat, including a Chinese called Evans. In my room, I have Captain Chippywood and Lieut. Tressider. Ian Blair and Mathers of the Punjabis bring along some chapatties, which go down well with butter and marmalade. Roy Haywood and Glasgow join us and spend a pleasant evening. Ken had been to Kai Tak on a working party, and been roughly handled by a sentry, but an officer apologised and gave him a tin of plums which he brings along.

Eighth. Shave my beard off and feel a new man. Florrie turns

[11] Donald's sister.

up and I get another good parcel. I had told her if she wanted to get a note to me to bore a hole in a bar of soap and put the note inside. She has made a good job of it. Poor kid, the Japs have turned her out of her home. I keep trying to stop her bringing me parcels, but she tells me to mind my own business.

Nineth [*sic*] and tenth. A Jap general is due to arrive, and after a two-hour wait on parade he arrives and goes in a few minutes. Florrie turns up again and I get within ten yards of her. She appears to be in tears. I get a note to her and tell her not to bring any more food, but she just smiles and says she will be here again Sunday. News bad, Japs having landed on Singapore Island. Things look grim.

Eleventh and twelfth. Another parade and we are kept standing for two hours and nearly freeze to death, several men pass out. One has to go to bed fully dressed to keep warm. Chippy keeps us constantly amused with his antics.

Thirteenth. Electricity is turned on and we find a bulb. What luxury. Still very cold, and news still bad. Had slight attack of stomach poisoning. Give men a lecture on discipline as some troops in camp, not RAF, are getting unruly. GOC says he will hand control over to Japs unless men snap out of it. My men behaving very well. On the evening parade, camp commandant asks if I miss the others and says that perhaps in two months I shall be with them. Bitterly cold, difficult to keep warm.

Fourteenth and fifteenth. Florrie brings a huge parcel including a Chinese mingoia blanket, sheet and pillowcase, and food. What an angel, and one day I hope to repay her. Another death from dysentry and many more sick.

Week ending twenty-second. Slightly warmer but was thankful for that blanket. Singapore has fallen which is a severe blow. Cholera outbreak in colony and we fear it will reach the camp as sanitary conditions are awful and men in very low state, especially Scots. Two men killed at Kai Tak in landslide. At GOC's conference, he gives us the daily news from BBC as there is still a set working. Japs shoot two Chinese who were marched through the camp onto the jetty where were shot in the back. Food bad and little of it, but worst of all practically no medical requisites.

Week ending twenty-ninth. Florrie turns up every few days, and tells me the Japs have turned her out of her flat and pinched all her jewellery. I wish I could help her, and I tell her to leave the colony. Governor's chief of staff and retinue visit the camp. Another two hours on parade. Much warmer, and Chippy, Tressider, and I cut each other's hair off. We look extremely funny but it feels cool. Two Scots escape and Japs have rigid check on evening parade. Wet and cold again and running short of footwear. Owing to fifth columnists in the camp, Japs suspect we have a wireless, so GOC orders it to be destroyed. A three-hour parade in the rain, and Japs search our rooms. They find a couple of wireless sets. No more BBC news now, just wild rumours. Two Scots who escaped have been shot. A proclamation is read to us forbidding escapes—all who are caught will be shot, and severe reprisals taken against our comrades. Malnutrition very noticeable. Personally I feel very fit, thanks to Florrie's parcels.

Week ending seventh March. Japs interview my wireless people, but I had prepared them for it and the Japs get nothing out of them. Florrie still sending parcels. Chippy also gets one from his wife. The women of HK are doing grand work; little do they know the difference their presence and gifts of food make to us. Usual two parades a day and life is becoming a little monotonous. Japs send for me, and I am escorted out by George, the Jap WO, and a Portuguese interpreter. I am taken to the camp commandant's office where the officers are very pleasant and give me some cigarettes. I ask the English-speaking guard commander about the RAF officers, and he says they will soon be back, being in Canton or HK.[12] The WO takes me to his flat where he proceeds to question me through the interpreter about the RAF, where we kept our stores, and how their air force compares to the RAF. He wants me [to] write my answers down on paper. I refuse to answer most questions, but I give my opinion of their air force which is far from complimentary. Am also asked if they could have reduced HK earlier by bombing indiscriminately. I write some lines of nonsense about raids on London e**.[13] Manage to pinch a handful of cigarettes before I go back to camp. Cigarettes run out and we smoke dried tea leaves, which are pretty foul. Another parcel including cigarettes and curry.

Week ending fourteenth. Getting warmer and diet beginning to have effect. Many men with beriberi or swelling of ankles and have difficulty in walking. Feel fairly fit but lack energy. Common sight to see several dead bodies in sea. George orders all ranks to salute him *a*sh**ep**sent**hem*k**o*we.

Twenty-first. Florrie turns up in her best effort looking charming. Suspect Rangoon has fallen, and Japs have a big celebration. Outlook looks decidedly grim. Troops put on an excellent concert and George attends. Have started brewing wine from raisins. Japs say officers are to be paid so shall be able to send some to Florrie. Wthr [weather] hot and acquire quite a tan. **e*ow***t*n*f*ur**sm**tada**ith*u**i*ex***a*f*n*as**cr**ours start to malign our people in the camp. Make most of a pair of wooden clogs as I only have v[ery] old pair of shoes.

Thirty-first. Japs have another search and confiscate all elec-

---

[12] They were in fact held in Shanghai.
[13] The remainder of the diary is incomplete, and some numbers cannot be deciphered.

trical kit, including Chippy's immersion heater. No meat for over a week and everyone gets one rice pot. Celebrate the twenty-fourth birthday of Ray and T

[The diary ends at this point. In the notebook, it is clear that several pages have been cut out.]

A Note on Sources

My research for this book depended heavily on the personal memories and written records of Donald Hill's family, and especially of his widow, Pamela. Her sisters, Mrs. Brigit Ferguson and Mrs. Sheila Froom, and family friends also helped with personal and often extremely vivid reminiscences. To fill in the gaps in Donald's experiences as a prisoner of war, I was aided by a piece of undeserved good fortune in having as a neighbor Mrs. Anne Sorby. She is a former Hong Kong resident; her knowledge of the place is formidable, and having spent an impressionable youth in two intelligence-gathering organizations, Britain's MI-5 and the Special Operations Executive, she possesses sleuthing skills beyond the ordinary. Thanks to her, I was introduced to a wealth of Hong Kong books and contacts, especially to a network of ex-prisoners of war whose help was invaluable. The Imperial War Museum's reference staff produced other diaries of Hong Kong prisoners, and those of Brigadier Cecil Templer and Captain A. White gave an especially clear picture of life in the camps.

At a late stage in writing, I had the luck to hear the tape recording which Donald Hill made in 1982 for his son, Christopher. It was not only full of detail about aspects of his life which I knew of only from others, but conveyed in the tone and timbre of his voice an immediate sense of the man he was and the struggle it cost him to keep his mind and life intact.

After the British edition was published, a call from Dr. Tony Goorney, a retired psychiatrist who had formerly worked at Ticehurst, the hospital where Donald was treated in his last years, enabled me to establish the real name of the heroic Florrie. During a rambling talk about the war, Donald had revealed that her name was Foo Ling. It seemed he had tried to find her after his release to acknowledge his debt to her, but could find no trace of her. It is probable that she did not survive the war. Like many Hong Kong Chinese, she suffered from malnutrition and ill-treatment by the occupying forces.

But of course the most puzzling and rewarding source of information was the notebook in which Donald Hill kept his coded diary. More often than not, it has seemed utterly baffling, but at times it offered great insights, as though the disguise itself were the man.

Acknowledgments

My debt to Pamela Hill, widow of Donald Hill, is so great that I have often felt that this book almost amounted to a collaboration. I shall always be deeply grateful to her, not only for her unstinting help but for her friendship. Her children, Joanna Wilkinson, Carolyn Morris, and Christopher Hill, have been equally generous with their time and memories, and I was also helped by a useful interview with Stuart Morris.

I am indebted to Brigit Ferguson and Sheila Froom, Pamela's sisters, who were informative, amusing, and vastly patient in providing recollection and comment. I owe thanks, too, to Philip Aston, who decrypted the diary, for his guidance, and to his wife, Linda, for her help. I am grateful for Barbara Waterworth's information about Iraq in the 1950s.

My friend and neighbor Anne Sorby not only

helped with reminiscence and books about Hong Kong but steered me toward crucial sources on the colony in wartime. Chief among them was Michael Wright, who generously talked about his experiences as a prisoner. I also acknowledge with gratitude the help of Arthur Gomes, MBE, of the Hong Kong Prisoners' Association, Group Captain Bennet, John Harris, Dr. Tony Goorney, and Dr. Peter Barham of the Wellcome Institute.

The book is the brainchild of my editor at Weidenfeld & Nicolson, Toby Mundy, who has overseen its genesis with a care and attention to detail for which I am continuingly grateful. I acknowledge the kindness of Russell Twisk, editor-in-chief of the *Reader's Digest* in the United Kingdom, and of Susannah Hickling, senior editor, in giving permission to use material that first appeared in an article I wrote for the magazine. I am grateful to Emma Baxter of Weidenfeld & Nicolson for her extremely cogent comments on an early draft. The American edition has benefited enormously from the imaginative contributions of my editor, Amy Scheibe.

I acknowledge the advice and help provided by the staff of the Imperial War Museum, the Public Record Office, the British Library, the London Library, and the Tunbridge Wells Public Library.

For the use of quotations, I acknowledge the following:

Five lines from "Sept. 1 1939" excerpted from *W. H. Auden Collected Poems* by W. H. Auden. Copyright © 1940 by W. H. Auden. Reprinted by permission of Random House, Inc.

Robert Graves, "She Tells Her Love While Half-Asleep": by permission of Carcanet Press.

My final acknowledgment must go to the extraordinary, tortured character of Donald Hill. I hope that I have done him justice, for he had firm tastes in books. Among those that came under his critical eye in prison camp was a book called *Juan in America* by Eric Linklater. This was my father's first best-seller, and one of his finest novels. Donald awarded it just three stars, meaning "Fair." I feel I have a lot to live up to.

14·8·16	20·5·6	15·4·1	4·2·5·2	3·5·5·1	8·1·8·1	2·1·4	5·1·15	5·4·...	
6·25·1·1	9·2·2·1	2·1·2·2	0·5·9·5	14·7·2	0·15·1	1·4·14	1·15·1	16·3·2	5·15
5·21·5·1	8·5·1·1	5·20·9	15·1·1	5·16·9	7·9·14	14·20	14·15	18·8·2	5·13
6·8·7·1·5	20·14	5·13·2	2·1·20	1·191	14·18·2	2·8·18	16·19	6·14·22	15·5
1·18·20	9·1·9·2	14·121	5·8·3·1	6·14·8	14·1·1·20	4·19	13·...	5·1·2·1	5·9
14·232	5·18·1	5·8·6·1	5·14·1	9·8·8·9	15·2·9	18·20	1·8·19	6·15·2	0·16
14·5·20	15·1·1	5·3·19	16·12	16·20	1·1·22	21·6·19	19·1	8·4·13	121
20·7·222	5·18·9	23·20	1·20·9·5	2·11	2·5·1·9	10·7·2	2·22·6	18·14	21·1
14·5·13·2	3·13·1	14·6·2	1·8·22	6·22·9	5·15·1	5·20·7	18·7·1	3·5·5·6	5·1
2·0·232	5·5·2·4	21·24	12·20	8·9·15	16·12	19·14	18·19	21·5·5	24
20·5·20·9	20·24	5·5·20	11·14	9·5·7·2	25·5·23·9·5·2	4·201	9·14·2	21	
1·14·23·9	21·9·5	20·19	21·19	18·7·2	0·14·1	8·111	8·23·5	5·19·1	8·2
2·0·5·39	5·7·14	21·9·1	8·7·12	4·9·21	13·1·5·1·9·20	24·5·4	13·25	1·16	
7·20·11	11·8·1	5·3·23	20·25	15·7·5	15·9·2	3·1·16	18·5·1	4·5·10	14·1
8·6·20·9	14·1·5	2·252	0·6·19	1·12·2	5·14·2	2·6·7·4	15·15	18·15	1·20
1·3·24·1	0·15·1	4·151	4·9·28	15·15	23·14	1·1·20·8·14·6	23·25	7·14	
1·8·14·1	2·18·8	8·131	14·14·1	8·1·9·1	9·9·15	16·20	12·15	19·3·1	9·1
00·12·2·1	14·122	5·1·5·4	3·5·1·5	15·24	1·191	6·24·2	5·5·3·1	19·22	18
13·14·5·5	16·6·1	4·131	5·20·5	11·2·9	19·9·2	120·5	20·14	4·16·6	3·1
5·20·0·9·5·5	15·15	15·20	14·24	18·15	15·3·6	23·14	12·8·1	14·7·19·9·5	
8·1·121	5·19·1	4·192	0·1·7·1	9·202	1·5·20	5·4·4·1	8·7·14	14·4·1	12
8·15·14	12·22	14·18	18·12	16·12	22·18	1·12·1	16·11	16·15	15·1
6·14·8·2	0·182	12·9·1	8·12·3	9·191	8·5·14	15·25	4·15·8	19·18	7·2
14·8·202	0·18·2	21·16	1·151	8·191	220·5	15·16	9·5·1·4	24·21	25
2·9·151	5·4·1·1	14·1·20	18·5·5	19·1·9	5·21·5	15·23	19·15	5·5·8·1	14·9
2·0·141	4·21·5	5·15·5	4·212	5·4·20	3·14·4	19·24	1·6·5·1	14·201	8·4
14·3·1·14	1·1·15	9·2·4·2	0·6·21	15·5·5	15·21	21·6·1	25·20	12·15	20
3·5·231	14·4·7·2	0·14·2	0·14·2	0·112	3·192	0·12·9	24·9·1	5·5·15	25
1·83·15·6·15·2	3·8·18	9·9·20	23·18	18·1·2	5·8·19	6·5·12	18·5·1	32	
20·20·8·5	19·1·3	6·5·2·1	220·4	14·13	9·191	8·14·8	20·14·1	4·18·9	5·5
1·6·15·2	0·16·5	15·14	5·201	9·20·8	8·192	2·8·5·1	5·12·3	14·9·8	5·5
1·3·3·1·1	4·131	5·9·23	21·18	1·2·11	5·19·8	14·5·1	9·14·1	6·191	9·2
21·2·125	21·12	8·201	5·242	3·191	9·251	9·5·2·1	9·151	1·2·1·1	5·5
14·1·18·7	16·6·9	4·12·5	1819	20·6·5	7·6·18	24·15	14·5·9	9·5·15	1·1
9·16·23	2·9·1·2	5·19·14	20·5·5	9·9·6·1	3·15·9	19·2·2	0·9·9·2	013·5	5·5
8·5·202	0·10·1	8·23·1	1·5·9·2	0·5·1·1	2·14·5	5·4·1·1	0·5·1·1	20·21	9
2·1·121	8·000	12·19	25·6·6	1·7·20	14·1·1	5·9·20·5·15·3	3·3·13	15	
5·6·16·8	2·9·2·9	1·11·8	3·181	8·9·19	1·201	8·141	1·8·21	1·5·20	9
14·9	14·14	20·20	15·5·7	21·7·2	1191	2·3·16	23·7·2	0·25·5	1·192	0·1
1·215·8	5·7·8·4	12·19	20·12	5·192	3·5·5·9	18·9·5	9·1·14·9	15·9·2	14
2·1·9·5·20	14·5·1	14·7·1·1	5·14·1	4·9·5·5	5·9·18	16·7·9·8·1·9·1	9·18·7	2	
14·1	5·8·18	14·9·1	9·5·18	8·121	5·5·23	12·4·1	5·131	6·2·14	15·3·1	2